HEALTHY Hometown Favorites

America's Best-Loved Recipes from Community Cookbooks—
Made Light by the Food Editors of **PREVENTION** Magazine

Compiled and Edited by Mary Jo Plutt

Rodale Press, Inc.
Emmaus, Pennsylvania

Copyright © 1995 by Rodale Press, Inc.
Cover Illustration copyright © 1995 by Beth Krommes
Interior Illustrations copyright © 1995 by Chris Van Dusen
Front Cover Photograph copyright © 1995 by Becky Lougast-Stayner
Back Cover Photographs (top and bottom) copyright © 1995 by
    Donna H. Chiarelli
Back Cover Photograph (middle) copyright © 1995 by Angelo Caggiano

Produced in cooperation with The Wimmer Companies, Inc.

Front Cover Recipe: Creamy Chocolate Roll (page 255); adapted from: *Cultivated Palate* by the Arboretum Foundation, Washington Park Arboretum

ISBN 0–87596–251–3 hardcover

Distributed in the book trade by St. Martin's Press

2 4 6 8 10 9 7 5 3 1 hardcover

——— OUR MISSION ———

We publish books that empower people's lives.

——— RODALE BOOKS ———

Healthy Hometown Favorites Editorial Staff
Editor: Mary Jo Plutt
Managing Food Editor: Jean Rogers
Contributing Writer: Paula M. Bodah
Associate Art Director: Faith Hague
Studio Manager: Joe Golden
Interior Designer: Joyce Weston
Interior Illustrator: Chris Van Dusen
Cover and Layout Designer: Eugenie Seidenberg Delaney
Cover Illustrator: Beth Krommes
Front Cover Photographer: Becky Lougast-Stayner
Front Cover Food Stylist: Marie Piraino
Back Cover Photographer (top and bottom): Donna H. Chiarelli
Back Cover Photographer (middle): Angelo Caggiano
Recipe Testing, Rodale Test Kitchen: JoAnn Brader; Kay Cernuska;
    Anita Hirsch, M.S., R.D.; Nancy Zelko
Nutrition Consultant: Linda Yoakam, M.S., R.D.
Copy Editor: Kathy Diehl
Production Manager: Helen Clogston
Manufacturing Coordinator: Melinda B. Rizzo

Prevention Magazine Health Books
Vice-President and Editorial Director: Debora T. Yost
Art Director: Jane Colby Knutila
Research Manager: Ann Gossy Yermish
Copy Manager: Lisa D. Andruscavage
Senior Vice-President and Editor-in-Chief, Rodale Books: Bill Gottlieb

To the countless children and teenagers
who inspire us with their relentless discipline.
Day in and day out, year after year, they are always
on guard in their quest to manage their diabetes.

GLEN WIMMER, PRESIDENT
THE WIMMER COMPANIES

Contents

Every recipe in Healthy Hometown Favorites includes a nutrient analysis to help you plan a healthful diet. We followed these guidelines when analyzing recipes.

• We used the first ingredient listed when an option is given.

• If a quantity range is given (such as two to three tablespoons), we used the first (smaller) amount.

• Ingredients described as optional or designated by "if desired" are omitted from the analysis.

• Ingredients not specifically listed in the recipe are not included, such as salt that the cook might add to the water when preparing pasta or rice.

• Figures given are for cooked meat, poultry and fish, with visible fat and skin removed when specified in the recipe.

• If a range of servings is given, the analysis is for the first number (for example, four servings in a recipe that makes four to six servings).

Health experts recommend a diet in which no more than 30 percent of the calories come from fat. And we heartily concur. But we freely admit that some of the recipes in this book do exceed the 30-percent limit. That's because some dishes, such as certain meat entrées, just naturally contain a higher percentage—but the total number of fat grams in them is acceptably low. Other foods, such as green salads and cooked vegetables, have so few calories that even a tiny amount of fat drives the percent figure way up.

The thing you need to remember is that the dietary recommendation applies to your total diet, not to individual foods. When you balance higher-percent foods with others that are very low—unbuttered bread, noodles or rice and beans, for example—your total diet will even itself out.

In addition, the recipes in this book are slimmed-down versions of America's favorite foods. So enjoy them in good health.

Introduction

Food does more than just nourish our bodies. It links us to our heritage, family and community. And the recipes we pass from generation to generation and share among friends become personal gifts we cherish forever. Community cookbooks are collections of these time-honored treasures. Most often the proceeds from the sale of these books are used to fund community causes, such as the training program for first-time parents in Worcester, Massachusetts, and the construction of the fine-arts auditorium for Lee-Scott Academy in Auburn, Alabama.

In *Healthy Hometown Favorites*, we're pleased to share with you nearly 200 hometown recipes selected from 77 community cookbooks nationwide—and updated for today's healthier lifestyle. In addition, we introduce you to the worthwhile causes that benefit from the efforts of these charitable organizations. You'll find the details in special "Our Cause" boxes scattered throughout the book.

When we set out to create this cookbook, our goal was to provide you with the healthiest, best-tasting appetizers, entrées, side dishes and desserts we could find. And we found plenty. Take the Greek Potato Wedges featured in *Rogue River Rendezvous* from the Junior Service League of Jackson County, Oregon. Or the Creamy Chocolate Roll from *Cultivated Palate*, which benefits the Arboretum Foundation Washington Park Arboretum. And then there's the Crispy Baked Chicken from the Junior League of Worcester's *A Taste of New England*.

Often the recipes that caught our fancy needed a little modification to trim a bit of fat, calories or sodium from them. So we made a few changes to increase their nutrient content—without sacrificing the quality and taste that made each of them so popular in the first place.

Some of the recipe modifications we made were minor, such as substituting light convenience products for their regular counterparts or replacing high-fat or high-sodium ingredients with slightly different ones that are lower in fat or sodium. Other changes were more dramatic, like using fruit puree (such as applesauce, mashed bananas or prune puree) in baked products to replace some of the fat. Sometimes we simply changed to a healthier cooking method, such as oven-frying instead of deep-fat frying.

In addition, as a service to today's smaller families, we scaled down many of the recipes to yield four to six servings. We also adjusted the portion sizes to bring them in line with the recommendations of today's health experts. That means, for instance, serving two to three ounces of cooked lean meat, fish or poultry at a meal instead of the larger quantities that used to be so common.

To make sure all of our culinary adjustments actually work, we enlisted the aid of the kitchen experts at the Rodale Test Kitchen to test—and retest, when necessary—each and every recipe. Above all, we want to assure you that you'll have success when you prepare the recipes for your family.

A special feature of this book is our chapter entitled "Potluck Potpourri." It pays homage to the always-popular covered-dish dinners and potluck suppers that bring together people united in a cause. Our collection of recipes features dishes that can be made ahead, that travel well and that never fail to please. And we give you lots of tips guaranteed to make your group's next social gathering a surefire success.

This book, like community cookbooks everywhere, reflects the character of the many people who shared their recipes. We heartily thank all of the organizations that participated in our project. And in following the spirit of community organizations nationwide, we're pleased to announce that a donation has been made on their behalf to the Juvenile Diabetes Foundation. That association is working tirelessly to find a cure for juvenile diabetes. For more details about their work, see the profile that begins on page 1.

We'd like to give extra-special thanks to Glen Wimmer and The Wimmer Companies for their participation in this project. Only with their help were we able to share with you this special collection of recipes and community causes from across the country.

Mary Jo Plutt
Cooking Editor
Prevention Magazine Health Books

Our Cause
Juvenile Diabetes
Foundation

Juvenile Diabetes Foundation: Dedicated to a Cure

*E*very year 13,000 American children and teenagers are diagnosed with juvenile diabetes. One in 400 of those children will die because a doctor won't recognize the symptoms of the disease in time to begin proper treatment.

Children are not alone in their risk. To date, each year 6,000 adults will lose their sight to diabetes, the number-one cause of blindness in adults.

This is tragic, of course. More heartbreaking, though, is the fact that all those deaths and almost all diabetes-related blindness could be prevented.

The Juvenile Diabetes Foundation International (JDF) wants you to know this because they need your help to end death from diabetes, to end blindness from diabetes and to end diabetes, period.

Kenneth Farber, executive director of JDF, has absolute faith in that last aim. "There's no question that a cure will be found," he says. "How soon it will happen is the question. We have set a goal of making this the Decade for the Cure."

The organization was founded in 1970 by a handful of parents of children with diabetes. Today, it is an international foundation with headquarters in New York City and more than 130 chapters all over the globe. Tens of thousands of volunteers do everything from organizing fund-raising events and working with the government on diabetes-related issues to promoting education and providing information.

JDF's primary purpose is to raise money for diabetes research. Last year, for example, the organization raised over $34 million, more than 83 percent of which went directly to research and education. That's more money than any other private health agency in the world raises for diabetes research. It's enough for JDF to fund about a third of the research proposals that it believes can lead to better treatment of diabetes and a cure for the disease.

The organization is scrupulous in choosing the research projects that it will fund, looking for the best and the brightest in the biomedical community. Proposals are carefully reviewed by a group of eminent physicians and researchers as well as a committee of JDF chapter members. Final approval comes from the Foundation's International Board of Directors.

Still, a cure is, as the saying goes, so close and yet so far. The Juvenile Diabetes Foundation cannot rest yet.

The past 15 years have brought a lot of good news for people with diabetes. The medical community has made enormous strides in understanding and treating the disease. New medications and treatments make it easier for people with diabetes to not only live but also live well and happily.

Some of the devastating complications of diabetes are now avoided or minimized, thanks to the research. Laser treatments, for example, help prevent, or at least slow, the loss of eyesight. Easy, accurate methods for measuring glucose mean people with diabetes can monitor their own blood sugar levels daily for consistently good health. Progress has been made in transplant research. Someday, a pancreas transplant or injection of insulin-producing cells might cure the illness. And gene research suggests that doctors will be able to predict who will get diabetes so it can be prevented before it starts.

JDF is not all money, medicine and science, though. While the cure is being sought, the organization is busy teaching kids and adults all over the world how to live well with diabetes. "What makes diabetes different from other diseases," says Farber, "is that the patient, not the doctor, is in control." The Foundation works hard to involve its members and to invite and encourage people with diabetes and their families and friends to join in the organization's many activities.

Diabetes plays no favorites, striking kids of all ages and ethnic backgrounds.

That's not hard, it turns out. Members are a committed bunch. Take the group's annual Walk for the Cure for diabetes. Last year, in 75 cities across America, on city blocks and in suburban neighborhoods, on boardwalks and in parks, on grass and pavement, nearly 60,000 people joined the walk, raising $9.7 million.

Kids are as important as adults at JDF, and the organization's younger members are as devoted and active as are the grown-ups. Casey Johnson, a 14-year-old New York City girl who has diabetes, chaired a competition to design a scarf and necktie to raise money for JDF. Children with or without diabetes were invited to enter, and hundreds of creative kids from all around the country answered the call.

The winner of the competition was a design by Dana Mangnuson, a 14-year-old from Grand Rapids, Michigan, who herself has diabetes. Her design incorporates the flags of many countries, emphasizing that diabetes does not discriminate in choosing its victims. People from all over the world, from every race and nationality and religion, can and do get diabetes. JDF hopes to raise more than $10,000 on sales of the scarves and neckties, which can be purchased in department stores throughout the country.

Casey Johnson and her dog, Oink, model the scarf and tie created to raise money for diabetes research.

Through such activities, the Juvenile Diabetes Foundation helps both those with diabetes and the people close to them understand the disease and take control over it. Diet and exercise, Farber reminds us, are the most important factors in preventing and controlling diabetes and in allowing people to lead long, healthy lives despite the illness.

The Juvenile Diabetes Foundation has become a crucial player in the fight against juvenile diabetes. But Farber looks forward to the day when the organization he heads will no longer be needed, to the day when diabetes will be conquered.

"We're not a complicated organization," he says. "All we want to do is go out of business."

For further information, contact the Juvenile Diabetes Foundation International, Diabetes Research Foundation, 432 Park Avenue South, New York, NY 10016-8013.

Potluck Potpourri

Dish Up a Perfect Potluck

Whether it's called a potluck, a covered-dish dinner or a BYOF (bring your own food) get-together, dinners where everyone pitches in are becoming more popular than ever. With today's busy lifestyles, these gatherings provide opportunities to enjoy good food along with good company—without a huge amount of work on the part of any one person.

At potlucks, everyone is a host as well as a guest. Here are some tips for creating and enjoying your next covered-dish dinner.

• What to bring? Something tasty, of course. But also something that can be transported easily and served simply. In this chapter you'll find dishes that are perfectly suited for a potluck affair. But don't be limited by our selection—there are plenty of other appetizers, main dishes, desserts and salads in later chapters that will work well, too.

• Plan the menu by food categories—appetizers, main dishes, vegetables and salads, desserts, breads and beverages. Assign one person to coordinate the food selections. The coordinator can make arbitrary assignments to individuals or let the other guests sign up for whatever they want to bring.

• Those who don't cook can still participate by bringing non-food items, such as plates, napkins, glasses, silverware and serving utensils.

• Write your name and telephone number on pieces of masking tape and use them to label your dishes and serving utensils. Also keep track of any other items, such as towels or pot holders, so you can carry them back home with you.

• To transport a casserole hot from the oven, immediately wrap it in foil. Then wrap the dish in several layers of newspaper or a quilted casserole cozy. Pack the dish in a shallow box with towels all around it to minimize movement. Time things so that the casserole gets served as soon as possible.

• Assume responsibility for keeping your dish at its proper temperature during the party. You can keep foods hot with a warming plate, electric skillet, chafing dish or Crock-Pot. And you can keep foods cold by using an insulated cooler or setting the serving bowl in a larger bowl of ice.

• Set out the appetizers as soon as they arrive. If you're bringing an appetizer, plan to arrive a few minutes early so that you have time to say hello and still get your food on the table before the other guests arrive.

• If you will need to reheat your food, check before the day of the party to make sure that there will be space available in the on-site microwave or oven.

• Serve the meal buffet-style, arranged in a logical linear fashion. Begin with the dinner plates and main entrées. Then proceed to side dishes, salads and breads. End with silverware, napkins and beverages.

• It may be helpful to place the desserts on a separate table. That way, guests who are ready for dessert can help themselves without disrupting others who are still getting their dinner.

• Be responsible for cutting, slicing or scooping your food before putting it on the buffet table so guests can easily serve themselves while going through the buffet line.

• Be a helper as well as a guest at the party. Share in the chores of setting out the food, taking dirty dishes and glasses to the kitchen and cleaning up afterwards.

• Potlucks are ideal for exchanging taste-tested recipes. Bring a few blank self-addressed, stamped postcards with you to the party. When you taste a recipe you would like to add to your collection and the other person agrees to share it, simply hand him or her a postcard. At home, the person can write the recipe on your postcard and just drop it in the mail.

Homemade Herb Cheese

Adapted from *Vintage Vicksburg*
VICKSBURG JUNIOR AUXILIARY

We left just enough margarine in this garlic-and-herb cheese spread to give it a rich, buttery flavor. We made up the difference with additional light cream cheese, a lower-fat alternative to margarine. Serve the spread with crackers, party breads or sliced baguettes.

2 containers (8 ounces each) soft-style light cream cheese
¼ cup tub-style reduced-calorie margarine or butter blend
3 cloves garlic, minced
1 tablespoon finely chopped fresh chives
1½ teaspoons finely chopped fresh chervil or ½ teaspoon dried chervil, crushed
1½ teaspoons finely chopped fresh tarragon or ½ teaspoon dried tarragon leaves, crushed
1 teaspoon finely chopped fresh parsley or ½ teaspoon dried parsley, crushed
½ teaspoon finely chopped fresh thyme or ¼ teaspoon dried thyme leaves, crushed
¼ teaspoon ground white pepper

In a medium bowl, stir together the cream cheese and margarine or butter blend until well-combined. Then stir in the garlic, chives, chervil, tarragon, parsley, thyme and pepper.

Transfer to a small crock or container. Cover tightly and chill in the refrigerator for at least 4 hours to blend the flavors.

Makes 2¼ cups; 18 servings.

❧ PER 2 TABLESPOONS: 55 calories, 4.5 g. total fat, 2.7 g. saturated fat, 9 mg. cholesterol, 144 mg. sodium

Dill Dip with Rye Bread

Adapted from *Lone Star Legacy*

AUSTIN JUNIOR FORUM

Yogurt cheese is a healthy alternative to regular sour cream and cream cheese. It's made by simply draining the liquid from yogurt. For this creamy and delicious dip, we replaced the usual sour cream with yogurt cheese and supplemented it with reduced-fat mayonnaise.

DILL DIP

1½   cups fat-free plain yogurt cheese (see tip on page 64)
1¼   cups reduced-fat mayonnaise
2   tablespoons dried minced onions
2   tablespoons finely chopped fresh parsley
2–2½   teaspoons dillweed or 2 tablespoons finely chopped fresh dill
¼   teaspoon seasoned salt
⅛   teaspoon garlic powder

BREAD BOWL

1   unsliced round loaf white or rye bread (6″–8″)

FOR THE DILL DIP: In a medium bowl, stir together the yogurt cheese, mayonnaise, onions, parsley, dill, salt and garlic powder. Cover and chill in the refrigerator for at least 2 hours to blend the flavors.

FOR THE BREAD BOWL: Insert the point of a sharp knife into the top of the loaf at a 45° angle and 1″ from the top edge. Cut around the top edge of the loaf, then remove the top. Remove the bread from inside the loaf, forming a ¼″-thick shell. Set the bowl aside and cut the bread into large cubes.

Just before serving, place the bread bowl on a large platter. Spoon the dip into the bowl and arrange the bread cubes around it.

Makes 24 servings.

❧ PER SERVING: 58 calories, 4.2 g. total fat, 0.8 g. saturated fat, 1 mg. cholesterol, 107 mg. sodium

Buffalo Chicken Wings

Adapted from *River Feast*
JUNIOR LEAGUE OF CINCINNATI

A few simple changes slimmed these hot and spicy wings nicely. We replaced butter in the marinade with chicken broth and used fat-free sour cream and reduced-fat mayonnaise in the dip.

BUFFALO WINGS

5 pounds chicken wings (about 20 wings)
1 cup defatted reduced-sodium chicken broth or unsweetened apple or pineapple juice
1 bottle (2½ ounces) hot-pepper sauce (or to taste)
⅛ teaspoon onion powder
⅛ teaspoon garlic powder

BLUE CHEESE DIP

¾ cup fat-free sour cream
¾ cup reduced-fat mayonnaise
⅓ cup crumbled blue cheese
1 tablespoon fresh lemon juice
Pinch of onion powder
Pinch of garlic powder
1–2 tablespoons skim milk (optional)

FOR THE BUFFALO WINGS: Preheat the oven to 400°. Split the wings and reserve the wing tips for another use (such as making chicken stock). Spread the remaining wing sections in a 15″ × 10″ baking pan. Bake about 20 minutes or until no longer pink. Then transfer the wing sections to a large tray or cutting board lined with paper towels. Blot the top of the chicken with additional paper towels. Cool slightly.

Transfer the chicken to a large resealable plastic bag. Add the broth or juice, hot-pepper sauce, onion powder and garlic powder. Seal the bag. Turn the bag to combine the mixture and coat the chicken. Marinate the chicken in the refrigerator for 6 to 12 hours, turning the bag occasionally.

FOR THE BLUE CHEESE DIP: Meanwhile, in a small bowl, stir together the sour cream, mayonnaise, blue cheese, lemon juice, onion powder and garlic powder. Cover and chill in the refrigerator for at

---

OUR CAUSE

Junior League of Cincinnati

The people of Cincinnati have a reputation for loving a good celebration. Maybe they're influenced by those rowdy Kentuckians just across the Ohio River! More likely, they simply take a righteous pride in their vital city on the busy river.

Whatever the reason, *River Feast* extols the city by presenting more than 350 recipes from both home cooks and chefs at the city's most prestigious restaurants. The innovative women of the Junior League of Cincinnati enlisted the help of Apple Computer in putting together this, their second cookbook.

The result is a good-looking book that shows off the city at its finest. Even better, the League saved money by using the desktop publishing capabilities available to them. And that enables a greater percentage of the price of each book to go directly to the League's favorite causes. Among those causes are projects and agencies that aid residents, especially women and children in crisis or just in need of a helping hand.

---

least 2 hours to blend the flavors. If desired, stir in enough of the milk to make a desired consistency.

Preheat the oven to 400°. Remove the chicken from the bag. Discard the marinade. (If desired, you may freeze the chicken for a later time.) Place the chicken on a baking sheet in a single layer. Bake for 5 minutes. Turn the chicken over and bake about 5 minutes more or until lightly browned. Serve with the dip.

TEST KITCHEN TIP: For an easy cool-down dip, use a store-bought fat-free or reduced-fat blue cheese or ranch-style salad dressing instead of making your own.

Makes 10 servings.

ટ▲ PER SERVING (2 PIECES CHICKEN WITH A SCANT 3 TABLE-
SPOONS DIP): 258 calories, 17.8 g. total fat, 5.3 g. saturated fat,
55 mg. cholesterol, 294 mg. sodium

Picadillo Dip

Adapted from *Land of Cotton*
JOHN T. MORGAN ACADEMY

When making this classic dip, take your choice of very lean
ground beef or ground venison. The venison gets only 18 percent
of its calories from fat, making it an excellent alternative to
regular beef and pork. To further reduce the fat and boost the
fiber in this dip, we decreased the amount of meat by half and
made up the volume with black beans.

8	ounces ground beef (95% lean) or venison
½	cup no-salt-added tomato sauce
6	tablespoons no-salt-added tomato paste
4	medium tomatoes, chopped
1	cup canned black beans, rinsed and drained
⅔	cup water
½	green pepper, chopped
½	cup light raisins
½	cup dark raisins
1	tablespoon dried minced onions or ¼ cup finely chopped onions
¼	teaspoon salt
¼	teaspoon dried oregano leaves, crushed Ground black pepper (to taste)
¼	cup slivered almonds, toasted (optional)

In a large skillet, cook the beef or venison until it is browned, stirring occasionally. Drain the meat in a strainer or colander, then transfer it to a large plate lined with paper towels. Blot the top of the meat with additional paper towels.

Wipe out the skillet with paper towels and return the meat to the skillet. Stir in the tomato sauce and tomato paste until combined. Then stir in the tomatoes, beans, water, green peppers, light raisins, dark raisins, onions, salt and oregano. Season to taste with the black pepper. Bring to a boil, then reduce the heat. Cover and simmer for 30 minutes. If necessary, stir in a small amount of additional water if the mixture is too thick for dipping chips.

To serve, transfer the dip to a large chafing dish to keep warm. If desired, sprinkle with the almonds to garnish.

TEST KITCHEN TIP: Serve this Mexican dip with no-oil baked tortilla chips. Look for them in the snack section of your supermarket or at health food stores. Or make your own. Here's how.

Preheat the oven to 400°. Coat a large baking sheet with no-stick spray. Stack several flour or corn tortillas, then cut the stack into 6 wedges. Place the wedges on the baking sheet in a single layer. Lightly mist them with no-stick spray. If desired, lightly sprinkle with salt. Bake for 10 minutes or until the chips are lightly browned and crisp.

Makes 4 cups; 16 servings.

ᓚ PER ¼ CUP: 83 calories, 2 g. total fat, 0.7 g. saturated fat, 9 mg. cholesterol, 94 mg. sodium

---

Salmon Filling for Hors d'Oeuvres

Adapted from *Family and Company*
JUNIOR LEAGUE OF BINGHAMTON

For this salmon filling, we substituted pureed cottage cheese for whipped heavy cream. The cottage cheese gives the filling a creamy, light texture without contributing a lot of fat. Serve the filling in opened fresh pea pods or hollowed-out cherry tomatoes. Or spoon it onto cucumber rounds, endive leaves or bias-sliced carrots.

      8   ounces salmon fillet or steak or 1 can (7½ ounces)
          pink salmon, drained, flaked and skin removed
      2   cups fat-free or 1% fat cottage cheese
    2–3   teaspoons finely chopped fresh dill
          Ground white pepper (to taste)

If using fresh salmon, measure the thickness of the fillet or steak. Pour about ½″ of water into a small skillet. Bring just to a boil. Add the salmon. Return just to a boil, then reduce the heat. Cover and gently simmer about 5 minutes per ½″ thickness of the salmon or until the fish flakes easily when tested with a fork. Drain, then remove and discard the skin and bones; flake the salmon.

In a blender or food processor, process the cottage cheese until smooth. Transfer to a medium bowl. If using canned salmon, crush

(continued)

the bones. Add the fresh or canned salmon with the bones to the cottage cheese. Stir in the dill, then season to taste with the pepper.

Makes 3 cups; 24 servings.

> ❧ PER 2 TABLESPOONS: 22 calories, 0.3 g. total fat, 0.1 g. saturated fat, 2 mg. cholesterol, 58 mg. sodium

---

Scramble Mix

Adapted from *Pow Wow Chow*
THE FIVE CIVILIZED TRIBES MUSEUM

Butter-flavored granules boost the flavor in this snack mix as well as lower the fat. If you want to reduce the fat even more, use the oyster crackers instead of the pecans.

4	packages (½ ounce each) butter-flavor mix
½	cup water
¼	cup canola oil
2	tablespoons Worcestershire sauce
2	teaspoons seasoned salt
1	teaspoon garlic powder
¼	teaspoon onion powder
1	box (15 ounces) bite-size wheat-square cereal (8 cups)
1	box (10 ounces) round toasted-oat cereal (11 cups)
1	package (12 ounces) unsalted pretzel sticks or twists (10 cups)
1	pound pecans (5 cups) or 5 cups oyster crackers

Preheat the oven to 250°. In a small saucepan, stir together the butter-flavor mix and water. Heat and stir just until the mix dissolves. Remove from the heat and stir in the oil, Worcestershire sauce, salt, garlic powder and onion powder. Set the butter-flavor mixture aside.

Coat a large, shallow roasting pan with no-stick spray. In the pan, combine the wheat cereal, oat cereal, pretzels and pecans or oyster crackers. Drizzle the butter-flavor mixture over the cereal mixture and gently stir until coated.

Bake for 2 hours, gently stirring the mixture every 15 minutes. Cool, stirring occasionally.

TEST KITCHEN TIP: To make a smaller batch of this favorite snack mixture, use 2 packages butter-flavor mix, ¼ cup water, 2 tablespoons oil, 1 tablespoon Worcestershire sauce, 1 teaspoon seasoned salt, ½ teaspoon garlic powder, ⅛ teaspoon onion powder, 4 cups wheat-square cereal, 5½ cups oat cereal, 5 cups pretzels and 2½ cups pecans or oyster crackers.

For impromptu parties, make a full batch and freeze it in large resealable plastic bags. The flavor will stay fresh in the freezer and the mixture will thaw quickly when you need some.

Makes 34 cups; 68 servings.

> ৯ PER ½ CUP: 104 calories, 5.7 g. total fat, 0.5 g. saturated fat, 0 mg. cholesterol, 112 mg. sodium

---

Little Links in Oriental Sauce

Adapted from *Rave Reviews*
JUNIOR LEAGUE OF NORTH LITTLE ROCK

Here's an appetizer from Rave Reviews *that'll receive rave reviews at your next potluck party. In our testing, we used lower-fat cocktail sausages. If these are not available in your area, use reduced-fat, fully cooked smoked turkey sausages and cut them diagonally into ½" slices.*

⅓   cup packed brown sugar
4   teaspoons all-purpose flour
1   teaspoon dry mustard
½   cup unsweetened pineapple juice
¼   cup cider vinegar
¾   teaspoon reduced-sodium soy sauce
1   pound cocktail wieners
1   pound reduced-fat smoked cocktail sausages

In a medium saucepan, stir together the brown sugar, flour and mustard. Then stir in the pineapple juice, vinegar and soy sauce. Bring to a boil. Reduce the heat. Gently boil and stir for 1 minute.

Add the wieners and sausages. Stir until coated. Then cook, uncovered, over medium-low heat about 5 minutes or until heated through, stirring occasionally.

(continued)

To serve, transfer to a chafing dish to keep warm. Serve with decorative toothpicks.

TEST KITCHEN TIP: To reduce the fat and calories even further, use 1 pound 97% fat-free hot dogs instead of the cocktail wieners and diagonally cut each hot dog into 5 pieces. You'll save an additional 18 calories and 2.4 grams total fat per serving.

Makes 100 pieces; 50 servings.

> PER 2 PIECES: 58 calories, 4.4 g. total fat, 1 g. saturated fat, 5 mg. cholesterol, 213 mg. sodium

---

Meatball Chowder

Adapted from *Come and Get It*
JUNIOR WELFARE LEAGUE OF TALLADEGA

Tomato juice is ideal for an easy soup base. In this recipe, we used its reduced-sodium counterpart and reduced-sodium beef broth instead of bouillon to keep the salt within healthful limits.

MEATBALLS

4	egg whites, lightly beaten
⅓	cup fine saltine cracker crumbs
2	teaspoons skim milk
¼	teaspoon salt
⅛	teaspoon pepper
2	pounds ground beef (95% lean)

SOUP

1   can (46 ounces) reduced-sodium tomato juice
3   cans (13¾ ounces each) reduced-sodium beef broth,
    defatted
3   small onions, each cut into eighths
¼   cup long-grain white rice
1   tablespoon sugar
2   bay leaves
1   teaspoon dried marjoram leaves, crushed
6   medium carrots, sliced
4   potatoes, diced
3   cups sliced celery
1   can (11 ounces) whole kernel corn with sweet peppers,
    drained

FOR THE MEATBALLS: Preheat the broiler. In a large bowl, stir together the egg whites, cracker crumbs, milk, salt and pepper. Add the beef and mix until well-combined. Form the meat mixture into 1″ balls. (You will have about 64 meatballs.)

Coat the unheated rack of a broiling pan with no-stick spray. Place the meatballs on the rack. Broil 4″ from the heat about 4 minutes or until they are lightly browned on the surface, turning the meatballs often for even browning. (The meatballs will not be cooked through.) Transfer the meatballs to a large plate or tray lined with paper towels. Blot the meatballs with additional paper towels.

FOR THE SOUP: In a large Dutch oven or 8-quart stockpot, stir together the tomato juice, broth, onions, rice, sugar, bay leaves and marjoram. Bring to a boil, then reduce the heat. Cover and simmer for 15 minutes. Add the meatballs, carrots, potatoes, celery and corn. Return to boil, then reduce the heat. Cover and simmer about 30 minutes more or until the vegetables are tender and the meatballs are no longer pink in the center. Remove and discard the bay leaves before serving.

Makes 12 main-dish servings.

❧ PER SERVING: 292 calories, 9.8 g. total fat, 3.7 g. saturated fat, 48 mg. cholesterol, 484 mg. sodium

Chili Supreme

Adapted from *Yesterday, Today and Tomorrow*
BADDOUR MEMORIAL CENTER

Sometimes when you make over a recipe, you can omit certain ingredients without a noticeable taste difference. In this chili, for instance, we eliminated butter and used defatted chicken broth instead of oil to sauté the vegetables.

3	cups chopped onions
4	medium green peppers, chopped
¼	cup defatted reduced-sodium chicken broth
2	cloves garlic, minced
2	pounds ground beef (95% lean)
12	ounces Italian-seasoned ground turkey sausage
3	cans (16 ounces each) no-salt-added tomatoes (with juice), cut up
¼	cup chopped fresh parsley or 2 tablespoons dried parsley
¼	cup chili powder
3	tablespoons cumin powder
1½	teaspoons ground black pepper
¾	teaspoon salt
3	cans (16 ounces each) pinto beans, rinsed and drained

Lightly coat an unheated Dutch oven or 6-quart stockpot with no-stick spray. Add the onions, green peppers, broth and garlic. Cook and stir over medium heat for 10 to 15 minutes or until the onions are tender.

Add the beef and sausage. Cook until the beef is browned and the sausage is no longer pink, stirring occasionally. Drain the beef mixture in a strainer or colander, then transfer it to a very large plate lined with paper towels. Blot the top of the beef mixture with additional paper towels.

Wipe out the Dutch oven or stockpot with paper towels and return the beef mixture to it. Stir in the tomatoes (with juice), parsley, chili powder, cumin, black pepper and salt. Bring to a boil, then reduce the heat. Cover and gently simmer for 30 minutes, stirring occasionally.

Baddour Memorial Center

The late Charles Baddour loved to cook. Mr. Charles, as he was known in the community of Senatobia, Mississippi, and in the city of Memphis, especially loved to bake. He was legendary for baking as many as 500 birthday cakes a year for family and friends.

When he compiled a collection of his favorite recipes in *Yesterday, Today and Tomorrow*, a cookbook to raise money for the Baddour Memorial Center for mentally disabled adults, you can be sure that the section on cakes was one of the best and biggest ever presented in a cookbook. The Baddour Memorial Center opened in 1978 and was the result of a bequest from Charles's brother Paul, who died in 1973.

Charles and the rest of the family established the center, and Charles took on the task of compiling the cookbook as a fund-raiser. The first copy came off the press in 1979. To date, about 80,000 books have been sold. The profits benefit 161 mentally disabled adults from 27 states who live at the center. For the residents and their families, the Baddour Center is a beacon of light and a testament to the value of the special people it helps.

Stir in the beans. Continue cooking about 5 minutes more or until the mixture is heated through.

Makes 14 main-dish servings.

ֹ PER SERVING: 292 calories, 12.3 g. total fat, 3.2 g. saturated fat, 40 mg. cholesterol, 600 mg. sodium

Delta Beef and Rice

Adapted from *Heart and Soul*
JUNIOR LEAGUE OF MEMPHIS

This rice casserole comes from the rich farmland of the Mississippi River delta via the Junior League of Memphis. According to many health experts, a healthy diet includes 6 to 11 servings of grain-based food, which includes rice. This dish will help you easily meet that requirement. And to make it even more healthful, we slightly decreased the amount of meat and increased the rice.

1½	pounds ground beef (95% lean)
1	cup sliced green onions
1	cup chopped celery
½	cup chopped green peppers
1	large clove garlic, minced
1	tablespoon + 1 cup defatted reduced-sodium beef broth
1	can (16 ounces) no-salt-added tomato sauce
1	can (15 ounces) no-salt-added tomato puree
¼	cup chopped fresh parsley
1	tablespoon dried oregano leaves, crushed
1	tablespoon dried basil, crushed
1	tablespoon Worcestershire sauce
¼	teaspoon seasoned salt
¼	teaspoon ground black pepper
3	cups cooked brown rice
¾	cup (3 ounces) finely shredded reduced-fat sharp Cheddar cheese (optional)

Preheat the oven to 350°. In a large skillet, cook the beef until it is browned, stirring occasionally. Drain the beef in a strainer or colander, then transfer it to a large plate lined with paper towels. Blot the top of the beef with additional paper towels. Set aside.

Wipe out the skillet with paper towels. To the skillet, add the onions, celery, green peppers, garlic and 1 tablespoon of the broth. Cook and stir over medium heat about 8 minutes or until the celery is tender.

Stir in the beef, tomato sauce, tomato puree, the remaining 1 cup broth, parsley, oregano, basil, Worcestershire sauce, salt and black pepper. Then add the rice and stir until well-combined.

Coat a 13″ × 9″ baking dish with no-stick spray. Transfer the beef mixture to the baking dish. Cover with foil. Bake about 30 minutes or until heated through. If desired, sprinkle with the Cheddar and bake about 5 minutes more or until the cheese is melted.

Makes 8 main-dish servings.

&. PER SERVING: 141 calories, 0.8 g. total fat, 0.2 g. saturated fat, 0 mg. cholesterol, 187 mg. sodium

Barbecued Pork on a Bun

Adapted from *Family and Company*
JUNIOR LEAGUE OF BINGHAMTON

Everyone will enjoy these great-tasting sandwiches at your next get-together. What's more, you can even prepare the meat mixture a day ahead and refrigerate it until the time of the party. You'll be spared last-minute preparation—and any surface fat in the dish will solidify upon chilling so you can easily lift it off.

4	green peppers, chopped
2	cups chopped sweet white onions
2	tablespoons + 1 cup water
2½	pounds boneless pork loin, trimmed of all visible fat and cut into 1″ cubes
1	can (6 ounces) no-salt-added tomato paste
½	cup cider vinegar
½	cup packed brown sugar
¼	cup mild chili powder
2	tablespoons prepared mustard
1	tablespoon Worcestershire sauce
1	teaspoon salt
14	whole-grain hamburger buns or 28 French rolls (about 3″ long), split and toasted

In a Dutch oven, cook and stir over medium heat the peppers and onions in 2 tablespoons of the water until tender, stirring often.

Add the remaining 1 cup water, pork, tomato paste, vinegar, brown sugar, chili powder, mustard, Worcestershire sauce and salt. Bring to a boil, then reduce the heat to low. Cover and gently simmer for 2½ to 3 hours or until the meat easily pulls apart when tested with a fork. Stir often during cooking.

Using 2 forks, shred the meat by pulling it apart. Cover and refrigerate the mixture about 3 hours or until the fat solidifies on the surface.

Lift the fat from the surface and discard. Heat the mixture over medium-high heat until hot, stirring often. Serve ½ cup of the mixture inside each hamburger bun or ¼ cup inside each French roll.

Makes 14 main-dish servings.

ช● PER SERVING: 274 calories, 8 g. total fat, 2.3 g. saturated fat, 36 mg. cholesterol, 493 mg. sodium.

Black-Eyed Pea Jambalaya

Adapted from *Talk about Good!*
JUNIOR LEAGUE OF LAFAYETTE

This dish combines two Southern stars—black-eyed peas and jambalaya, the traditional Creole rice dish—into one main feature that's high in fiber and low in fat.

1	medium onion, chopped
½	cup finely chopped green peppers
8	ounces ground pork loin or ground beef (95% lean)
1	cup diced low-sodium, 96% fat-free cooked ham
2¼	cups long-grain white rice
1	can (14½ ounces) reduced-sodium chicken broth, defatted
3	cups water
2	teaspoons steak sauce
2	teaspoons Worcestershire sauce
1	can (15 ounces) black-eyed peas, rinsed and drained

Lightly coat an unheated large skillet with no-stick spray. Add the onions and peppers. Cook and stir over medium heat about 3 minutes or until the onions are tender.

Add the pork or beef and ham. Cook and stir for 1 minute. Then add the rice. Continue cooking and stirring until the pork is no longer pink or the beef is browned.

Stir in the broth, water, steak sauce and Worcestershire sauce. Bring to a boil, then reduce the heat. Cover and simmer about 20 minutes or until the rice is tender.

Stir in the peas and heat through.

TEST KITCHEN TIP: Jambalaya often contains tomatoes. If you'd like to add some, stir 1 can (16 ounces) recipe-style stewed tomatoes (with juice) into the rice mixture when you add the black-eyed peas. Then heat through and serve.

Makes 8 main-dish servings.

    PER SERVING: 313 calories, 4 g. total fat, 1.3 g. saturated fat, 23 mg. cholesterol, 515 mg. sodium

Chicken Tetrazzini

Adapted from *The Pasquotank Plate*
CHRIST EPISCOPAL CHURCHWOMEN

We used sharp reduced-fat Cheddar in this dish instead of mild Cheddar to intensify the cheese flavor. Lower-fat cheeses often have less flavor than their regular counterparts, so it pays to use the most piquant version you can find.

1	cup chopped onions
½	cup chopped green peppers
1	clove garlic, minced
1	tablespoon + 1 cup defatted reduced-sodium chicken broth
8	ounces fresh mushrooms, sliced
2	tablespoons cornstarch
1	can (12 ounces or 1½ cups) evaporated skim milk
½	teaspoon salt
¼	teaspoon ground black pepper
1⅓	cups finely shredded reduced-fat sharp Cheddar cheese
2	cups cooked and cubed chicken breasts
2	tablespoons sherry or 1 teaspoon sherry extract
8	ounces spaghetti, cooked

Preheat the oven to 350°. Lightly coat an unheated medium saucepan with no-stick spray. Add the onions, green peppers, garlic and 1 tablespoon of the broth. Cook and stir over medium heat about 5 minutes or until the onions are tender. Then add the mushrooms and cook and stir for 1 minute more. Using a slotted spoon, transfer the vegetables to a large bowl and set aside.

Using a wire whisk, stir the cornstarch into the liquid in the saucepan. Then stir in the remaining 1 cup broth, milk, salt and black pepper. Cook and stir over medium heat until the mixture begins to thicken and just comes to a boil.

Stir 1 cup of the cheese into the milk mixture. Cook and stir until melted. Remove from the heat. Stir in the chicken and sherry or sherry extract.

Add the cheese mixture to the vegetables in the bowl. Then add the spaghetti. Toss until combined.

OUR CAUSE

Christ Episcopal Churchwomen

The community of Elizabeth City, North Carolina, is small; fewer than 15,000 people live there. The parish of Christ Episcopal Church is even smaller, with only about 300 communicants. Still, the parish and its Episcopal Churchwomen have a large presence in their town.

The congregation is an old one, first designated a parish in 1701 by the North Carolina Assembly. The current church building was constructed in 1857 and, with its medieval-style architecture, has become one of Elizabeth City's most familiar landmarks. Over the years, the close-knit members of the parish have put their hearts and souls into their church and their community.

Thanks to parishioners, the church has a beautiful collection of stained-glass windows, needlepoint kneeler-cushions designed and handmade by women in the parish and a lovely garden to memorialize deceased members of the parish. Lately, the Episcopal Churchwomen of Christ Church have turned their attention to the community, with the special goal of helping children in need. Sales of *The Pasquotank Plate*, which highlights the good cooking of the Carolina Coast, will help them in those efforts.

Coat a 2-quart casserole with no-stick spray, then transfer the mixture to the casserole. Cover and bake for 30 minutes. Sprinkle with the remaining ⅓ cup cheese. Bake, uncovered, for 5 minutes more or until the cheese is melted.

Makes 8 main-dish servings.

&. PER SERVING: 272 calories, 4.5 g. total fat, 2 g. saturated fat, 34 mg. cholesterol, 537 mg. sodium

Chicken Lasagna

Adapted from *Uptown Down South*
JUNIOR LEAGUE OF GREENVILLE

Here's a new twist on the ever-so-popular potluck dish, lasagna. This version uses mafalda, narrow ruffled-edge noodles, instead of lasagna noodles. They're less fuss to cook and layer in the dish. When buying noodles, always read the labels and choose those made without egg yolks.

8	ounces mafalda or wide yolk-free egg noodles
¼	cup tub-style reduced-calorie margarine
4¼	cups (34 ounces total) defatted reduced-sodium chicken broth
½	cup all-purpose flour
½	teaspoon dried basil leaves, crushed
½	teaspoon ground black pepper
¼	teaspoon salt
5	cups cooked and cubed chicken breasts
4	egg whites, lightly beaten
1	container (24 ounces) fat-free cottage cheese
2	cups (8 ounces) finely shredded reduced-fat mozzarella cheese
¼	cup grated Parmesan cheese

Preheat the oven to 350°. Cook the pasta according to the package directions, but without adding salt. Drain, rinse with water and drain again. Set aside.

Meanwhile, in a medium saucepan, melt the margarine. Using a wire whisk, stir in ¼ cup of the broth. Then stir in the flour, basil, pepper and salt until smooth. Stir in the remaining 4 cups broth. Cook and stir over medium heat until the mixture begins to thicken and just comes to a boil. Stir in the chicken and set aside.

In medium bowl, stir together the egg whites and cottage cheese. Coat a 13″ × 9″ baking dish with no-stick spray.

To assemble the lasagna, spoon about a third of the chicken-sauce mixture into the dish. Then layer half the noodles, half the cottage cheese mixture, half the mozzarella and another third of the chicken-sauce mixture. Repeat layers with the remaining noodles, cottage cheese mixture, mozzarella and chicken-sauce mixture. Sprinkle with the Parmesan.

Bake, uncovered, for 45 to 60 minutes or until heated through.
Let stand for 10 minutes before serving.

Makes 12 main-dish servings.

> 🥄 PER SERVING: 299 calories, 9 g. total fat, 1.7 g. saturated fat,
> 42 mg. cholesterol, 512 mg. sodium

Scrambled Egg Casserole

Adapted from *Two and Company*
ST. THOMAS CHURCH

*No need to banish eggs from your brunch menu. By using half the
standard amount of whole eggs and combining them with egg
substitute, we cut way back on cholesterol. The main reason we
didn't opt for using only egg substitute is that some whole eggs
were necessary to keep the dish light and fluffy.*

SCRAMBLED EGGS
    1½   cups fat-free egg substitute
    6   eggs
    3   tablespoons skim milk

SAUCE
    ¼   cup chopped onions
    1   can (10¾ ounces each) condensed cream of
         mushroom soup with ⅓ less salt and 99% fat-free
         (see tip on page 28)
    ¼   cup sherry, nonalcoholic wine or skim milk
    1   cup (4 ounces) finely shredded reduced-calorie sharp
         Cheddar cheese

Preheat the oven to 300°. Coat a 2-quart casserole with no-stick
spray and set aside.

FOR THE SCRAMBLED EGGS: In a medium bowl, beat together the egg substitute, eggs and milk.

Lightly coat an unheated, large no-stick skillet with no-stick
spray. Then heat the skillet over medium heat. Add the egg mixture
to the skillet. Cook, stirring occasionally, until the eggs are set, but
still moist. Remove from the heat and set aside.

(continued)

FOR THE SAUCE: Coat a small saucepan with no-stick spray. Add the onions. Cook and stir over medium heat about 3 minutes or until the onions are tender. Stir in the soup and the sherry, wine or milk. Cook and stir over medium heat until warm.

To assemble, in the prepared casserole, layer half each of the eggs, sauce and Cheddar. Then repeat layers with the remaining eggs, sauce and Cheddar.

Bake, uncovered, about 45 minutes or until heated through.

TEST KITCHEN TIP: As another flavor option, use condensed cream of chicken soup (again, in the reduced-fat and reduced-sodium version) in place of the mushroom soup. The chicken soup will also give the dish more of a yellow color.

Makes 10 main-dish servings.

❧ PER SERVING: 116 calories, 5.2 g. total fat, 1.9 g. saturated fat, 134 mg. cholesterol, 380 mg. sodium

---

Overnight Chicken Soufflé

Adapted from *Virginia Seasons*
JUNIOR LEAGUE OF RICHMOND

By using low-fat products, we were able to whittle away fat and cholesterol in this stratalike dish. For a heart-healthy holiday brunch, serve the soufflé with a big bowl of fresh fruit.

    8   cups French bread cubes, slightly dried
    1   pound cooked and cubed chicken breasts
    1   cup chopped celery
    ¾   cup finely chopped onions
    ¾   cup finely chopped green peppers
    ½   cup reduced-fat mayonnaise
    3   cups skim milk
    1   cup fat-free egg substitute
    2   teaspoons cornstarch
    1   can (10¾ ounces) condensed cream of mushroom or
        chicken soup with ⅓ less salt and 99% fat-free
    1   cup (4 ounces) finely shredded reduced-fat sharp
        Cheddar cheese

Junior League of Richmond

Back in 1926 the Junior League of Richmond consisted of just 59 young women, all dedicated to helping make life better for the citizens of their historic Virginia city. Today, the League has more than 1,400 members who contribute 30,000 volunteer hours every year to causes that serve families, children and education.

The busy group initiates projects and helps fund and run existing programs that it believes are important in the community. The $1.5 million that the League has raised since it was founded has gone to many projects. Current favorites include the Metro Literacy Council of Richmond and Sacred Heart Family Resource Center.

In an area whose bounty was literally a lifesaver for settlers from the time that Captain John Smith arrived in 1607, the League's cookbook has naturally been an important part of the group's fund-raising activities. Since its first printing in 1984, more than 60,000 copies of *Virginia Seasons* have been sold to help the League continue its good work.

Coat a 13″ × 9″ baking pan or dish with no-stick spray. Evenly spread 2½ cups of the bread cubes in the bottom of the pan.

In a medium bowl, stir together the chicken, celery, onions, peppers and mayonnaise. Spread the mixture on top of the bread cubes in the pan. Then top with the remaining 5½ cups bread cubes.

In the medium bowl, stir together the milk, egg substitute and cornstarch. Then pour the mixture over the bread and chicken in the pan. Cover with plastic wrap and refrigerate for 12 to 16 hours.

Preheat the oven to 350°. Uncover and bake for 15 minutes. Pour the soup over the egg mixture in the pan, then bake for 30 minutes. Sprinkle with the Cheddar and bake about 10 minutes more or until the cheese melts.

Makes 12 main-dish servings.

   PER SERVING: 208 calories, 7.5 g. total fat, 2 g. saturated fat, 19 mg. cholesterol, 503 mg. sodium.

Paella Salad

Adapted from *Thymes Remembered*
JUNIOR LEAGUE OF TALLAHASSEE

This salad originally got its pretty color from a yellow rice mix. Unfortunately, the mix also had a high amount of sodium. But you can make rice yellow without extra sodium by using saffron or turmeric.

SEASONED SHRIMP
- 1 cup water
- ½ teaspoon Old Bay seasoning or seasoned salt
- ⅛ teaspoon dry mustard
- 4 ounces small shrimp, shelled and deveined

SALAD DRESSING
- ¼ cup defatted reduced-sodium chicken broth
- 2 tablespoons olive or canola oil
- 2 tablespoons tarragon vinegar

RICE
- 2½ cups water
- 1¼ cups long-grain white rice
- ¼ teaspoon ground saffron or turmeric
- ⅛ teaspoon onion powder

SALAD
- 2 cups cooked and cubed chicken breasts
- 4 ounces fully cooked smoked turkey sausage, halved lengthwise and sliced
- 1 cup frozen small peas, thawed
- 1 tomato, seeded and chopped
- 1 small green pepper, chopped
- ½ cup finely chopped onions
- ⅓ cup thinly sliced celery

FOR THE SEASONED SHRIMP: In a medium saucepan, bring the water, seasoning or seasoned salt and mustard to a boil. Add the shrimp. Return to a boil, then reduce the heat. Simmer, uncovered, for 1 to 3 minutes or until the shrimp turn pink, stirring occasionally. Drain and chill.

NO TIME TO COOK?

When you're rushed, look to these fast and easy suggestions for potluck ideas.

• Cut a loaf or two of Italian or French bread into serving-size pieces. Brush with a little bit of olive oil and sprinkle with Parmesan or Romano cheese. Wrap in foil and heat.

• Slice a platterful of cucumbers and tomatoes (or use cherry tomatoes for extra ease).

• Prepare a plate of julienned vegetables. Do the slicing yourself or buy the veggies at your supermarket's salad bar.

• Cut pita bread into wedges and serve with hummus from your supermarket's deli counter.

• Arrange whole-grain crisp bread or fat-free crackers with reduced-fat Cheddar, Monterey Jack or Swiss cheese cubes on a bread board. If desired, place a bowl of green or black olives on the board.

• Mix a jar of citrus sections, peach slices and pineapple chunks. Chill before serving. If desired, sprinkle some fresh raspberries or blueberries over the top.

FOR THE SALAD DRESSING: In a small bowl, use a wire whisk to stir together the broth, oil and vinegar until well-combined.

FOR THE RICE: In a medium saucepan, combine the water, rice, saffron or turmeric and onion powder. Bring to a boil, then reduce the heat. Cover and simmer about 20 minutes or until the rice is tender and the liquid is absorbed.

Transfer the rice to a large bowl. Add the dressing, then cool to room temperature.

FOR THE SALAD: Add the shrimp, chicken, sausage, peas, tomatoes, peppers, onions and celery to the rice. Toss until combined. Cover and chill for at least 4 hours to blend the flavors.

Makes 4 main-dish servings.

&. PER SERVING: 510 calories, 15.8 g. total fat, 2.3 g. saturated fat,
   111 mg. cholesterol, 409 mg. sodium

Chicken Cashew Salad

Adapted from *Heart and Soul*
JUNIOR LEAGUE OF MEMPHIS

When eating healthy, you can still enjoy nuts in your favorite dishes by cooking smart. In this salad, we reduced the amount of cashews from 2 cups to 1 cup and chopped them so that the flavor is better distributed throughout the salad.

CHICKEN

3 pounds skinless, boneless chicken breasts

SALAD

2½ cups chopped celery
2 cans (8 ounces each) sliced water chestnuts, drained
1 can (15¼ ounces) pineapple chunks (packed in juice), drained
¾ cup snipped dates
1½ cups reduced-fat mayonnaise
1–2 tablespoons reduced-sodium soy sauce
2 teaspoons curry powder
Lettuce leaves
1 cup cashews, coarsely chopped

FOR THE CHICKEN: Bring about 1" of water to a boil in a large skillet. Carefully add the chicken. Cover and simmer for 15 to 20 minutes or until the chicken is tender and no longer pink. Drain and chill.

FOR THE SALAD: Cut the chicken into bite-size pieces, then transfer it to a large bowl. Add the celery, water chestnuts, pineapple and dates.

In a small bowl, stir together the mayonnaise, soy sauce and curry powder. Add the mayonnaise mixture to the chicken mixture and toss until coated. Cover and chill in the refrigerator for up to 6 hours.

To serve, line a large serving bowl with the lettuce. Stir ¾ cup of the cashews into the salad, then transfer the salad to the serving bowl. Top with the remaining ¼ cup cashews.

TEST KITCHEN TIP: At first glance, this salad may appear high in fat (in fact, 40% of the calories do come from fat). But when you serve the salad with pita bread or rolls—for a hearty entrée—the percent of calories from fat falls. Remember that it's your overall diet that's important, not the percentage of a single dish.

Makes 12 main-dish servings.

❧ PER SERVING: 397 calories, 17.7 g. total fat, 3.6 g. saturated fat, 45 mg. cholesterol, 269 mg. sodium

---

Apricot Nectar Salad

Adapted from *Thymes Remembered*
JUNIOR LEAGUE OF TALLAHASSEE

Oranges, grapes and apples pack lots of fiber into this salad that comes from the Junior League of Tallahassee.

1 package (4-serving-size) sugar-free lemon-flavored gelatin
1 can (12 ounces or 1½ cups) apricot nectar
⅓ cup cold water
1 tablespoon fresh lemon juice
1 can (11 ounces) mandarin orange sections
   (packed in water), drained
¾ cup seedless green grapes, cut in half
½ cup diced unpeeled apples
   Sliced apples, small grape clusters or mandarin
   orange sections (optional)

Place the gelatin in a medium bowl. In a small saucepan, bring the apricot nectar to a boil. Stir the nectar into the gelatin. Stir until the gelatin is dissolved.

Stir in the water and lemon juice. Chill in the refrigerator about 1½ hours or until partially set (the consistency of unbeaten egg whites).

Gently stir in the oranges, grapes and diced apples. Lightly coat a 4-cup mold with no-stick spray, then transfer the gelatin mixture to the mold. Cover and chill about 3 hours or until firm.

To serve, unmold the salad onto a serving platter or plate. If desired, garnish with the additional fruit.

Makes 8 side-dish servings.

❧ PER SERVING: 59 calories, 0.1 g. total fat, 0 g. saturated fat, 0 mg. cholesterol, 34 mg. sodium

Russian Raspberry Cream Mold

Adapted from *A Taste of Aloha*
JUNIOR LEAGUE OF HONOLULU

*The sweetened sour-cream topping is the trademark of this salad.
We used skim milk and reduced-fat sour cream to keep the fat
down to only 1 gram per serving.*

GELATIN LAYER

    1   package (4-serving-size) sugar-free raspberry-flavored
         gelatin

    1   cup boiling water

  ½   cup cold water

    1   cup fresh or frozen unsweetened red raspberries, thawed

SOUR CREAM LAYER

  ¼   cup sugar

    1   envelope unflavored gelatin

  ½   cup water

    1   container (8 ounces) reduced-fat sour cream

    1   cup skim milk

    1   teaspoon clear vanilla

FOR THE GELATIN LAYER: Place the gelatin in a medium
bowl. Stir in the boiling water until the gelatin is dissolved. Then stir
in the cold water. Chill in the refrigerator about 1 hour or until partially set (the consistency of unbeaten egg whites).

Gently stir in the raspberries. Lightly coat a 6-cup mold or an
8" × 8" baking dish with no-stick spray. Then transfer the gelatin
mixture to the mold or baking dish. Cover and chill in the refrigerator about 1 hour or until firm.

FOR THE SOUR CREAM LAYER: Meanwhile, in a small saucepan, stir together the sugar and gelatin. Then stir in the water. Cook
and stir over low heat until the sugar and gelatin are dissolved. Remove from the heat.

Using a wire whisk, stir in the sour cream until smooth. Then stir
in the milk and vanilla until combined. Slowly pour the sour cream
mixture over the gelatin layer. Then chill in the refrigerator about 4
hours or until firm.

To serve, unmold the molded salad onto a serving platter or plate
or cut the salad in the baking dish into squares.

TEST KITCHEN TIP: If you're a strawberry lover, *A Taste of Aloha* suggests using strawberry-flavored gelatin and strawberries instead of the raspberries.

Makes 12 side-dish servings.

🍴 PER SERVING: 56 calories, 1 g. total fat, 0.6 g. saturated fat, 0 mg. cholesterol, 52 mg. sodium

---

Layered Strawberry Gelatin Salad

Adapted from *Land of Cotton*

JOHN T. MORGAN ACADEMY

This popular layered salad can also double as a dessert.

CRUST

6½	ounces unsalted pretzels
3	tablespoons tub-style reduced-calorie margarine
3	tablespoons apricot all-fruit spread

CREAM CHEESE LAYER

2	containers (8 ounces each) soft-style light cream cheese
½	cup sugar
1¼	cups (4 ounces) thawed reduced-calorie frozen whipped topping

STRAWBERRY LAYER

2	packages (4-serving-size each) sugar-free strawberry-flavored gelatin
1	cup boiling water
1	cup cold water
5	cups (20 ounces) frozen unsweetened strawberries, thawed and sliced

FOR THE CRUST: Preheat the oven to 350°. Lightly coat a 13″ × 9″ baking dish with no-stick spray and set aside.

In a blender or food processor, process small batches of the pretzels until finely ground. (You should have 2½ cups of crumbs.) Set the crumbs aside.

In a small saucepan, heat and stir the margarine and apricot

(continued)

spread until melted. Remove from the heat. Stir in the pretzels. Pat the mixture on the bottom of the prepared baking dish. Bake for 10 minutes. Cool on a wire rack.

FOR THE CREAM CHEESE LAYER: Meanwhile, stir together the cream cheese and sugar until well-blended. Gently stir in the whipped topping. Spread the cheese mixture on top of the cooled crust. Cover and refrigerate until you are ready to top it with the strawberry layer.

FOR THE STRAWBERRY LAYER: Place the gelatin in a medium bowl. Stir in the boiling water. Continue stirring until the gelatin is dissolved. Then stir in the cold water.

Add the strawberries and stir. Chill in the refrigerator about 45 minutes or until partially set (the consistency of unbeaten egg whites).

Spoon the strawberry mixture on top of the cheese layer. Then cover and chill in the refrigerator about 2 hours or until firm. Cut into squares to serve.

TEST KITCHEN TIP: For a smaller party, the ingredients for this salad can be easily halved and put into an 8″ × 8″ baking dish.

Makes 12 side-dish servings.

  PER SERVING: 261 calories, 13.7 g. total fat, 5.8 g. saturated fat, 30 mg. cholesterol, 463 mg. sodium

Crystal's Coleslaw

Adapted from *Candlelight and Wisteria*
LEE-SCOTT ACADEMY

The secret to this tasty coleslaw is in its dressing—it's slightly sweet with a touch of tanginess. Just cutting back a little on the sugar reduced calories without affecting the flavor.

DRESSING

½	cup sugar
1	tablespoon cornstarch
⅔	cup water
⅓	cup cider vinegar
2	egg whites, lightly beaten
1	egg, lightly beaten

SALAD

4	cups chopped red or green cabbage (see tip)
2½	cups chopped cauliflower
6	green onions, thinly sliced
4	slices turkey bacon, finely cut up, cooked and drained

FOR THE DRESSING: In a small heavy saucepan, stir together the sugar and cornstarch. Then stir in the water, vinegar, egg whites and eggs. Cook and stir over low heat until the mixture begins to thicken and just comes to a boil. Remove from the heat and cool to room temperature, stirring occasionally.

FOR THE SALAD: In a large bowl, combine the cabbage, cauliflower and onions.

Pour the dressing over the cabbage mixture and toss until coated. Sprinkle the bacon on top. Cover and chill in the refrigerator for at least 2 hours to blend the flavors.

TEST KITCHEN TIP: This salad is very pretty with red cabbage. But if you use red cabbage, do not chill the salad for more than 2 or 3 hours. As this salad stands, the red from the cabbage bleeds onto the cauliflower.

Makes 14 side-dish servings.

 PER SERVING: 56 calories, 1.1 g. total fat, 0.3 g. saturated fat, 17 mg. cholesterol, 20 mg. sodium

Layered Salad Supreme

Adapted from *Uptown Down South*
JUNIOR LEAGUE OF GREENVILLE

Traditional recipes for this salad call for a lot more nuts. But water chestnuts are a wonderfully crunchy and low-fat substitute for nuts. To reduce the fat even more, omit the pecans altogether.

1	package (10 ounces) fresh spinach, stems removed and torn
3	teaspoons sugar
5	slices turkey bacon, finely cut up, cooked and drained
4	hard-cooked egg whites (discard yolks), chopped
2	cups torn iceberg lettuce
2	cups sliced fresh mushrooms
1	can (8 ounces) water chestnuts, drained and coarsely chopped
1	package (10 ounces) frozen peas, thawed and well-drained
1½	cups reduced-fat mayonnaise
1	cup (4 ounces) finely shredded reduced-fat Swiss or Cheddar cheese
1	cup seeded and chopped tomatoes
½	cup toasted and chopped pecans

To assemble the salad, place the spinach in a 13″ × 9″ casserole or baking dish. Sprinkle with 1 teaspoon of the sugar. Then layer on top the bacon, egg whites and lettuce. Sprinkle with another 1 teaspoon of the sugar. Finally, layer on top the mushrooms, water chestnuts and peas. Sprinkle with the remaining 1 teaspoon sugar.

Carefully spread the mayonnaise on top. Cover and chill in the refrigerator for up to 24 hours.

Just before serving, top the salad with the Swiss or Cheddar, tomatoes and pecans.

TEST KITCHEN TIP: To turn this into a main-dish salad, add a layer of cubed smoked chicken or turkey breast.

Makes 18 side-dish servings.

❧ PER SERVING: 173 calories, 11.2 g. total fat, 1.7 g. saturated fat, 7 mg. cholesterol, 155 mg. sodium

Black-Eyed Pea Salad

Adapted from *Deep in the Heart*
DALLAS JUNIOR FORUM

For this salad, the Dallas Junior Forum jazzed up a store-bought salad dressing with a Southwest flavor. In this low-fat version, we used zesty herb dressing. But reduced-fat Italian, red-wine-and-vinegar or French dressing would also be delicious.

DRESSING

1 package (0.9 ounces) fat-free zesty herb salad dressing mix

1 jalapeño pepper, seeded and finely chopped (wear disposable gloves when handling)

½ teaspoon dried basil, crushed

½ teaspoon chili powder

½ teaspoon ground black pepper

⅛ teaspoon hot-pepper sauce

SALAD

1 can (15 ounces) black-eyed peas, rinsed and drained

¾ cup sliced green onions

¾ cup chopped green peppers

4 ounces fully cooked, reduced-fat smoked sausages, chopped

¾ cup peeled, seeded and chopped cucumbers

¾ cup seeded and coarsely chopped tomatoes

FOR THE DRESSING: Prepare the dressing mix according to the package directions. In a large bowl, stir together ½ cup of the dressing, jalapeño peppers, basil, chili powder, black pepper and hot-pepper sauce. (Reserve the remaining portion of salad dressing for another use.)

FOR THE SALAD: Add the peas, onions, peppers and sausages to the dressing mixture. Toss until coated. Cover and chill in the refrigerator for 24 hours.

One hour before serving, add the cucumbers and tomatoes. Toss until coated. Cover and chill. Then toss again just before serving.

Makes 12 side-dish servings.

&. PER SERVING: 54 calories, 0.9 g. total fat, 0.3 g. saturated fat, 6 mg. cholesterol, 433 mg. sodium

Sour Cream Potato Salad

Adapted from *Sea Island Seasons*
BEAUFORT COUNTY OPEN LAND TRUST

Whether it's a picnic, family reunion or church social, potato salad always finds a place at the table. To lighten up this old-time favorite without compromising its taste and texture, we simply switched to reduced-fat and fat-free products and discarded 2 of the 4 hard-cooked egg yolks.

7	medium potatoes (2¼ pounds total)
4	hard-cooked eggs
1	cup reduced-fat mayonnaise
¾	cup sliced celery
½	cup fat-free sour cream
⅓	cup clear reduced-fat French or fat-free Italian salad dressing
⅓	cup sliced green onions
1½	teaspoons prepared horseradish mustard
¼	teaspoon salt
¼–½	teaspoon celery seeds
⅓	cup peeled, seeded and diced cucumbers
	Thinly sliced green onion tops or chopped fresh chives (optional)

In a large covered saucepan, cook the potatoes in boiling water for 20 to 25 minutes or just until tender.

Meanwhile, for the dressing, separate the yolks from the egg whites. Discard 2 of the yolks. Sieve the remaining 2 yolks into a medium bowl. Chop the egg whites, then add them to the bowl. Stir in the mayonnaise, celery, sour cream, salad dressing, onions, mustard, salt and celery seeds. Set the dressing mixture aside.

Drain the potatoes well. Using a sharp knife, slice the potatoes ¼" thick and transfer them to a very large bowl. Pour the dressing mixture over the warm potatoes. Gently toss until coated. Cover and chill in the refrigerator for at least 2 hours, but not longer than 12 hours.

Beaufort County Open Land Trust

If you saw the movie *The Prince of Tides*, you know how beautiful South Carolina's historic Low Country is. The movie was filmed there, and the residents of this area, which stretches between Charleston and Hilton Head, are justifiably proud of their domain, with its marshes and its stunning views of the Intercoastal Waterway.

Back in 1971, three concerned citizens formed the Beaufort County Open Land Trust, the first such trust in South Carolina. Today, the land trust owns 20 properties and has protected countless acres of open space and sweeping vistas for South Carolinians and visitors alike to enjoy. The earnings from the *Sea Island Seasons* cookbook help fund the trust's efforts.

Beaufort is a traditional southern town with a population of only 12,000, but that hasn't stopped the trust from selling 55,000 copies of its book. The reasons for its success are twofold: The book is faithful to the culinary traditions of the Low Country, and purchasers know that the proceeds support a group that Beaufort County residents consider guardians of the area's beauty.

Just before serving, add the cucumbers and gently toss. If desired, sprinkle with the onion tops or chives to garnish.

Makes 16 side-dish servings.

> PER SERVING: 122 calories, 5 g. total fat, 1.2 g. saturated fat, 27 mg. cholesterol, 224 mg. sodium

Chili Corn

Adapted from *Seasoned with Sun*
JUNIOR LEAGUE OF EL PASO

Sometimes it can be a give-and-take situation when substituting lower-fat and reduced-sodium products for their regular counterparts, as in this scalloped corn dish. We chose to use fat-free saltines in this recipe—they contain about 120 milligrams of sodium per 5 crackers. Opting for low-sodium saltines would have cut sodium but increased fat. So if sodium is a major concern in your diet, you may want to use the crackers that are lowest in sodium.

¼	cup skim milk
¼	teaspoon cornstarch
3	cans (16 ounces each) white shoepeg corn, drained
3 – 4	cans (4 ounces each) diced green chili peppers, drained
1	can (12 ounces or 1½ cups) evaporated skim milk
1½	cups (5 ounces) finely shredded reduced-fat sharp Cheddar cheese
¼	cup tub-style reduced-calorie margarine, melted
2	cups fat-free saltine crackers, crushed into fine crumbs

Preheat the oven to 350°. Coat a 3-quart casserole with no-stick spray and set aside.

In a large bowl, use a wire whisk to stir together the skim milk and cornstarch. Stir in the corn, chili peppers, evaporated milk, Cheddar and margarine. Then stir in 1¼ cups of the cracker crumbs until well-combined.

Transfer the corn mixture to the prepared casserole. Sprinkle with the remaining ¾ cup crumbs. Bake about 50 minutes or until a knife inserted in the center comes out clean.

TEST KITCHEN TIP: Shoepeg corn is creamy white in color and sweeter than yellow corn. For a more colorful but less sweet side dish, try using whole kernel baby corn. If you like, stir in 1 cup chopped sweet red peppers.

Makes 24 side-dish servings.

PER SERVING: 141 calories, 3.2 g. total fat, 0.9 g. saturated fat, 5 mg. cholesterol, 528 mg. sodium

Three-Bean Bake

Adapted from *Between Greene Leaves*
GREENE COUNTY HOMEMAKERS EXTENSION ASSOCIATION

These calico baked beans will be a hit at any potluck affair. To save on fat calories, we reduced the amount of bacon and used the turkey version. If you prefer a bigger fat savings or if there will be vegetarians at the gathering, omit the bacon entirely and use a little more liquid smoke for flavor.

8	ounces turkey bacon, cut up
2	medium onions, chopped
½	cup packed brown sugar
¼	cup cider vinegar
1	teaspoon dry mustard
	Dash of liquid smoke
1	can (16 ounces) vegetarian beans in tomato sauce
1	can (15¼ ounces) butter beans, rinsed and drained
1	can (15 ounces) no-salt-added red kidney beans, rinsed and drained

Preheat the oven to 350°. Lightly coat an unheated medium skillet with no-stick spray. Add the bacon. Cook until done, stirring occasionally. Transfer the bacon to a plate lined with paper towels and blot the top of the bacon with additional paper towels.

Add the onions to the skillet. Cook and stir over medium heat about 3 minutes or until the onions are tender. Stir in the brown sugar, vinegar, mustard and liquid smoke. Gently simmer, uncovered, for 10 minutes. Then remove from the heat.

In a 2½-quart casserole, gently stir together the bacon, onion mixture, vegetarian beans, butter beans and kidney beans until well-combined. Cover and bake for 1 hour.

Makes 14 side-dish servings.

ॐ PER SERVING: 174 calories, 4.8 g. total fat, 1.3 g. saturated fat, 16 mg. cholesterol, 277 mg. sodium

Baked White Beans

Adapted from *Still Gathering*
AUXILIARY TO THE AMERICAN OSTEOPATHIC ASSOCIATION

What's loaded with dietary fiber, yet low in calories, fat and sodium? Beans, of course! To keep these baked beans healthy, we used turkey bacon instead of pork bacon and added a dash of liquid smoke for flavor. To cut back on sodium, we discarded the salty brine from the canned beans and replaced the liquid with fruit juice.

    4   cans (15 ounces each) Great Northern beans, rinsed and drained
    2   small onions, chopped
  ⅔   cup unsweetened pineapple or apple juice
    8   ounces turkey bacon, cut up, cooked and drained
    2   tablespoons packed brown sugar
    2   tablespoons molasses
       Dash of liquid smoke

Preheat the oven to 325°. In a 2½-quart casserole, stir together the beans, onions, pineapple or apple juice, bacon, brown sugar, molasses and liquid smoke until well-combined. Cover and bake for 1 hour.

Makes 16 side-dish servings.

  PER SERVING: 171 calories, 4.4 g. total fat, 1.2 g. saturated fat, 14 mg. cholesterol, 601 mg. sodium

Auxiliary to the
American Osteopathic Association

Still Gathering is a bit of a play on words. It does, certainly, refer to the fact that the American Osteopathic Association has been gathering annually since 1897 for meetings. But it is also a tribute to Dr. Andrew Taylor Still, who in 1892 established the first school of osteopathy in Kirksville, Missouri.

Now, there are more than 30,000 osteopathic physicians in the United States. The Auxiliary to the American Osteopathic Association formed in 1939 to promote and support public health education, to provide scholarships for students and funds for research and to foster volunteerism in hospitals and community health programs. The auxiliary is dedicated to health education nationally. On local levels, programs help prevent child abuse and substance abuse.

Still Gathering is a collection of recipes from auxiliary members nationwide. Sales of the book enable the group to continue projects such as Care-A-Van, a free health-screening van that has served 65,000 people around the country.

Hash Brown Potato Casserole

Adapted from *The Pasquotank Plate*
CHRIST EPISCOPAL CHURCHWOMEN

Not all hash brown potatoes are created equal—some are loaded with fat. In making over this popular potluck side dish, we made a major fat savings by simply using hash brown potatoes with no added oil.

1   can (10¾ ounces) 99% fat-free condensed cream of chicken soup with ⅓ less salt
1   container (8 ounces) reduced-fat sour cream
¼   cup skim milk
¼   teaspoon salt
1   package (2 pounds) refrigerated or frozen hash brown potatoes with no fat, thawed
2   cups (8 ounces) finely shredded reduced-fat sharp Cheddar cheese
¼   cup chopped onions
1¼   cups crushed corn flakes

Preheat the oven to 350°. Coat a 3-quart casserole with no-stick spray and set aside.

In a large bowl, stir together the soup, sour cream, milk and salt. Then gently stir in the potatoes, Cheddar and onions.

Transfer the mixture to the prepared casserole. Sprinkle with the corn flakes.

Bake for 45 to 60 minutes or just until the potatoes are tender.

Makes 16 side-dish servings.

& PER SERVING: 141 calories, 3 g. total fat, 1.6 g. saturated fat, 6 mg. cholesterol, 430 mg. sodium

Pennsylvania Dutch Potato Dressing

Adapted from *Recipe Jubilee!*
JUNIOR LEAGUE OF MOBILE

Here's an ever-so-popular dish from the heartland of Pennsylvania. We lowered fat and calories by replacing the standard butter with butter-flavor mix and a little margarine. It gives this mashed potato casserole a rich, buttery taste with a fraction of the calories.

8 medium potatoes (about 2½ pounds total), quartered
2 stalks celery, chopped
1 small green pepper, chopped
1 medium onion, chopped
½ cup prepared butter-flavor mix
1 cup + 2 tablespoons plain stuffing croutons, slightly crushed
⅛ teaspoon salt
⅛ teaspoon ground black pepper
1 can (5 ounces or ⅔ cup) evaporated skim milk
½ cup skim milk
3 teaspoons tub-style reduced-calorie margarine

Place the potatoes in a large saucepan. Cover with water. Bring to a boil, then reduce the heat. Cover and gently boil about 20 minutes or until tender.

Meanwhile, in a medium skillet, combine the celery, green peppers, onions and butter-flavor mix. Cook and stir over medium heat about 10 minutes or until the celery is tender. Remove from the heat and stir in the croutons. Set the vegetable mixture aside.

Preheat the oven to 325°. Coat a 1½-quart casserole with no-stick spray and set aside. Drain the potatoes. Use a potato masher to mash the potatoes or beat them with an electric mixer on low speed. Add the salt and black pepper. Then gradually beat in the evaporated milk and skim milk until smooth.

Gently stir the vegetable mixture into the potato mixture. Then transfer to the prepared casserole. Dot the top with the margarine, using ½-teaspoon portions. Bake about 1 hour or until lightly browned.

Makes 14 side-dish servings.

PER SERVING: 103 calories, 0.9 g. total fat, 0.1 g. saturated fat, 1 mg. cholesterol, 84 mg. sodium

Sweet Potato Casserole

Adapted from *Merrymeeting Merry Eating*
MID COAST HOSPITAL/BRUNSWICK AUXILIARY

To satisfy your sweet tooth nutritiously, try this slimmed-down version of a Southern favorite. We used dark brown sugar instead of light brown sugar to achieve the same level of sweetness with less sugar.

TOPPING

¼   cup all-purpose flour
1   tablespoon packed dark brown sugar
1   tablespoon tub-style reduced-calorie margarine
¼   cup chopped pecans

POTATO CASSEROLE

2   egg whites, lightly beaten
1   egg, lightly beaten
½   cup evaporated skim milk
⅓   cup packed dark brown sugar
2   tablespoons tub-style reduced-calorie margarine, melted
2   teaspoons vanilla
1   teaspoon finely shredded orange peel (optional)
¼   teaspoon salt
3   cups cooked and mashed sweet potatoes (see tip)

FOR THE TOPPING: In a small bowl, stir together the flour and brown sugar. Then use your fingers to rub the margarine into the flour mixture until crumbly. Stir in the pecans and set aside.

FOR THE POTATO CASSEROLE: Preheat the oven to 350°. Coat a shallow 2-quart casserole or an 8″ × 8″ baking dish with butter-flavored no-stick spray and set aside.

In a medium bowl, stir together the egg whites, eggs, milk, brown sugar, margarine, vanilla, orange peel (if desired) and salt until well-combined. Then gently stir in the sweet potatoes.

Transfer the potato mixture to the prepared casserole. Sprinkle with the topping mixture. Then generously coat the topping with the butter-flavored no-stick spray. Bake about 35 minutes or until heated through and golden on top.

OUR CAUSE

Mid Coast Hospital/Brunswick Auxiliary

Maine is famed for its wild, rocky seacoast. But it also holds a wealth of rivers, many with picturesque names. Native Americans bestowed such names as the Abagadusset, the Androscoggin, the Cathance, the Kennebec and the Muddy rivers. Merrymeeting Bay is the cheerful name of the point at which these five rivers converge, and it is here that the town of Brunswick was incorporated more than 250 years ago.

The members of the Mid Coast Hospital/Brunswick Auxiliary named their cookbook *Merrymeeting Merry Eating* to salute the historic and natural beauty of their surroundings and to celebrate the wonderful fact that the best eating seems, happily, to coincide with the merriest of occasions. These are the events that call for good food and drink and the sharing of affection, laughter and joy.

The 250 men and women of the auxiliary devote their energy to raising funds for Mid Coast Hospital. Money also goes toward health-career scholarships for worthy area students as well as hospital employees who want to further their education.

TEST KITCHEN TIP: To make 3 cups of mashed sweet potatoes, begin with 5 medium sweet potatoes (about 1¾ pounds). Peel and cut off any woody portions and ends. Then cut the potatoes into quarters and cook them in boiling water about 30 minutes or until tender. Drain well and mash with a potato masher or beat with an electric mixer on low speed.

Makes 8 side-dish servings.

~ PER SERVING: 263 calories, 7 g. total fat, 0.8 g. saturated fat, 26 mg. cholesterol, 162 mg. sodium

Danish Apple Bars

Adapted from *Merrymeeting Merry Eating*
MID COAST HOSPITAL/BRUNSWICK AUXILIARY

These bars taste just like apple pie but are a lot easier to serve at a potluck party. We made this flaky but sturdy pastry with half butter and half light cream cheese instead of all butter to cut back on fat.

PASTRY

- 3 ounces light cream cheese
- ⅓ cup stick margarine (not reduced-calorie)
- 2½ cups all-purpose flour
- ⅛ teaspoon salt
- ⅓ cup + 3 tablespoons skim milk
- ¾ cup fine corn flake crumbs

APPLE FILLING

- 9 cups cored, peeled and sliced cooking apples
- 1 cup sugar
- 1½ teaspoons ground cinnamon
- 1 egg white, lightly beaten

ICING

- ½ cup powdered sugar
- 1 teaspoon stick margarine (not reduced-calorie), melted
  A few drops of almond extract
- 2–3 teaspoons skim milk

FOR THE PASTRY: In a large bowl, use an electric mixer to beat together the cream cheese and margarine just until blended. Add the flour and salt. Using a pastry blender, cut the flour and salt into the cream cheese mixture until the mixture resembles coarse crumbs.

Add ⅓ cup of the milk. Using a fork, toss and stir lightly until moistened. If necessary, add enough of the remaining 3 tablespoons milk to moisten all of the flour mixture.

Divide the mixture in half. Then, using your hands, gently shape each half into a ball. On a lightly floured surface, roll 1 ball of the dough into a 17½" × 12½" rectangle.

Generously coat a 15″ × 10″ baking pan with no-stick spray. Carefully transfer and fit the rectangle-shaped dough into the baking pan. Sprinkle the corn flake crumbs evenly over the dough.

FOR THE APPLE FILLING: Place the apples in another large bowl. In a small bowl, stir together the sugar and cinnamon. Sprinkle the mixture over the apples and toss until coated. Spread the apples evenly on top of the corn flake crumbs in the pan.

Preheat the oven to 350°. On a lightly floured surface, roll the remaining portion of dough into a 15½″ × 10½″ rectangle. Place the dough on top of the apples. Press the edges together to seal. Prick the top several times to vent the steam. Brush the top with the egg white.

Bake for 35 to 45 minutes or until golden. Cool in the pan on a wire rack.

FOR THE ICING: Meanwhile, in another small bowl, stir together the powdered sugar, margarine, almond extract and enough of the milk to make a drizzling consistency.

Drizzle the icing over the top of the pastry. Cut into bars.

Makes 25.

ᴥ PER BAR: 150 calories, 3.5 g. total fat, 0.9 g. saturated fat, 1 mg. cholesterol, 96 mg. sodium

Praline Cheesecake

Adapted from *Gracious Goodness . . . Charleston!*

BISHOP ENGLAND HIGH SCHOOL

Here's a nutty cheesecake that's so rich and creamy, your guests will never believe each serving has only 248 calories and 11 grams of fat. To make it healthier without compromising its good taste, we used a combination of light and fat-free cream cheese. For the crust, we used apple jelly and margarine instead of butter to hold the graham cracker crumbs together.

CRUST

2	tablespoons apple jelly
1	tablespoon reduced-calorie margarine
1½	cups fine cinnamon graham cracker crumbs

FILLING

2	packages (8 ounces each) light cream cheese, softened
1	package (8 ounces) fat-free cream cheese, softened
⅔	cup packed brown sugar
2	tablespoons all-purpose flour
2	teaspoons vanilla
2	eggs
2	egg whites
⅓	cup toasted and finely chopped pecans

TOPPING

¾	cup thawed, reduced-fat frozen whipped topping (optional)
12	pecan halves (optional)

FOR THE CRUST: In a small saucepan, heat and stir the jelly and margarine just until melted. Remove from the heat. Stir in the cracker crumbs until well-combined.

Coat a 9″ springform pan with no-stick spray. Lightly press the crumb mixture in the bottom and about 2″ up the sides of the pan and set aside.

FOR THE FILLING: Preheat the oven to 350°. In a medium bowl, use an electric mixer to beat together the light cream cheese, fat-free cream cheese, brown sugar and flour. Beat in the vanilla.

Add the eggs and egg whites. Beat just until combined. Stir in the pecans.

Pour the filling into the crust. Bake for 40 to 45 minutes or until the filling is almost set in the center. Cool the cheesecake in the pan on a wire rack for 10 minutes. Then loosen the sides of the pan, but do not remove the sides. Cool the cake completely. Remove the sides of the pan and chill the cake in the refrigerator for at least 8 hours before serving.

FOR THE TOPPING: If desired, top each serving with a spoonful of the whipped topping and a pecan half.

Makes 12 servings.

&. PER SERVING: 248 calories, 11 g. total fat, 4.7 g. saturated fat, 52 mg. cholesterol, 417 mg. sodium

---

Cookies and Cream Cheesecake
Adapted from *The Golden Taste of South Carolina*
SOUTH CAROLINA FARM BUREAU FEDERATION

Thanks to reduced-fat commercial products, you can enjoy a delicious cheesecake like this and still have it fit into your healthy lifestyle.

CRUST

1   tablespoon stick margarine (not reduced-calorie)
1   cup reduced-fat chocolate sandwich cookies crushed into fine crumbs

FILLING

2   packages (8 ounces each) light cream cheese, softened
1   package (8 ounces) fat-free cream cheese, softened
⅔   cup sugar
2   tablespoons all-purpose flour
1   teaspoon vanilla
2   eggs
1   egg white
¾   cup coarsely chopped reduced-fat chocolate sandwich cookies

FOR THE CRUST: Preheat the oven to 325°. In a small saucepan, melt the margarine. Remove from the heat. Stir in the cookie crumbs until well-combined.

Lightly coat the bottom of a 9″ springform pan with no-stick spray. Then press the crumb mixture on the bottom. Bake for 10 minutes. Cool on a wire rack.

FOR THE FILLING: In a medium bowl, use an electric mixer to beat together the light cream cheese, fat-free cream cheese, sugar and flour. Then beat in the vanilla.

Add the eggs and egg white. Then beat just until combined. Fold or gently stir in the cookies. Pour the filling over the crust in the pan. Bake in the 325° oven for 45 to 50 minutes or until the filling is almost set in the center.

Cool the cheesecake in the pan on a wire rack for 10 minutes. Then loosen the sides of the pan, but do not remove the sides. Cool the cake completely. Remove the sides of the pan and chill the cake in the refrigerator for at least 8 hours before serving.

Makes 12 servings.

    🍃 PER SERVING: 227 calories, 10.4 g. total fat, 5 g. saturated fat, 52 mg. cholesterol, 423 mg. sodium

Party-Time Tidbits

Caramel Apple Dip

Adapted from *The League Sampler*
CLARKSBURG LEAGUE FOR SERVICE

*Here's a trick-and-treat snack for little goblins on Halloween.
Instead of layering the cream cheese and the caramel topping,
we stirred the two together. This trick makes the dip go farther so
that each apple wedge gets a thin coating of this gooey mixture
rather than a big scoop.*

1   container (8 ounces) soft-style light cream cheese
⅓   cup caramel ice-cream topping
1–2   tablespoons skim milk (optional)
2   tablespoons toasted and chopped almonds or
     chopped peanuts
5   large tart apples, cored and cut into 8 wedges each
     (see tip)

In a small serving bowl, stir together the cream cheese and
caramel topping. If necessary, stir in enough of the milk to make the
mixture a dipping consistency. Sprinkle the almonds or peanuts on
top to garnish.

To serve, place the bowl on a large serving plate and arrange the
apple wedges around the bowl.

TEST KITCHEN TIP: The Clarksburg League for Service recommends serving this dip with Granny Smith apples. We also found
the varieties of Jonathan, McIntosh, Winesap and Golden Delicious
to be delicious with it.

Makes 10 servings.

≈ PER SERVING (2 TABLESPOONS DIP WITH 4 APPLE WEDGES):
   131 calories, 5.1 g. total fat, 2.5 g. saturated fat, 8 mg. cholesterol,
   154 mg. sodium

Florentine Dip

Adapted from *A Taste of Aloha*
JUNIOR LEAGUE OF HONOLULU

Most spinach dips are seasoned with an envelope of vegetable soup mix, making the dips very high in sodium. This tasty version uses Beau Monde—a commercial salt, onion and celery seed seasoning (look for it in the spice section of your market). Although it, too, contains salt, you only use ¾ teaspoon compared with an entire package of soup mix.

1	cup reduced-fat mayonnaise
1	container (8 ounces) fat-free sour cream or fat-free plain yogurt
1	teaspoon reduced-sodium Worcestershire sauce
¾	teaspoon Beau Monde seasoning
1	clove garlic, minced
1	package (10 ounces) frozen chopped spinach, thawed
¾	cup chopped green onions

In a medium bowl, stir together the mayonnaise, sour cream or yogurt, Worcestershire sauce, Beau Monde and garlic.

Drain and squeeze the spinach to remove excess moisture. Add the spinach and onions to the mayonnaise mixture. Stir until well-combined. Cover and chill in the refrigerator for at least 4 hours to blend the flavors.

TEST KITCHEN TIP: For added color and crunch, stir in a small amount of chopped sweet red peppers, shredded carrots and chopped water chestnuts.

Makes 2¾ cups; 22 servings.

❧ PER 2 TABLESPOONS: 50 calories, 3.6 g. total fat, 0.7 g. saturated fat, 0 mg. cholesterol, 84 mg. sodium

Hummus

Adapted from *Gracious Goodness . . . Charleston!*
BISHOP ENGLAND HIGH SCHOOL

Most chick-pea spreads are made with a large amount of tahini, a peanut butter–like paste made from sesame seeds that's high in fat. But this recipe from Gracious Goodness *uses only 2 tablespoons. Serve the hummus with pita bread wedges or baguette slices.*

1	can (15 ounces) chick-peas (garbanzo beans), rinsed and drained
¼	cup (4 tablespoons) fresh lemon juice (see tip)
2	tablespoons tahini (sesame seed paste)
1	clove garlic
	Pinch of salt
1–4	teaspoons water (optional)
	Pinch of paprika, sliced green onions or chopped fresh parsley (optional)

In a blender or food processor, process the chick-peas, lemon juice, tahini, garlic and salt until smooth and creamy. If necessary, stir in enough of the water to make a spreading consistency.

Transfer the mixture to a small serving bowl. If desired, sprinkle with the paprika, onions or parsley to garnish.

TEST KITCHEN TIP: If you prefer less lemon flavor in your hummus, use 2 tablespoons lemon juice and 2 tablespoons water instead of the full amount of lemon juice.

Makes 2 cups; 16 servings.

PER 2 TABLESPOONS: 38 calories, 1.5 g. total fat, 0.1 g. saturated fat, 0 mg. cholesterol, 114 mg. sodium

Crab Ball

Adapted from *The Shadows-on-the-Teche Cookbook*
THE SHADOWS SERVICE LEAGUE

Cream cheese is the base for this cheese ball and critical to its overall flavor. We found that light cream cheese, rather than its fat-free counterpart, gives a better taste. Serve the ball with baguette or party bread slices or pita breads cut into wedges.

1	package (8 ounces) light cream cheese, softened
1½–2	tablespoons prepared horseradish
1	tablespoon reduced-calorie, reduced-sodium ketchup
2	teaspoons finely chopped onions
1½	teaspoons Worcestershire sauce
1	teaspoon fresh lemon juice
8	ounces lump crab meat, flaked; or 1 can (6 ounces) crab meat, drained and flaked; or 6 ounces surimi (imitation crab meat), chopped
	Hot-pepper sauce (to taste)

In a medium bowl, combine the cream cheese, horseradish, ketchup, onions, Worcestershire sauce and lemon juice. Stir or beat with an electric mixer until well-blended.

Add the crab or surimi and stir until combined. Season to taste with the hot-pepper sauce. Form the mixture into a ball. Cover and refrigerate for at least 6 hours before serving.

Makes 2¼ cups; 18 servings.

≈ PER 2 TABLESPOONS: 41 calories, 2.5 g. total fat, 1.4 g. saturated fat, 16 mg. cholesterol, 129 mg. sodium

Rich Hot Crab Dip

Adapted from *Candlelight and Wisteria*
LEE-SCOTT ACADEMY

This hot dip takes full advantage of the quality of today's lower-fat products, such as mayonnaise and cream cheese. And even with these substitutes, the dip is still very creamy and packed with flavor—but it contains only about 3 grams of fat per serving.

1 package (8 ounces) light cream cheese
⅓ cup fat-free mayonnaise
1 teaspoon onion powder
¾ –1 teaspoon dry mustard
Dash of garlic powder
6 ounces crab meat, flaked
2 tablespoons dry sherry, or 2 tablespoons skim milk + ½ teaspoon sherry extract
1 tablespoon finely chopped green peppers (optional)
1 tablespoon drained and finely chopped pimento (optional)
Paprika

In a small heavy saucepan, combine the cream cheese, mayonnaise, onion powder, mustard and garlic powder. Cook and stir over low heat just until the cream cheese is melted.

Stir in the crab and sherry or the mixture of milk and sherry extract. If desired, stir in the peppers and pimento. Cook and stir over low heat until heated through.

To serve, transfer the mixture to a small chafing dish. Lightly sprinkle with the paprika. Keep warm.

TEST KITCHEN TIP: Serve this elegant dip with an assortment of low-salt or fat-free crackers, such as wheat, cracked pepper or sesame. Or serve 1½"-long bias-sliced pieces of celery to scoop up the dip.

Makes 1⅔ cups; 13 servings.

PER 2 TABLESPOONS: 59 calories, 3.3 g. total fat, 1.8 g. saturated fat, 19 mg. cholesterol, 214 mg. sodium

Lee-Scott Academy

The charming Cary-Pick House in Auburn, Alabama, was surely an inspiration for *Candlelight and Wisteria*. Since its 1840 construction, the Greek Revival home has been a sterling example of both elegant Southern living and warm Southern hospitality.

Alice Cary Pick Gibson's family has owned the house since the 1890s, and Mrs. Gibson has continued the home's long tradition of hospitality. Many visitors and dignitaries have enjoyed the warmth of the house and the bounties of its authentic country kitchen. The recipes in *Candlelight and Wisteria* embrace the love of good food—and of romance—associated with the deep South.

Proceeds from the book go toward construction of a fine-arts auditorium at the Lee-Scott Academy, a college preparatory school of about 540 students from preschool through grade 12, of which Mrs. Gibson is a founder. An added bonus: The book is sprinkled liberally with pretty illustrations of the Cary-Pick House drawn by Lee-Scott Academy art teacher Cheryl Mann Hardin.

Tortilla Pinwheels

Adapted from *Seasoned with Sun*
JUNIOR LEAGUE OF EL PASO

When you're in a hurry and need a quick snack, try these lunchmeat roll-ups from the Junior League of El Paso. We recommend using roasted or baked chicken breasts to keep the fat low, but almost any low-fat lunchmeat will be delicious.

¼	cup (2 ounces) soft-style light cream cheese
1	can (4 ounces) diced green chili peppers, drained
¼	cup rinsed and chopped ripe pitted olives or finely chopped sweet red peppers
1	small clove garlic, crushed to a paste
2–3	dashes of hot-pepper sauce
4–5	flour tortillas (8″ in diameter)
1	package (2½ ounces) very thinly sliced roasted chicken breast

In a small bowl, stir together the cream cheese, chili peppers, olives or red peppers, garlic and hot-pepper sauce until well-combined.

Spread the cream cheese mixture onto 1 side of each tortilla. Then place the chicken on top. Roll up tightly, jelly-roll fashion. Wrap each tortilla roll in plastic wrap. Chill in the refrigerator for at least 2 hours before serving.

To serve, unwrap and cut each roll into 1″ slices.

Makes 32 or 40 pinwheels; 16 or 20 servings.

❀ PER 2 PINWHEELS: 41 calories, 1.4 g. total fat, 0.4 g. saturated fat, 4 mg. cholesterol, 188 mg. sodium

Croutons with Tomato and Pesto

Adapted from *Sensational Seasons*
JUNIOR LEAGUE OF FORT SMITH

This new-fashioned pesto from the Junior League of Fort Smith is made with only a fraction of the olive oil that a traditional pesto contains. When served on baguette slices with tomatoes, it makes a wonderfully delicious appetizer or accompaniment to soup or salad.

1   loaf (24") baguette
2   tablespoons olive oil
2   cups packed fresh basil leaves with stems removed
1   cup packed fresh parsley with stems removed
¼   cup pine nuts, toasted
¼   cup defatted reduced-sodium chicken broth
3   tablespoons finely shredded fresh Parmesan cheese
1   clove garlic, halved
4   plum or small tomatoes, thinly sliced
48   small fresh basil leaves

Preheat the oven to 350°. Diagonally slice the bread into 48 slices, cutting each ½" thick. Place the slices on a large baking sheet. Brush one side of the slices with 1 tablespoon of the oil. Bake about 14 minutes or until golden. Set aside.

For the pesto, in a food processor, process the 2 cups basil, parsley, pine nuts, broth, Parmesan, the remaining 1 tablespoon oil and garlic until the pesto mixture is smooth. If necessary, stop and scrape down the sides of the container. (If using a blender, blend the ingredients in two batches.)

To serve, place a tomato slice on top of each toasted bread slice. Then top each with 1 teaspoon of the pesto mixture and a basil leaf.

TEST KITCHEN TIP: For a small party or get-together, you can easily cut this recipe in half. Prepare as above, but use ½ baguette loaf, 3 teaspoons oil, 1 cup basil leaves, ½ cup parsley, 2 tablespoons pine nuts, 2 tablespoons broth, 1½ tablespoons cheese, 1 small clove garlic, 2 plum or small tomatoes and 24 basil leaves.

Makes 48; 24 servings.

ðŸ–‰ PER 2 CROUTONS: 80 calories, 2.9 g. total fat, 0.4 g. saturated fat,
1 mg. cholesterol, 132 mg. sodium

Vegetable Pizza

Adapted from *Family and Company*
JUNIOR LEAGUE OF BINGHAMTON

One way to get your daily recommended share of vegetables is with this popular appetizer. We use refrigerated pizza dough, which is lower in fat than the crescent dough often used for this pizza. We also use yogurt cheese rather than cream cheese as a nonfat base for the vegetables.

1	can (10 ounces) refrigerated pizza dough
1	cup fat-free plain yogurt cheese (see tip), fat-free ricotta cheese or pureed fat-free cottage cheese
¼	cup reduced-fat mayonnaise
1	clove garlic, minced
1½	teaspoons chopped fresh dill or ½ teaspoon dillweed
1½	teaspoons finely chopped fresh chives or ½ teaspoon chopped dried chives
2	cups desired fresh vegetable toppings (finely chopped broccoli, cauliflower and green peppers; coarsely shredded carrots; sliced mushrooms; and seeded and chopped tomatoes)
⅓	cup finely shredded reduced-fat sharp Cheddar or colby cheese
⅓	cup alfalfa sprouts

Preheat the oven to 425°. Coat a baking sheet with no-stick spray. Unroll the pizza dough onto the baking sheet. Press or roll the dough to a 12" × 10" rectangle. Pinch the edges to form a ridge. Bake about 8 minutes or until lightly browned. Cool.

Meanwhile, in a medium bowl, stir together the yogurt cheese or ricotta or cottage cheese, mayonnaise, garlic, dill and chives.

Spread the cheese mixture on the pizza crust. Then top with the desired vegetables, Cheddar or colby cheese and sprouts.

TEST KITCHEN TIP: The advantage of yogurt cheese on this pizza instead of fat-free or light cream cheese is that the yogurt cheese has more flavor.

To make 1½ cups yogurt cheese, begin with 32 ounces fat-free plain yogurt (made without gelatin). Line a strainer with a double layer of cheesecloth or a coffee filter. Place the strainer over a deep bowl.

OUR CAUSE

Junior League of Binghamton

Manhattan may get all the credit as the seat of New York's culture, but the women of the Junior League of Binghamton are—rightfully—proud of all that their city has to offer. Binghamton sits at the meeting point of the Susquehanna and Chanango rivers in southern New York. Like most cities lucky enough to be situated on the water, it has long been a haven for families with the creativity and will to prosper. The result is a city with two colleges, several museums and an abundance of craftspeople and artists who bring vitality and excitement to the community.

For 63 years, Binghamton's Junior League has been an important element in the life of the city. *Family and Company* offers traditional dishes of the area with a contemporary flair. Look for recipes from both local and national celebrities, from Carol Burnett to Elizabeth Taylor and from Willard Scott to Mario Cuomo.

The cookbook serves as a fund-raiser for the League's many causes, particularly those helping women and children. Among the League's pet projects are a hands-on museum for children and the Children's Center, a shelter for abused children.

Spoon the yogurt into the strainer. Cover with plastic wrap. Place the bowl in the refrigerator and let the whey from the yogurt drain into the bowl. Let stand for 14 to 24 hours or until the yogurt is quite thick. Discard the whey and transfer the yogurt cheese to a plastic or glass container. Cover and store in the refrigerator for up to 3 days.

Makes 20 servings.

   PER SERVING: 66 calories, 1.7 g. total fat, 0.3 g. saturated fat, 1 mg. cholesterol, 128 mg. sodium

Baked Stuffed Mushrooms

Adapted from *Savoring the Southwest*
ROSWELL SYMPHONY GUILD

Many stuffed mushrooms are filled with fatty sausage. This recipe from the Roswell Symphony Guild has a savory, low-fat bread-crumb filling instead.

16 large fresh mushrooms (with caps about 1½″ in diameter)
1   tablespoon reduced-calorie butter blend
2   tablespoons + 3 teaspoons dry white wine or nonalcoholic white wine
¼   cup finely chopped fresh parsley
4   teaspoons finely shredded fresh Parmesan cheese
2   teaspoons fine dry bread crumbs
1   clove garlic, minced
¼   teaspoon dried thyme leaves, crushed
¼   teaspoon dried oregano leaves, crushed
    Pinch of salt
    Pinch of freshly ground black pepper

Preheat the oven to 375°. Coat a 13″ × 9″ baking pan with no-stick spray and set aside.

Gently wash the mushrooms and remove their stems. Place the mushroom caps on paper towels to drain. Finely chop the stems.

Melt the butter blend in a medium skillet. Remove the skillet from the heat and stir in 2 tablespoons of the wine. Then remove 1 tablespoon of the butter-wine mixture and set aside.

Add the chopped mushrooms to the remaining butter-wine mixture in the skillet. Cook and stir over low heat until the mixture is dry.

Stir in the parsley, Parmesan, bread crumbs, garlic, thyme, oregano, salt and pepper. Stir in enough of the remaining 3 teaspoons wine to moisten.

Spoon the mushroom mixture into the mushroom caps. Arrange the filled mushrooms in the prepared pan. Bake for 15 to 20 minutes or until heated through and slightly tender, basting occasionally with the remaining butter-wine mixture. Serve hot.

Makes 16.

   ❧ PER MUSHROOM: 15 calories, 0.9 g. total fat, 0.2 g. saturated fat, 0 mg. cholesterol, 18 mg. sodium

Oven-Fried Vegetables

Adapted from *Still Gathering*
AUXILIARY TO THE AMERICAN OSTEOPATHIC ASSOCIATION

*You don't need a deep-fat fryer to make these crispy vegetables.
The Auxiliary to the American Osteopathic Association shows us
an easy low-fat method.*

1   cup fine, dry seasoned bread crumbs
2   tablespoons grated Parmesan cheese
¼   teaspoon garlic powder
¼   teaspoon ground black pepper
1   egg white
2   tablespoons water
1   small zucchini (about 4 ounces), cut into ¼"-thick slices
½   small eggplant (about 4 ounces), cut into ¼"-thick slices
    and quartered
4   ounces small fresh mushrooms
½   large sweet white onion or medium green pepper,
    cut into ¼"-thick slices

Preheat the oven to 450°. Coat a large no-stick baking sheet with
no-stick spray. Set the baking sheet aside.

In a shallow dish or pie plate, combine the bread crumbs, cheese,
garlic powder and black pepper. In another shallow dish or pie plate,
use a fork to beat together the egg white and water.

Using the fork, dip the zucchini, eggplant, mushrooms and
onions or green peppers in the egg white mixture, then in the bread
crumb mixture.

Arrange the coated vegetables on the prepared baking sheet in a
single layer. Bake for 12 to 15 minutes or until the vegetables are tender and the coating is crisp and golden. Serve immediately.

TEST KITCHEN TIP: If you'd like to simplify things, pare
down the list of vegetable choices to 2 and use 4 cups total.

Makes 6 servings.

ᨒ PER SERVING: 94 calories, 1.6 g. total fat, 0.5 g. saturated fat,
    2 mg. cholesterol, 173 mg. sodium

Chinese Dumplings

Adapted from *Settings*
JUNIOR LEAGUE OF PHILADELPHIA

The simple dipping sauce used here adds a finishing touch to these low-fat delights.

DIPPING SAUCE

¼   cup reduced-sodium soy sauce
¼   cup rice wine vinegar
2   teaspoons chopped green onions

DUMPLINGS

27   wonton wrappers
1   egg white, lightly beaten
8   ounces ground pork loin (see tip)
4   ounces cooked and deveined shrimp, finely chopped
1   tablespoon finely chopped water chestnuts, celery or carrots
1½   green onions, finely chopped
¾   teaspoon dry white wine, nonalcoholic white wine or water
¼   teaspoon garlic powder

FOR THE SAUCE: In a small saucepan, stir together the soy sauce, vinegar and onions. Bring to a boil. Then remove from the heat and set aside to cool while preparing the dumplings.

FOR THE DUMPLINGS: Bring the wrappers to room temperature. Meanwhile, in a medium bowl, stir together the egg white, pork, shrimp, water chestnuts, celery or carrots, onions, wine or water and garlic powder. Cover and refrigerate the filling for 30 minutes.

To assemble the dumplings, place one wrapper on the work surface (cover the remaining wrappers to prevent them from drying out). Spoon ½ to 1 tablespoon of the filling in the center of the wrapper. Bring 2 opposite corners to the center and pinch the corners together to seal. Then bring the remaining 2 corners to the center and pinch together to seal. Pinch the 4 edges to seal. Set the dumpling aside on a piece of wax paper. Repeat making more dumplings with the remaining wrappers and filling. Fold the ends toward the middle and pinch closed at the top.

In a large skillet with a rack, bring ½" of water to a boil. Place the dumplings on the rack, making sure the dumplings sit above the water. Cover tightly and steam for 4 to 5 minutes or until the pork mixture is no longer pink. (Or, use a wok and steam according to the manufacturer's directions.)

Serve the dumplings with the dipping sauce.

TEST KITCHEN TIP: Ground pork usually gets a very high percentage of its calories from fat. To get leaner ground pork, ask the butcher to grind a pork tenderloin for you. Another way to reduce fat in recipes calling for ground pork is to replace half the meat with ground turkey breast, which is very lean.

Makes 27; 9 servings.

&❧ PER 3 DUMPLINGS (WITH 2½ TEASPOONS SAUCE): 129 calories, 2.3 g. total fat, 0.7 g. saturated fat, 34 mg. cholesterol, 332 mg. sodium

Yippee Yogurt Pops

Adapted from *The League Sampler*
CLARKSBURG LEAGUE FOR SERVICE

Satisfy your children's mid-afternoon hunger pangs with these good-for-you treats from the Clarksburg League for Service.

1 container (16 ounces) fat-free plain yogurt or fat-free and sugar-free vanilla-flavored yogurt
1 can (6 ounces) frozen apple juice, pineapple juice, pink lemonade or grape juice concentrate, thawed
8 3-ounce paper drink cups
8 wooden ice-pop sticks

In a medium bowl, stir together the yogurt and juice concentrate until well-blended.

Pour the mixture into the paper cups. Cover each with foil and freeze about 1 hour or until partially frozen.

Insert an ice-pop stick in the center of each and freeze at least 4 hours or until completely frozen.

To serve, let the pops stand at room temperature for 5 minutes. Then gently peel the paper cups from the frozen pops.

Makes 8.

28 PER POP: 87 calories, 0.1 g. total fat, 0 g. saturated fat, 0 mg. cholesterol, 40 mg. sodium

*Favorite
Breads*

Lemon-Glazed Muffins

Adapted from *Settings*
JUNIOR LEAGUE OF PHILADELPHIA

Yogurt contributes to the moistness and richness of these low-fat muffins from the Junior League of Philadelphia. In testing, we also trimmed away some fat by using only half the amount of walnuts and toasting them for a nuttier flavor. Serve these cakelike muffins for a midmorning break or pack them in a bag lunch for a healthy dessert.

MUFFINS

2 cups all-purpose flour
¾ cup sugar
1 teaspoon baking powder
½ teaspoon baking soda
¼ teaspoon salt
2 egg whites, lightly beaten
1 egg, lightly beaten
1 cup fat-free plain yogurt
2 tablespoons butter or margarine, melted
2 tablespoons prepared butter-flavor mix or unsweetened applesauce
1 tablespoon finely shredded lemon peel
¼ cup toasted and finely chopped walnuts

GLAZE

⅓ cup sugar
⅓ cup fresh lemon juice
1½ tablespoons water

FOR THE MUFFINS: Preheat the oven to 375°. Coat twelve 2½″ muffin cups with no-stick spray. Set the muffin cups aside.

In a large bowl, stir together the flour, sugar, baking powder, baking soda and salt.

In a small bowl, stir together the egg whites, eggs, yogurt, butter or margarine, butter-flavor mix or applesauce and lemon peel. Add the yogurt mixture to the flour mixture. Stir just until moistened. (The batter will be lumpy.) Fold in the walnuts.

Spoon the batter into the prepared muffin cups, filling each cup about three-quarters full. Bake about 20 minutes or until a toothpick inserted in the center comes out clean. (Do not overbake.) Cool the muffins in the pan on a wire rack for 5 minutes.

FOR THE GLAZE: Meanwhile, in a small saucepan, combine the sugar, lemon juice and water. Bring to a boil. Boil, uncovered, for 1 minute.

Using the tines of a fork, gently pierce the muffins tops several times. Then spoon about 2 teaspoons of the glaze over the top of each muffin.

Cool the muffins in the pan for 5 minutes more. Then remove the muffins from the pan. Serve warm.

Makes 12.

ิ₈ PER MUFFIN: 196 calories, 4 g. total fat, 1.5 g. saturated fat, 23 mg. cholesterol, 155 mg. sodium

---

Carrot-Orange Muffins

Adapted from *Some Like It Hot*
JUNIOR LEAGUE OF MCALLEN

It took only one minor change to make these muffins a bit healthier: We replaced half of the oil with applesauce.

1   cup unbleached flour
1   cup whole-wheat flour
2   teaspoons baking powder
1   teaspoon ground cinnamon
¼   teaspoon salt
2   egg whites, lightly beaten
1   teaspoon finely shredded orange peel
½   cup + 2 tablespoons fresh orange juice
½   cup skim milk
2   tablespoons canola oil
2   tablespoons unsweetened applesauce or prepared butter-flavor mix
2   tablespoons honey
1   cup coarsely shredded carrots

Preheat the oven to 400°. Coat twelve 2½" or thirty-six 1¾" muffin cups with no-stick spray or line them with paper baking cups. Set the muffin cups aside.

In a large bowl, stir together the unbleached flour, whole-wheat flour, baking powder, cinnamon and salt.

In a small bowl, stir together the egg whites, orange peel, orange juice, milk, oil, applesauce or butter-flavor mix and honey. Beat with a fork until well-combined. (The mixture will look curdled.) Then stir in the carrots.

Add the carrot mixture to the flour mixture. Stir just until moistened. (The batter will be lumpy.) Spoon the batter into the prepared muffin cups, filling each cup about three-quarters full.

Bake for 14 to 16 minutes for the smaller muffins or 20 to 22 minutes for the larger muffins, or until a toothpick inserted in the center comes out clean. (Do not overbake.) Cool the muffins in the pan on a wire rack for 5 minutes. Then remove the muffins from the pan. Serve warm.

TEST KITCHEN TIP: For variety, the Junior League of McAllen suggests substituting 1 cup coarsely grated zucchini for the carrots.

Makes 12 regular-size or 36 miniature-size muffins.

&❧ PER REGULAR-SIZE MUFFIN: 121 calories, 2.6 g. total fat, 0.2 g. saturated fat, 0 mg. cholesterol, 118 mg. sodium

&❧ PER MINIATURE-SIZE MUFFIN: 40 calories, 0.9 g. total fat, 0.1 g. saturated fat, 0 mg. cholesterol, 39 mg. sodium

Northwest Blueberry Muffins

Adapted from *Rogue River Rendezvous*
JUNIOR SERVICE LEAGUE OF JACKSON COUNTY

Wild blueberries are very small and are ideal for these muffins. If all you can find are cultivated blueberries, choose ones that are tiny. Larger blueberries are heavy and will sink to the bottom of these low-fat muffins.

2	cups all-purpose flour
⅓	cup sugar
1	tablespoon baking powder
¼	teaspoon salt
¼ – ½	teaspoon ground cinnamon (optional)
1	egg, lightly beaten
1	cup skim milk
¼	cup unsweetened applesauce
¼	cup stick margarine (not reduced-calorie), melted
1	cup wild or small domestic fresh or canned blueberries

Preheat the oven to 400°. Line twelve 2½″ muffin cups with paper baking cups. Set the muffin cups aside.

In a large bowl, stir together the flour, sugar, baking powder, salt and cinnamon, if desired.

In a small bowl, stir together the eggs, milk, applesauce and margarine. Add the egg mixture to the flour mixture. Stir just until moistened. (The batter will be lumpy.) Fold in the blueberries.

Spoon the batter into the prepared muffin cups, filling each cup about two-thirds full. Bake for 24 to 26 minutes or until a toothpick inserted in the center comes out clean. (Do not overbake.) Cool the muffins in the pan on a wire rack for 5 minutes. Then remove the muffins from the pan. Serve warm.

Makes 12.

> ❧ PER MUFFIN: 153 calories, 4.5 g. total fat, 0.9 g. saturated fat, 18 mg. cholesterol, 188 mg. sodium

Boston Brown Bread

Adapted from *Specialties of the House*
KENMORE ASSOCIATION

This low-fat bread from the Kenmore Association is made with a variety of grains—rye and whole-wheat flours and cornmeal.

1	tablespoon all-purpose flour
	Boiling water
1	cup dark raisins
1	cup whole-wheat flour
1	cup rye flour
¾	cup yellow cornmeal
2	teaspoons baking soda
¼	teaspoon salt
1½	cups skim milk
¾	cup dark molasses
½	cup fat-free egg substitute

Preheat the oven to 350°. Coat two 8" × 4" loaf pans with no-stick spray, then sprinkle with the all-purpose flour. Shake the pans, tilting them back and forth, until they are coated with a light dusting of the flour. Remove and discard the excess flour. Set the pans aside.

Pour enough boiling water over the raisins to cover. Let stand about 10 minutes or until plump.

Meanwhile, in a large bowl, stir together the whole-wheat flour, rye flour, cornmeal, baking soda and salt. In a small bowl, stir together the milk, molasses and egg substitute. Add the milk mixture to the flour mixture. Stir until combined. Then stir in the raisins.

Spoon the batter into the prepared pans. Bake about 35 minutes or until a toothpick inserted in the center comes out clean. (Do not overbake.) Cool the loaves in the pans on a wire rack for 10 minutes. Then remove the loaves from the pans. Serve warm.

TEST KITCHEN TIP: Boston brown bread freezes well, but if you'd rather make just one loaf, use ½ cup raisins, ½ cup whole-wheat flour, ½ cup rye flour, ¼ cup + 2 tablespoons cornmeal, 1 teaspoon baking soda, ⅛ teaspoon salt, ¾ cup skim milk, ¼ cup + 2 tablespoons molasses and ¼ cup egg substitute.

Makes 2 loaves; 32 slices.

PER ½" SLICE: 36 calories, 0.1 g. total fat, 0 g. saturated fat, 0 mg. cholesterol, 44 mg. sodium

Banana Bread

Adapted from *Our Favorite Recipes*
ST. JOHN'S GUILD

Pureed fruits, such as bananas, apples and pears, are a popular fat-replacer for baked products. The fruits contribute the moistness and flavor usually achieved by fat. For this bread, we added an extra mashed banana to replace ⅓ cup of butter.

- 2 cups all-purpose flour
- 1 cup sugar
- 1 teaspoon baking powder
- 1 teaspoon baking soda
- ¼ teaspoon salt
- ¼ cup nonfat buttermilk
- 2 egg whites
- 1 egg
- 4 ripe medium bananas, mashed (1⅓ cups)
- ½ cup toasted and coarsely chopped walnuts

Preheat the oven to 350°. Coat an 8″ × 4″ loaf pan with no-stick spray. Set the pan aside.

In a large bowl, stir together the flour, sugar, baking powder, baking soda and salt.

In a small bowl, use a wire whisk to beat together the buttermilk, egg whites and egg until well-combined. Press the bananas through a potato ricer or use a potato masher to create a finer texture. Stir the bananas into the buttermilk mixture.

Add the banana mixture to the flour mixture. Stir just until moistened. (The batter will be lumpy.) Fold in the walnuts.

Spread the batter in the prepared loaf pan. Bake for 45 to 50 minutes or until a toothpick inserted in the center comes out clean. (Do not overbake.) Cool the bread in the pan on a wire rack for 10 minutes. Then remove the bread from the pan and cool completely before slicing.

Makes 1 loaf; 16 slices.

❧ PER ½″ SLICE: 160 calories, 2.8 g. total fat, 0.3 g. saturated fat, 13 mg. cholesterol, 121 mg. sodium

Cranberry–Orange Bread

Adapted from *Our Country Cookin'*
JUNIOR SOCIAL WORKERS OF CHICKASHA

This tasty holiday bread is the ideal way to give the gift of better health to the ones you love. It uses only 2 tablespoons of oil, so it's really low in fat.

2	cups all-purpose flour, sifted
¾	cup sugar
1½	teaspoons baking powder
½	teaspoon baking soda
½	teaspoon salt
2	egg whites, lightly beaten
1	teaspoon finely shredded orange peel
¾	cup fresh orange juice
2	tablespoons canola oil
1	cup coarsely chopped cranberries
⅓	cup toasted and coarsely chopped walnuts

Preheat the oven to 350°. Coat an 8″ × 4″ loaf pan with no-stick spray. Set the pan aside.

In a large bowl, stir together the flour, sugar, baking powder, baking soda and salt.

In a small bowl, stir together the egg whites, orange peel, orange juice and oil. Add the orange mixture to the flour mixture. Stir just until moistened. (The batter will be lumpy.) Fold in the cranberries and walnuts.

Spread the batter in the prepared pan. Bake for 55 to 60 minutes or until a toothpick inserted in the center comes out clean. (Do not overbake.) Cool the bread in the pan on a wire rack for 10 minutes. Then remove the bread from the pan and cool it completely before slicing.

Makes 1 loaf; 16 slices.

PER ½″ SLICE: 133 calories, 3.3 g. total fat, 0.2 g. saturated fat, 0 mg. cholesterol, 131 mg. sodium

Pumpkin Mincemeat Bread

Adapted from *Cordonbluegrass*
JUNIOR LEAGUE OF LOUISVILLE

A combination of applesauce and buttermilk replaces butter in this recipe and still keeps the bread moist and tender.

1¾	cups + 1 tablespoon all-purpose flour
¾	cup sugar
½	cup packed brown sugar
1	tablespoon pumpkin pie spice
2½	teaspoons baking powder
¼	teaspoon baking soda
¼	teaspoon salt
⅔	cup canned pumpkin
4	egg whites
⅓	cup nonfat buttermilk
⅓	cup unsweetened applesauce
1	tablespoon canola oil
¾	cup condensed mincemeat

Preheat the oven to 350°. Coat an 8″ × 4″ loaf pan with no-stick spray. Set the pan aside.

In a large bowl, stir together 1¾ cups of the flour, sugar, brown sugar, pumpkin pie spice, baking powder, baking soda and salt.

Add the pumpkin, egg whites, buttermilk, applesauce and oil. Use an electric mixer to beat on low speed just until blended, then on medium-high speed for 2 minutes.

Place the mincemeat in a small bowl. Sprinkle with the remaining 1 tablespoon flour and toss until coated. Then stir the mincemeat mixture into the batter.

Spread the batter in the prepared pan. Bake for 55 to 60 minutes or until a toothpick inserted in the center comes out clean. (Do not overbake.) Cool the bread in the pan on a wire rack for 10 minutes. Then remove the bread from the pan and cool it completely before slicing.

Makes 1 loaf; 16 slices.

&ae; PER ½″ SLICE: 139 calories, 1.1 g. total fat, 0.1 g. saturated fat, 0 mg. cholesterol, 129 mg. sodium

Papaya-Coconut Bread

Adapted from *Specialties of the House*

KENMORE ASSOCIATION

Coconut extract is a great way to reduce the fat and calories in some foods and still keep the nutty flavor. In this tropical bread, we replaced half the coconut with the extract and saved a total of 176 calories and 12 grams of fat. We left in some coconut for its unique texture.

1	cup raisins
¼	cup rum or bourbon (see tip)
½	cup sugar
¼	cup stick margarine (not reduced-calorie), softened
1	cup mashed papaya (about 1 large papaya), see tip
¼	cup unsweetened applesauce
¼	cup nonfat buttermilk
¼	teaspoon coconut extract
2	egg whites
2	cups all-purpose flour
1	teaspoon baking powder
1	teaspoon baking soda
¼	teaspoon salt
½	cup unsweetened flaked coconut

In a small bowl, combine the raisins and rum or bourbon. Let stand for 30 minutes, stirring occasionally.

Preheat the oven to 350°. Coat an 8″ × 4″ loaf pan with no-stick spray; set aside. In a large bowl, use an electric mixer to beat together the sugar and margarine until well-combined. Then beat in the papaya, applesauce, buttermilk and coconut extract until just combined.

Drain the raisins well and discard the liquid. Stir the raisins into the papaya mixture. Set the fruit mixture aside.

Wash and dry the small bowl and beaters. Add the egg whites to the bowl and beat with the electric mixer on high speed until the egg whites form soft peaks. Fold the egg whites into the fruit mixture.

In the small bowl, stir together the flour, baking powder, baking soda and salt. Then stir in the coconut. Add the flour mixture to the fruit mixture. Gently stir until well-combined.

Spread the batter in the prepared loaf pan. Bake for 55 to 60 minutes or until a toothpick inserted in the center comes out clean. (Do not overbake.) Cool the bread in the pan on a wire rack for 10

┌───┐

OUR CAUSE

Kenmore Association

The gingerbread that visitors to Kenmore are served—from George Washington's mother's recipe—is just one of the many special things about this museum house. Built before the American Revolution and opened as a museum in 1922, Kenmore was the home of George Washington's sister, Betty Lewis. It is one of the country's oldest museum houses.

The beautiful Georgian mansion has a long history of hospitality. It was here that the Marquis de Lafayette made a surprise visit and found Mary Washington baking her now-famous gingerbread. It was here that, in 1777, Mrs. Lewis entertained a group of imprisoned Hessian officers with music, tea, wine and cakes.

By 1922, when the first organization to restore Kenmore was formed, the old house had been through two major wars and was a bit the worse for the wear. Tireless efforts—and countless fund-raising luncheons, teas and dinners—have returned Kenmore to its early glory. Now this treasure sponsors lectures, workshops and educational, musical and theatrical programs for the Fredericksburg community and visitors. Hands-on programs bring the joys of Kenmore closer to children and the visually impaired. *Specialties of the House* helps keep Kenmore glorious.

└───┘

minutes. Then remove the bread from the pan and cool completely before slicing.

TEST KITCHEN TIP: If you prefer not to use alcohol in this bread, soak the raisins in 3 tablespoons water mixed with 1 tablespoon rum extract.

For variety, the Kenmore Association suggests substituting 1 cup mashed mango for the papaya.

Makes 1 loaf; 16 slices.

> PER ¹/₂" SLICE: 154 calories, 3.8 g. total fat, 1.3 g. saturated fat, 0 mg. cholesterol, 151 mg. sodium

Mr. Tim's Baked Hush Puppies

Adapted from *The Black Family Dinner Quilt Cookbook*
NATIONAL COUNCIL OF NEGRO WOMEN

Hush puppies are cornmeal dumplings that are traditionally deep-fried. This innovative recipe from the National Council of Negro Women has trimmed them down considerably. The secret: baking the hush puppies in mini-muffin tins instead of immersing them in fat.

¼	cup all-purpose flour
¼	cup yellow cornmeal
¾	teaspoon baking powder
¼	teaspoon salt
¼	teaspoon sugar
¼	teaspoon garlic powder
¼	teaspoon celery flakes
⅛	teaspoon ground red pepper
1	egg white, lightly beaten
2	tablespoons milk
2	teaspoons canola oil
2	tablespoons finely chopped green onions
1	tablespoon minced fresh parsley

Preheat the oven to 425°. Coat eight 1½″ muffin cups with nostick spray. Set the muffin cups aside.

In a medium bowl, stir together the flour, cornmeal, baking powder, salt, sugar, garlic powder, celery flakes and pepper.

In a small bowl, stir together the egg whites, milk and oil. Add the milk mixture to the flour mixture. Stir just until moistened. (The batter will be lumpy.) Fold in the onions and parsley.

Spoon 1 tablespoon of the batter into each prepared muffin cup. Bake for 15 to 20 minutes or until a toothpick inserted in the center of a hush puppy comes out clean. (Do not overbake.) Remove the hush puppies from the pan and serve immediately.

Makes 8; 4 servings.

&⬤ PER 2 HUSH PUPPIES: 88 calories, 2.8 g. total fat, 0.4 g. saturated fat, 1 mg. cholesterol, 216 mg. sodium

Chocolate Chip Coffee Cake

Adapted from *California Kosher*
WOMEN'S LEAGUE OF ADAT ARI EL SYNAGOGUE

Chocolate-lovers, this mid-morning treat is sure to satisfy your yearnings. We used miniature chocolate chips instead of regular chips so that each bite is loaded with lots of chocolate flavor. And because the smaller chips get distributed through the cake better, we were able to use fewer chips.

1	tablespoon + 1¾ cups all-purpose flour
1½	teaspoons baking powder
½	teaspoon baking soda
1	cup sugar
¼	cup stick margarine (not reduced-calorie), softened
1	container (8 ounces) fat-free sour cream
4	egg whites
⅔	cup mini chocolate chips
½	cup toasted and finely chopped walnuts or pecans (optional)
1–2	teaspoons powdered sugar (optional)

Preheat the oven to 350°. Lightly coat a 6-cup Bundt pan or an 8" × 4" loaf pan with no-stick spray. Then sprinkle with 1 table-spoon of the flour. Shake the pan, tilting it back and forth, until it is coated with a light dusting of flour. Remove and discard the excess flour. Set the baking pan aside.

In a small bowl, stir together the remaining 1¾ cups flour, baking powder and baking soda. In a large bowl, use an electric mixer to beat together the sugar and margarine until well-combined. Add the sour cream and egg whites. Beat until well-combined. Add the flour mix-ture and beat on low speed just until combined. Fold in the chocolate chips and walnuts or pecans, if desired.

Evenly spread the batter in the prepared pan. Bake for 45 to 55 minutes or until no imprint remains when lightly touched in the cen-ter. (Do not overbake.) Cool in the pan on a wire rack for 10 minutes. Loosen the edges of the cake from the pan. Remove from the pan and cool. If desired, sift the powdered sugar on top before serving.

Makes 12 servings.

❧ PER SERVING: 245 calories, 7.5 g. total fat, 0.8 g. saturated fat, 0 mg. cholesterol, 162 mg. sodium

Raisin Harvest Coffee Cake

Adapted from *Forum Feasts*
FRIENDS OF THE FORUM SCHOOL

When a recipe calls for cutting butter or margarine into a flour mixture, as in this apple-and-raisin cake, you can substitute light cream cheese as a lower-fat alternative. Be sure to use the cream cheese that comes in a block, because its texture is more like the texture of butter. The tub form will be too soft.

1½ cups all-purpose flour
¾ cup sugar
3¾ teaspoons baking powder
¼ teaspoon salt
6 tablespoons cold stick margarine (not reduced-calorie), cut into small pieces
3 ounces cold light cream cheese, cut into small pieces
2 egg whites
1 egg
2 cups peeled and finely chopped cooking apples
1½ cup raisins
2 tablespoons sugar (optional)

Preheat the oven to 350°. Generously coat a 9″ × 9″ baking pan with no-stick spray. Set the pan aside.

In a large bowl, stir together the flour, ¾ cup sugar, baking powder and salt. Using a pastry blender, cut the margarine and cream cheese into the flour mixture until it forms coarse crumbs.

In a small bowl, use a fork to beat together the egg whites and egg until well-combined. Add the egg mixture to the flour mixture. Using the fork, stir just until the flour mixture is moistened.

Stir in the apples and raisins until well-combined. (The batter will be stiff.) Spread the batter in the prepared pan. If desired, sprinkle with the 2 tablespoons sugar.

Bake for 55 to 60 minutes or until a toothpick inserted in the center comes out clean. (Do not overbake.) Cool the cake in the pan on a wire rack for 15 minutes. Then cut into squares to serve.

TEST KITCHEN TIP: If you have leftover coffee cake, store it in the freezer. Low-fat baked goods can go stale when stored at room temperature—even for 1 day. To thaw and reheat the pieces, set the

Friends of the Forum School

The first *Forum Feasts* cookbook was published in 1968. Through the years, the collection of recipes featuring good home cooking (what we call comfort food nowadays) has been an undeniably important source of support for the Forum School.

This Waldwick, New Jersey, school serves children who have autism, schizophrenia and other disorders. The nonprofit school, a pioneer in special education and one of the first of its kind in the country, began modestly in 1954 with four students in two rooms borrowed from a VFW Hall.

Today, the school has its own campus with 17 classrooms, therapy rooms, a conference room, a cafeteria and a swimming pool. Programs for the children, who range in age from 3 to 16, include art and speech therapy, therapeutic swimming and gym classes, nutritional lunch programs, preschool and a pre-vocational class for the older students.

The Forum School is a godsend to the 100 or so students who attend, but there is still a waiting list of children who need the services that the school provides. The latest edition of *Forum Feasts* will continue to help the school expand to help those special children.

coffee cake on a paper towel and place in a microwave oven. Two pieces will heat in 15 to 20 seconds on high power; four pieces will take 45 to 60 seconds.

Makes 16 servings.

> PER SERVING: 187 calories, 5.7 g. total fat, 1.5 g. saturated fat, 15 mg. cholesterol, 204 mg. sodium

Praline French Toast Casserole

Adapted from *Still Fiddling in the Kitchen*

NATIONAL COUNCIL OF JEWISH WOMEN

This dish is like having dessert for breakfast! A praline topping crowns fluffy French toast. To lighten this special dish without sacrificing its goodness, we substituted egg whites for a few of the whole eggs in the toast portion and used reduced-calorie butter and syrup in the praline topping.

FRENCH TOAST

  4   egg whites
  2   eggs
  1   can (5 ounces or ⅔ cup) evaporated skim milk
1½ teaspoons packed brown sugar
  1   teaspoon vanilla
  6   slices French or Italian bread, cut ¾" thick
      (about 2" in diameter)

PRALINE TOPPING

 ¼ cup packed brown sugar
  3 tablespoons reduced-calorie maple-flavored syrup
  1 tablespoon reduced-calorie margarine
 ¼ cup toasted and chopped pecans

FOR THE FRENCH TOAST: In a medium bowl, use a wire whisk to beat together the egg whites, eggs, milk, brown sugar and vanilla.

Pour half the egg mixture into an 8" × 8" baking pan or plastic container. Then place the bread slices in the pan in a single layer. Pour the remaining egg mixture on top. Cover and refrigerate for 3 to 8 hours.

Preheat the oven to 350°. Coat an 8" × 8" baking dish or shallow casserole with no-stick spray and set aside.

OUR CAUSE

National Council of Jewish Women

The National Council of Jewish Women, Greater Detroit Section, (NCJW-GDS) supports so many causes that you have to wonder how they found time to publish a cookbook. *Still Fiddling in the Kitchen* is this active group's second cookbook, and it has already sold nearly 10,000 copies. There is no segment of society in the Detroit area that does not benefit from the work of the NCJW-GDS.

The group's concerns cover everyone from children to the elderly, from local to international. Some of the special programs they support are: Dor l' Dor, a program pairing senior citizens and sixth-graders in song and friendship; Space for Changing Families, a program providing support to families in transition; Up and Out, a service arranging activities with transportation to senior citizens; CASA (Court Appointed Special Advocates), specially trained volunteers working with the probate court; Meals on Wheels; and interest free educational assistance to Jewish students.

Proceeds from the book benefit all the group's projects, particularly those meeting the needs of children and families in our changing world.

FOR THE PRALINE TOPPING: Meanwhile, in a small saucepan, stir together the brown sugar, syrup and margarine. Heat until the margarine is melted. Stir in the pecans. Then spread the mixture on the bottom of the prepared baking dish.

Carefully transfer the soaked bread slices to the baking dish, placing them on top of the nut mixture in a single layer. Pour any of the remaining egg mixture over the bread.

Bake for 30 to 35 minutes or until set and very lightly browned. Let stand about 10 minutes before cutting. Cut into pieces to serve.

Makes 6 servings.

❧ PER SERVING: 260 calories, 7 g. total fat, 1.2 g. saturated fat, 72 mg. cholesterol, 318 mg. sodium

Apple Pancakes with Apricot Butter

Adapted from *Hospitality*
NORTH SHORE MEDICAL CENTER AUXILIARY

Apricot butter is the glimmering jewel for these delicious apple-filled pancakes. Rather than using a 1-to-1 ratio of preserves to butter, we used a 2-to-1 ratio and replaced the butter with tub-style margarine to cut back on saturated fat.

APRICOT BUTTER

½   cup apricot all-fruit spread
¼   cup tub-style reduced-calorie margarine
¼   teaspoon finely shredded lemon peel

PANCAKES

1   tablespoon sugar
½   teaspoon finely shredded lemon peel
½   teaspoon ground cinnamon
⅛   teaspoon ground cloves
1   medium tart apple, peeled, cored and coarsely shredded
½   cup all-purpose or white whole-wheat flour
½   teaspoon baking soda
¼   teaspoon salt
2   egg whites, lightly beaten
1   egg, lightly beaten
1   container (8 ounces) fat-free sour cream
1   tablespoon canola oil

FOR THE APRICOT BUTTER: In a small saucepan, combine the apricot spread, margarine and lemon peel. Cook and stir over low heat until melted. Remove from the heat and set aside.

FOR THE PANCAKES: In a small bowl, stir together the sugar, lemon peel, cinnamon and cloves. Add the apples and toss until coated. Set the apples aside.

In a medium bowl, stir together the flour, baking soda and salt. In another small bowl, stir together the egg whites, eggs, sour cream and oil.

Add the sour cream mixture to the flour mixture. Stir just until moistened. Fold in the apple mixture. Cover and refrigerate for 15 minutes.

Coat an unheated griddle or large skillet with no-stick spray. Heat the griddle over medium heat. Make 16 pancakes by spooning 2 tablespoons of the batter onto the hot griddle for each pancake and spreading the batter to about a 3" circle. Cook about 3 minutes or until the pancakes are bubbly and slightly dry around the edges. Carefully turn over and cook about 1 to 2 minutes more or until lightly browned.

If desired, transfer the pancakes to a baking sheet, cover with foil and keep warm in a 250° oven while cooking the remaining batter. Serve with the warm apricot butter.

TEST KITCHEN TIP: To reduce your fat intake even further, serve these pancakes with reduced-calorie maple-flavored syrup or fruit syrup. Or make your own fat-free topping by just melting the apricot all-fruit spread and thinning it with a small amount of apricot nectar or orange juice.

Makes 4 servings.

    PER SERVING: 398 calories, 15 g. total fat, 1.7 g. saturated fat, 53 mg. cholesterol, 475 mg. sodium

Blueberry–Corn Cakes

Adapted from *RSVP*
JUNIOR LEAGUE OF PORTLAND

*This specialty highlights one of Maine's finest—wild blueberries.
We liked the blueberry flavor so much that we slightly increased
the amount of berries. For a healthful topping, we suggest serving
these morning cakes with fat-free vanilla yogurt and additional
berries.*

¾   cup cornmeal
¼   cup all-purpose flour
1   teaspoon sugar
1   teaspoon baking powder
½   teaspoon baking soda
¼   teaspoon salt
1   egg, lightly beaten
1⅓ cups buttermilk
1   tablespoon canola oil
⅔   cup small fresh or frozen blueberries
    (wild or cultivated berries)
1   slice turkey bacon, finely cut up, cooked and drained
1¼ cups fat-free and sugar-free vanilla-flavored yogurt or
    1 cup reduced-calorie maple-flavored syrup

In a medium bowl, stir together the cornmeal, flour, sugar, baking powder, baking soda and salt.

In a small bowl, stir together the eggs, buttermilk and oil. Add the buttermilk mixture to the flour mixture. Stir just until moistened. (The batter will be lumpy.) Fold in the blueberries and bacon.

Coat an unheated griddle or large skillet with no-stick spray. Heat the griddle over medium heat. For each pancake, spoon about 1 heaping tablespoon of the batter onto the hot griddle, spreading them to about a 3½″ circle.

Cook about 3 minutes or until the pancakes are bubbly and slightly dry around the edges. Carefully turn over and cook about 2 to 3 minutes more or until lightly browned. Serve with the yogurt or syrup.

TEST KITCHEN TIP: Pancakes make a great on-the-go breakfast. If you have leftovers, wrap them individually in plastic wrap. Then place in a freezer bag and freeze.

To thaw and reheat the pancakes, place them in a single layer on a paper towel. Microwave on high power for 30 to 40 seconds for 1 pancake; do 4 pancakes for 1 to 1½ minutes.

Makes 20 pancakes; 5 servings.

ᘔ PER 4 PANCAKES: 224 calories, 5.5 g. total fat, 1.1 g. saturated fat, 46 mg. cholesterol, 379 mg. sodium

---

Good-Taste Waffles

Adapted from *Cranbrook Reflections*
CRANBROOK HOUSE & GARDENS AUXILIARY

These waffles are filled with good taste—even though they have practically no fat or cholesterol and very modest amounts of sodium.

3   egg whites
1   cup all-purpose flour
1   cup skim milk

Place the egg whites in a medium bowl. Let stand at room temperature for 30 minutes.

Generously coat the unheated grids of a no-stick waffle iron with no-stick spray. Preheat according to the manufacturer's directions.

Meanwhile, in another medium bowl, stir together the flour and milk and set the batter aside. Using an electric mixer, beat the egg whites on high speed until stiff peaks form. Fold the egg whites into the batter.

Spoon enough batter onto the bottom grids of the waffle iron to cover two-thirds of it. Quickly close the waffle iron and bake according to the manufacturer's directions. Do not open during baking.

When done, use a fork to lift and remove the waffle and repeat making more waffles with the remaining batter.

TEST KITCHEN TIP: An easy way to reheat leftover waffles and make them crispy again is to pop them into the toaster.

Makes 6 (7"-round) waffles; 3 servings.

ᘔ PER 2 WAFFLES: 197 calories, 0.5 g. total fat, 0.1 g. saturated fat, 1 mg. cholesterol, 97 mg. sodium

Challah

Adapted from *California Kosher*
WOMEN'S LEAGUE OF ADAT ARI EL SYNAGOGUE

*Our major adjustment to this sweet bread was with the salt—
we decreased the amount from 2 teaspoons to 1 teaspoon. But
because salt controls the rising action of yeast, we could not
eliminate it entirely. The flavor and structure of the bread would
have been affected.*

1	package active dry yeast
1	cup warm water (105°–115°)
3	tablespoons sugar
1	tablespoon canola oil
1	teaspoon salt
½	teaspoon vanilla
4¾ – 5¼	cups all-purpose flour
½	cup raisins (optional)
2	egg whites, lightly beaten
3	eggs
1	tablespoon water
1	teaspoon sesame seeds

In a large bowl, dissolve the yeast in ¼ cup of the warm water.
Cover and let stand for 5 minutes.

Stir in the remaining ¾ cup warm water, sugar, oil, salt and
vanilla. Then stir in 1 cup of the flour and, if desired, raisins until
well-combined.

Stir in the egg whites. Lightly beat 2 of the eggs. Add them along
with enough of an additional 3½ cups flour to make a soft dough.

Transfer the dough to a lightly floured work surface. Then knead
in enough of the remaining ¾ cups flour as you can until the dough is
smooth and elastic (3 to 5 minutes).

Coat a clean, dry large bowl with no-stick spray. Place the dough
in the bowl. Lightly coat the top of the dough with no-stick spray.
Cover and let rise, free from drafts, about 1 hour or until double in
size.

Punch the dough down. Cover and let rise again about 45 minutes or until nearly double in size. Meanwhile, coat a baking sheet
with no-stick spray.

Preheat the oven to 350°. Transfer the dough to a lightly floured work surface. To shape the loaf, divide the dough into fourths. Form 3 of the portions each into a 16″ inch rope. Place the ropes on the prepared baking sheet, 1″ apart. Starting in the middle, braid by bringing the left rope underneath the center rope. Then bring the right rope underneath the new center rope. Continue braiding to the end. To braid the other side, repeat as before, except bring the ropes over the center rope. Pinch the ends together to seal, then tuck under.

Divide the fourth rope into three portions. Roll each portion into a 14″ rope. Then braid as before. Place the smaller braid on top of the larger braid. Cover and let rise about 30 minutes or until nearly double in size.

Lightly beat the remaining egg with the 1 tablespoon water. Brush a small amount of the mixture over the loaf, then sprinkle with the sesame seeds. Discard any remaining egg mixture.

Bake for 25 minutes. Loosely cover with foil, then continue baking for 20 to 25 minutes more or until the loaf sounds hollow when tapped with your fingers. Remove the bread from the pan and let cool on a wire rack.

Makes 1 loaf; 30 slices.

&. PER ½″ SLICE: 91 calories, 1.2 g. total fat, 0.2 g. saturated fat, 21 mg. cholesterol, 81 mg. sodium

Light Yogurt Crescent Rolls

Adapted from *The Pasquotank Plate*
CHRIST EPISCOPAL CHURCHWOMEN

These dinner rolls are so rich and tender, you'll think you're eating croissants. But you'll be getting a lot less fat and calories.

1	package active dry yeast
½	cup warm water (105°–115°)
½	cup fat-free plain yogurt
¼	cup sugar
3	tablespoons fat-free egg substitute
2	tablespoons canola oil
3¾	cups all-purpose flour
½	teaspoon salt

In a medium bowl, dissolve the yeast in the water. Let stand for 5 minutes.

Stir in the yogurt, sugar, egg substitute and oil. Add 1 cup of the flour and salt. Use an electric mixer and beat on medium speed about 3 minutes. Using a spoon, stir in the remaining 2¾ cups flour to make a soft, sticky dough. Cover and refrigerate about 5 hours or until double in size.

Punch the dough down. Transfer the dough to a lightly floured work surface. Divide it in half. Roll each portion into a 10″ circle.

Lightly coat the dough with no-stick spray. Then cut each circle into 12 wedges. Beginning at the wide end of each wedge, roll up toward the point.

Coat a baking sheet with no-stick spray. Place the rolls, point side down, on the baking sheet 3″ apart. Cover and let rise, free from drafts, about 40 minutes or until doubled in size.

Meanwhile, preheat the oven to 375°.

Bake the rolls for 10 to 12 minutes or until golden brown. Remove the rolls from the baking sheet. Serve warm.

TEST KITCHEN TIP: For variety, shape the dough into round balls instead of crescents. After punching the dough down and halving it, divide each half into 12 pieces. Shape each piece into a ball. Let the balls rise as directed and bake them according to the recipe.

Makes 24.

    PER ROLL: 93 calories, 1.3 g. total fat, 0.1 g. saturated fat, 0 mg. cholesterol, 51 mg. sodium

Breakfast Ring

Adapted from *Our Country Cookin'*
JUNIOR SOCIAL WORKERS OF CHICKASHA

A recipe like this traditionally calls for the dough balls to be dunked into a bowl of melted butter, then rolled in a mixture of cinnamon and sugar. To eliminate the extra fat, we simply sprayed the dough with butter-flavored no-stick spray.

½ cup packed brown sugar
¼ cup stick margarine (not reduced-calorie)
¼ cup toasted and chopped pecans
⅔ cup sugar
2 teaspoons ground cinnamon
1 package (25 ounces or 24 dough balls) frozen white dinner-roll dough (see tip)

Generously coat a 12-cup Bundt pan with butter-flavored no-stick spray and set aside.

In a small saucepan, heat and stir the brown sugar and margarine until melted and well-combined. Stir in the pecans, then pour the mixture into the prepared pan.

In a shallow bowl, stir together the sugar and cinnamon. Generously spray each frozen dough ball with the butter-flavored no-stick spray. Then roll the balls in the sugar-and-cinnamon mixture.

Arrange the coated balls on top of the pecan mixture in the pan. Sprinkle any of the remaining sugar-and-cinnamon mixture on top. Cover and let rise, free from drafts, at room temperature for 3 to 4 hours or in the refrigerator for 8 to 10 hours, or until nearly double in size.

Preheat the oven to 325°. Uncover and bake for 40 to 45 minutes or until golden. Cool the cake in the pan on a wire rack for 5 minutes. Then invert it onto a serving plate and remove the pan. Cool for 10 minutes more before serving.

TEST KITCHEN TIP: There are two types of frozen dinner-roll dough on the market. One does not require thawing and rising; the other does require those steps. For this recipe to work properly, purchase the frozen dough balls that do require thawing and rising.

Makes 24 rolls; 12 servings.

❧ PER 2 ROLLS: 317 calories, 9.8 g. total fat, 1.8 g. saturated fat, 0 mg. cholesterol, 374 mg. sodium

Health Bread

Adapted from *Pow Wow Chow*
THE FIVE CIVILIZED TRIBES MUSEUM

This good-for-you bread from the Five Civilized Tribes Museum is packed with fiber and good taste!

1	package active dry yeast
2	cups warm water (105°–115°)
2	tablespoons sugar
½	teaspoon salt
4	cups unbleached flour
½	cup very warm water (120°–130°)
¼	cup molasses
3	tablespoons unsalted sunflower nuts
3	tablespoons toasted wheat germ
2	tablespoons canola oil
2	egg whites, lightly beaten
1	egg, lightly beaten
3¼ – 4	cups whole-wheat flour

In a large bowl, dissolve the yeast in half the warm water. Stir in the remaining 1½ cups warm water, sugar and salt. Then stir in the unbleached flour. Let stand, free from drafts, about 20 minutes or until bubbly.

Stir in the very warm water, molasses, sunflower nuts, wheat germ, oil, egg whites and eggs. Then stir in as much of the whole-wheat flour as you can.

On a lightly floured work surface, knead in enough of the remaining whole-wheat flour to make a dough that is smooth and elastic (8 to 10 minutes).

Coat a clean, dry large bowl with no-stick spray. Place the dough in the bowl. Lightly coat the top of the dough with no-stick spray. Cover and let rise, free from drafts, about 1½ hours or until double in size.

Punch the dough down. Then transfer the dough to a lightly floured work surface. Divide it in half. Cover it and let it rest for 10 minutes.

Coat two 9″ × 5″ loaf pans with no-stick spray. To shape the loaves, roll each portion of dough into a 12″ × 8″ rectangle. Beginning at a short end, tightly roll up each rectangle, jelly-roll fashion. Pinch the ends together to seal. Place in the prepared loaf pans with

The Five Civilized Tribes Museum

The Five Civilized Tribes Museum was dedicated in April 1966 to "those pioneer Indians whose courage and fortitude, perseverance and achievement sustained them through travail and disaster and earned for them the name of the Five Civilized Tribes."

The tribes laid the foundation for the state of Oklahoma. Their forced removal from their homeland—the southeastern quarter of the United States—in the 1830s to what is now Oklahoma is one of the most tragic episodes in American history and is known as the Trail of Tears.

The museum was established in the Old Union Agency, the first building ever erected to house the superintendency of the tribes. The making of the museum is the story of the inspired vision, the unswerving determination and the selfless effort of many people over the years. And the story of raising private donations to restore the building for museum purposes is one of hope, faith and goodness on the part of many people throughout Oklahoma as well as the rest of the United States.

Fund-raising plans and projects continue to carry out a dream of a new museum building to house art collections and other items of tribal history and culture. The *Pow Wow Chow* cookbook is one of the fund-raising efforts. The first edition sold out soon after its 1984 publication. The current second edition contains not only new recipes but also charming original drawings by Cherokee master artist Joan Brown.

the seam side down. Cover and let rise about 30 minutes or until nearly double in size.

Preheat the oven to 350°. Bake for 40 to 45 minutes or until the loaves sound hollow when tapped with your fingers. Remove the bread from the pans and let cool on a wire rack.

Makes 2 loaves; 36 slices.

&. PER ½" SLICE: 112 calories, 1.7 g. total fat, 0.2 g. saturated fat, 6 mg. cholesterol, 37 mg. sodium

Dilly Cheese Bread

Adapted from *Only in California*
CHILDREN'S HOME SOCIETY OF CALIFORNIA

*Here's a low-fat batter bread made even healthier by the use of
1 percent fat cottage cheese instead of its fattier counterpart.*

2¼ cups all-purpose flour
1 package active dry yeast
⅔ cup 1% fat cottage cheese
½ cup water
2 tablespoon sugar
2 tablespoons dillweed
1 tablespoon finely chopped onions
1 tablespoon tub-style reduced-calorie margarine
½ teaspoon salt
1 egg

In a large bowl, stir together 1 cup of the flour and yeast. Set the flour mixture aside.

In a small saucepan, cook and stir over medium-low heat the cottage cheese, water, sugar, dillweed, onions, margarine and salt until very warm (120°–130°).

Add the cottage cheese mixture and egg to the flour mixture. Use an electric mixer to beat on low speed just until blended, then on high speed for 3 minutes. Using a spoon, stir in the remaining 1¼ cups flour. (The dough will be sticky.)

Generously coat a 1½-quart round casserole with no-stick spray. Transfer the dough to the casserole. Cover and let rise, free from drafts, for 50 to 60 minutes or until nearly double in size.

Preheat the oven to 350°. Bake, uncovered, for 40 to 50 minutes or until golden. Remove the bread from the casserole and cool slightly on a wire rack before slicing. Cut into wedges and serve warm.

Makes 1 loaf; 15 wedges.

ð PER ½″ WEDGE: 95 calories, 1.3 g. total fat, 0.3 g. saturated fat,
15 mg. cholesterol, 125 mg. sodium

Pepperoni Bread

Adapted from *Preserving Our Italian Heritage*
SONS OF ITALY FLORIDA FOUNDATION

*Both pepperoni and cheese are snuggled in the center of this
yeast bread. To keep the filling low in fat, we used just enough
pepperoni for flavor and added some roasted red peppers to
extend the amount of filling.*

1	loaf (1 pound) homemade or frozen white, whole-wheat or whole-grain bread dough
½	cup (2 ounces) finely shredded reduced-fat mozzarella cheese
½	cup (2 ounces) finely shredded fat-free mozzarella cheese
½	cup drained and chopped bottled roasted red peppers (see tip)
3	ounces pepperoni, finely chopped (about ¾ cup)

If using frozen dough, thaw it according to the package directions.
Raise the dough until it is double in size. (Follow the recipe for
homemade dough and the package directions for frozen dough.)

Punch the dough down. Transfer the dough to a lightly floured
work surface. Cover and let rest for 10 minutes. Meanwhile, coat a
baking sheet with no-stick spray.

Preheat the oven to 350°. Roll the dough into a 14″ × 8″ rectangle. Combine the reduced-fat and fat-free mozzarella. Sprinkle the
cheese mixture, peppers and pepperoni evenly on top of the dough
to within 1″ of its edges. Roll up, jelly-roll fashion, starting at one of
the long sides. Pinch the ends together to seal. Transfer the roll, seam
side down, to the prepared baking sheet. Shape the roll into a horseshoe. Spray the roll with olive oil no-stick spray.

Bake for 30 to 40 minutes or until golden. (If necessary, loosely
cover with foil to prevent overbrowning.) Transfer the loaf from the
baking sheet to a wire rack. Let cool for 15 minutes before slicing.
Store leftovers, tightly wrapped, in the refrigerator for up to 1 day or
in the freezer for up to 1 month.

TEST KITCHEN TIP: To roast your own peppers instead of
using bottled ones, cut red peppers in half lengthwise and remove the
stems, seeds and inner membranes. Line a large baking sheet with
foil. Place the pepper halves, cut side down, on the sheet. Broil 5″

(continued)

from the heat for 10 minutes or until the skins begin to blister. Remove the peppers from the oven, place them in a clean paper bag and let them cool. Use a knife to remove the skin. Then chop the peppers as needed.

Makes 1 loaf; 28 slices.

&‑ PER ¹/₂" SLICE: 64 calories, 2.8 g. total fat, 0.7 g. saturated fat, 3 mg. cholesterol, 184 mg. sodium

---

Garlic Bread Twists

Adapted from *Gracious Goodness . . . Charleston!*
BISHOP ENGLAND HIGH SCHOOL

When you need bread sticks in a hurry, try these cheese-flavored ones from the Bishop England High School. They're made with refrigerated pizza dough to save you time. We also used an egg white mixture, instead of butter, to cut fat and calories.

1   can (10 ounces) refrigerated pizza dough
1   egg white
1   tablespoon water
½   teaspoon garlic powder or garlic-and-herb salt-free seasoning
2   teaspoons grated Parmesan cheese or 2 teaspoons sesame seeds or poppy seeds

Preheat the oven to 375°. Coat a baking sheet with no-stick spray.
Remove the pizza dough from its package but do not unroll it. Cut the dough crosswise into 12 slices. Then unroll each slice. Cut each piece in half. Twist each piece 3 or 4 times, then place on the prepared baking sheet about 1" apart.
In a small bowl, use a fork to lightly beat together the egg white and water. Brush a small amount of the mixture on the dough. Sprinkle the twists with the garlic powder or seasoning. Then sprinkle with the Parmesan, sesame seeds or poppy seeds. Bake for 12 to 15 minutes or until golden brown. Remove the bread twists from the baking sheet and serve warm.

Makes 24; 12 servings.

&‑ PER 2 BREAD TWISTS: 63 calories, 0.8 g. total fat, 0.1 g. saturated fat, 0 mg. cholesterol, 127 mg. sodium

Heartwarming Soups and Stews

Cream of Fresh Asparagus Soup

Adapted from *Yesterday, Today and Tomorrow*
BADDOUR MEMORIAL CENTER

Pureeing the asparagus gives this soup a full body, making it possible to switch from light cream to evaporated milk without a noticeable difference. The result is a thick side-dish soup that's almost fat-free.

2 pounds fresh asparagus (see tip)
1 can (14½ ounces) reduced-sodium chicken broth, defatted
½ cup evaporated skim milk
½ teaspoon fresh lemon juice
⅛ teaspoon ground white pepper
⅛ teaspoon salt (optional)
1 tablespoon finely chopped fresh parsley

To prepare the asparagus, break and discard the woody ends from the asparagus. Using a vegetable peeler, scrape and discard the scales from the base of the stalks. Then cut the stalks into ½″ pieces.

Transfer the asparagus to a large saucepan. Add the broth. Bring to boil, then reduce the heat. Cover and simmer for 10 to 15 minutes or until the asparagus is very tender.

Transfer the asparagus mixture, in small batches, to a blender or food processor. Process until smooth. Return the mixture to the saucepan. Stir in the milk, lemon juice, pepper and salt, if desired. Heat the soup until warm.

To serve, ladle the soup into small soup bowls and sprinkle with the parsley to garnish.

TEST KITCHEN TIP: When selecting asparagus, choose stalks that are crisp, long and slender and have tightly closed tips. For another treat, try this soup with white asparagus. Look for fresh white asparagus in specialty produce markets between March and June.

Makes 4 side-dish servings.

PER SERVING: 85 calories, 0.7 g. total fat, 0.2 g. saturated fat, 1 mg. cholesterol, 258 mg. sodium

Mexican Cheese Soup

Adapted from *Family Secrets*
LEE ACADEMY

Many times, reduced-fat cheeses do not melt as smoothly as their fattier counterparts. To overcome this, we recommend finely shredding the cheese and tossing it with a small amount of cornstarch before adding it to the soup.

½	cup finely chopped onions
½	cup finely chopped celery
3	tablespoons finely chopped green peppers
1	can (14½ ounces) reduced-sodium chicken broth, defatted
¾	cup (3 ounces) finely shredded reduced-fat sharp Cheddar cheese
1	teaspoon cornstarch
1	can (12 ounces or 1½ cups) evaporated skim milk
½	cup skim milk
⅓	cup reduced-sodium or regular mild salsa
2	tablespoons fat-free plain yogurt
8–10	drops hot-pepper sauce
1	tablespoon chopped fresh chives
	No-oil, unsalted tortilla chips (optional)

Lightly coat an unheated large skillet with no-stick spray. Add the onions, celery, green peppers and 2 tablespoons of the broth. Cook and stir over medium heat about 8 minutes or until the celery is tender. (If necessary, add more broth during cooking.)

Add the remaining broth. Bring to a simmer.

Meanwhile, place the Cheddar in a small bowl and sprinkle with the cornstarch. Toss until coated.

Slowly stir the cheese mixture into the broth mixture. Cook and stir over low heat just until the cheese is melted. Then stir in the evaporated milk, skim milk, salsa, yogurt and hot-pepper sauce. Heat just until warm, stirring occasionally. Ladle the soup into small soup bowls. Top each with some of the chives to garnish. If desired, serve with the tortilla chips.

Makes 4 side-dish servings.

🖎 PER SERVING: 163 calories, 3.8 g. total fat, 1.9 g. saturated fat, 13 mg. cholesterol, 722 mg. sodium

Roasted Pepper and Tomato Soup

Adapted from *Peachtree Bouquet*
JUNIOR LEAGUE OF DEKALB COUNTY

*Surprisingly, sweet peppers are a fantastic source of vitamin C.
And red peppers contain large quantities of vitamin A. Combined
with tomatoes—another great source of vitamin C—this side-dish
soup is a delicious way to meet your daily requirement of these es-
sential vitamins.*

4   medium sweet red peppers
2   cups peeled, seeded and chopped tomatoes (see tip)
    or 1 can (20 ounces) no-salt-added tomatoes, drained and
    cut up
1   teaspoon olive oil
2   small cloves garlic, minced
3   cups (24 ounces) defatted reduced-sodium chicken broth
    Pinch of salt
¼   teaspoon freshly ground black pepper
2   tablespoons red wine vinegar
2   tablespoons finely chopped fresh basil or 1½ teaspoons
    dried basil, crushed

To roast the red peppers, cut each pepper in half lengthwise and
remove the stems, seeds and inner membranes. Line a large baking
sheet with foil. Place the pepper halves, cut side down, on the baking sheet. Broil 5″ from the heat about 10 minutes or until the skin
begins to blister. Remove the peppers from the baking sheet and
cover with plastic wrap or place them in a clean paper bag, close it,
and let the peppers stand for 20 to 30 minutes.

Using a knife, pull the skin from the peppers. Discard the skin.
In a blender or food processor, puree the peppers and tomatoes.

Heat the oil in a medium saucepan. Add the garlic. Cook and stir
over medium heat for 30 seconds. Stir in the tomato-pepper mixture
and broth. Bring to a gentle boil, then reduce the heat. Simmer, uncovered, for 10 to 15 minutes or until the mixture is slightly thickened, stirring occasionally. Remove from the heat and stir in the salt
and black pepper. Let stand about 30 minutes to cool to room temperature before serving.

Just before serving, stir in the vinegar and basil.

TEST KITCHEN TIP: To easily peel tomatoes, bring a saucepan of water to a boil. Pierce a tomato with the tines of a fork, plunge it into the boiling water for 30 seconds, then lift it out and cool it under cold running water. Using a paring knife, pull the loosened skin from the tomato.

Makes 4 side-dish servings.

ॐ PER SERVING: 64 calories, 1.6 g. total fat, 0.2 g. saturated fat, 0 mg. cholesterol, 362 mg. sodium

Carrot-Ginger Soup

Adapted from *California Sizzles*
JUNIOR LEAGUE OF PASADENA

The Junior League of Pasadena says "This soup is worth its weight in gold." We agree—it's elegant, flavorful and packed with an ample serving of vitamin A. We kept the fat low by cooking the carrots in water and adding just enough butter for a rich flavor.

1	tablespoon butter
1	pound carrots, peeled and thinly sliced
1	large onion, chopped
2½	cups (20 ounces total) reduced-sodium chicken broth, defatted
1½	teaspoons finely shredded orange peel
¾	teaspoons ground ginger
¼	teaspoon ground coriander
¼	cup skim milk
¼	cup evaporated skim milk (see tip)
	Ground black pepper (to taste)
6	teaspoons grated Parmesan cheese
4	small fresh parsley sprigs

Melt the butter in a medium saucepan. Add the carrots, onions and 2 tablespoons water. Cover and cook over medium heat about 15 minutes or until the vegetables begin to soften, stirring occasionally.

Stir in 1 cup of the broth, orange peel, ginger and coriander. Reduce the heat to medium-low. Cover and simmer the mixture about 20 minutes or until the carrots are very tender.

In a blender or food processor, puree the carrot mixture in small batches. Transfer the mixture to the saucepan. Stir in the remaining 1½ cups broth, skim milk and evaporated milk. Season to taste with the pepper. Cook just until warm, stirring occasionally.

To serve, ladle the soup into small soup bowls. Sprinkle each with 1½ teaspoons of the Parmesan and garnish with a sprig of parsley.

TEST KITCHEN TIP: If you don't have evaporated skim milk on hand, use ½ cup skim milk instead. However, expect the consistency of this soup to be slightly thinner.

Makes 4 side-dish servings.

    🐟 PER SERVING: 133 calories, 4.1 g. total fat, 2.4 g. saturated fat, 11 mg. cholesterol, 449 mg. sodium

Wild Rice Soup

Adapted from *Desert Treasures*
JUNIOR LEAGUE OF PHOENIX

A small amount of whole milk gives this soup a creamy texture without contributing the extra fat that the half-and-half normally used in the recipe would.

1   tablespoon reduced-calorie butter blend
¼   cup very finely chopped carrots
1   tablespoon very finely chopped onions
1   can (14½ ounces) reduced-sodium chicken broth, defatted
3   tablespoons low-sodium 96% fat-free fully cooked ham, very finely chopped
¼   cup all-purpose flour
½   cup whole milk
1   cup cooked wild rice (see tip)
1   tablespoon dry sherry or ½ teaspoon sherry extract
    Finely chopped fresh parsley

Melt the butter blend in a medium saucepan. Add the carrots and onions. Cook and stir over medium heat about 3 minutes or until the onions are tender.

Stir in the broth and ham. Bring to a boil.

Meanwhile, in a small bowl, use a wire whisk to stir the flour into the milk.

Slowly stir the milk mixture into the broth mixture. Add the rice. Cook and stir over medium heat until the mixture begins to thicken and just comes to a boil. Reduce the heat to low. Cook and stir for 1 minute more. Stir in the sherry or sherry extract.

To serve, ladle the soup into small soup bowls. Sprinkle with the parsley to garnish.

TEST KITCHEN TIP: To get 1 cup of cooked wild rice, begin with ½ cup uncooked wild rice. Rinse the rice well under cold running water, then add it to a pan of boiling water. Simmer the rice about 40 minutes, or until tender. Drain the rice before adding it to the soup.

Makes 4 side-dish servings.

&. PER SERVING: 136 calories, 4.1 g. total fat, 1.3 g. saturated fat, 6 mg. cholesterol, 301 mg. sodium

Wonton Soup

Adapted from *Hospitality*
NORTH SHORE MEDICAL CENTER AUXILIARY

*To save on fat and calories, we made these pork-filled wontons
with ground pork loin. Many markets do not label their ground
meat products according to how much fat they contain. So you
may be wise to ask the butcher to grind a pork loin especially for
you. You'll end up with more than the 4 ounces you need here.
So freeze the remaining meat in 4- and 8-ounce packages to use in
other recipes.*

WONTONS

4   ounces ground pork loin
1   small green onion, sliced
1   teaspoon reduced-sodium soy sauce
¼   teaspoon cornstarch
½   teaspoon grated fresh ginger
1   egg white
1   tablespoon water
12 wonton wrappers

SOUP

2   cans (14½ ounces each) reduced-sodium chicken broth,
    defatted
2   green onions, sliced
1   tablespoon reduced-sodium soy sauce

FOR THE WONTONS: In a small skillet, cook the pork and
onions until the pork is no longer pink, stirring occasionally. Drain
the mixture, then transfer it to a plate lined with paper towels. Blot
the top of the mixture with additional paper towels.

Wipe out the skillet and return the pork mixture to it. Stir in the
soy sauce, cornstarch and ginger.

In a custard cup, lightly beat together the egg white and water.

To fill the wontons, spoon 1 teaspoon of the pork mixture in the
center of each wonton wrapper. Moisten the edges of the wrapper
with the egg white mixture. Fold the wonton wrapper in half, forming a triangle and enclosing the filling. Press the edges together to
seal. Then fold the right- and left-hand corners of the wrapper down
below the filling; moisten with the egg white mixture and press the
corners together securely to seal. Set the filled wontons aside.

OUR CAUSE

North Shore Medical Center Auxiliary

Witch trials aside, the lovely town of Salem, Massachusetts, on Boston's North Shore, has long been noted for its warmth toward visitors. The town has a reputation to uphold, after all, as the site of the seventeenth-century House of Seven Gables, the mansion made famous by Nathaniel Hawthorne's classic book of the same name.

In 1873 a sea captain named John Bertram solidified the town's caring persona when he founded the Salem Hospital to care for ill or injured seamen. Today, the 580-bed nonprofit hospital gets help from the Salem Hospital Aid Association, 650 men and women who, since 1939, have raised more than a million dollars and devoted countless hours to the care of the hospital's patients.

In a town as rich in history as Salem, it is not surprising that the members of the association found a wealth of recipes to include in their cookbook. Money raised by *Hospitality* will help the Salem Hospital Aid Association provide diagnostic and lifesaving equipment for the hospital and its health care affiliates.

FOR THE SOUP: In a medium saucepan, combine the broth, onions and soy sauce. Bring to a boil. Gently add the wontons. Reduce the heat and gently simmer, uncovered, for 2 minutes. (Do not boil or the wontons will split open.)

To serve, spoon three wontons into each soup bowl, then ladle the broth mixture over the wontons.

Makes 4 side-dish servings.

ᔐ PER SERVING: 136 calories, 2.5 g. total fat, 0.8 g. saturated fat, 17 mg. cholesterol, 129 mg. sodium

Springtime Vegetable Soup

Adapted from *Bay Leaves*

JUNIOR SERVICE LEAGUE OF PANAMA CITY

What can you do with all those vegetables when your garden is at its peak? Try this creamy soup, which is low in fat but full of body. The secret is replacing the standard heavy cream and egg yolk with evaporated skim milk and cornstarch.

1	teaspoon margarine
5	green onions, thinly sliced
2	cans (14½ ounces each) reduced-sodium chicken broth, defatted
1½	cups fresh green beans cut into 1″ pieces
2	teaspoons chopped fresh parsley
¼	teaspoon sugar
¼	teaspoon dried marjoram leaves, crushed
	Pinch of ground dried sage
¾	cup sliced celery
¾	cup bias-sliced carrots
1	can (5 ounces or ⅔ cup) evaporated skim milk
2	tablespoons cornstarch
1	small yellow summer squash, sliced ¼″ thick
	Ground black pepper (to taste)

Lightly coat an unheated medium saucepan with no-stick spray. Add the margarine and heat until melted. Add the onions. Cook and stir over medium heat about 3 minutes or until the onions are tender.

Stir in the broth, beans, parsley, sugar, marjoram and sage. Bring to a boil, then reduce the heat. Cover and simmer for 10 minutes.

Add the celery and carrots and return to a boil. Reduce the heat and simmer for 10 minutes. Meanwhile, in a small bowl, use a wire whisk to stir together the milk and cornstarch.

Slowly stir the milk mixture into the broth mixture. Add the squash. Cook and stir over medium heat until the mixture begins to thicken and just comes to a boil. Cook and stir for 2 minutes more. Season to taste with the pepper and serve.

Makes 4 main-dish servings.

&▲   PER SERVING: 107 calories, 1.4 g. total fat, 0.3 g. saturated fat, 1 mg. cholesterol, 507 mg. sodium

Tortilla Turkey Soup

Adapted from *Tropical Seasons*

BEAUX ARTS OF THE LOWE ART MUSEUM OF THE UNIVERSITY OF MIAMI

We added extra tomatoes and corn to this Mexican-style soup to increase its fiber content.

½ cup chopped onions
2 tablespoons diced green chili peppers
½ teaspoon chili powder (or to taste)
½ teaspoon ground cumin
1 small clove garlic, minced
¼ teaspoon dried oregano leaves, crushed
⅛ teaspoon ground red pepper
3 cups (24 ounces) defatted reduced-sodium chicken broth
1 can (16 ounces) no-salt-added tomatoes (with juice), cut up
6 ounces boneless turkey breast, cut into bite-size ½"-wide strips
1 cup frozen whole kernel corn
2 tablespoons chopped cilantro
Ground black pepper (to taste)
½ cup (2 ounces) finely shredded reduced-fat Monterey Jack cheese
½ cup no-oil, unsalted tortilla chips, broken into large pieces

Lightly coat an unheated medium saucepan with olive oil no-stick spray. Add the onions. Cook and stir over medium heat about 3 minutes or until the onions are tender.

Stir in the chili peppers, chili powder, cumin, garlic, oregano and red pepper. Cook and stir for 1 minute more. Then add the broth and tomatoes (with juice). Bring to a boil. Add the turkey and corn. Simmer, uncovered, about 3 minutes or until the turkey is tender and no longer pink. (If necessary, add a small amount of water or additional broth if the soup is too spicy.)

Stir in the cilantro. Season to taste with the black pepper. Top each serving with some of the Monterey Jack and chips.

Makes 4 main-dish servings.

PER SERVING: 196 calories, 4.8 g. total fat, 1.6 g. saturated fat, 45 mg. cholesterol, 457 mg. sodium

Black Bean Soup

Adapted from *Seasoned with Sun*

JUNIOR LEAGUE OF EL PASO

Salt pork is often used to flavor bean dishes. Unfortunately, it's almost pure fat, so it's not really desirable from a health standpoint. This soup contains lean ham in place of the salt pork, which gives a similar flavor with much less fat and sodium.

6	cups water
2	cups (24 ounces) defatted reduced-sodium beef broth
1½	cups dried black beans, sorted and rinsed
4	ounces low-sodium 96% fat-free fully cooked ham, chopped
½	cup chopped onions
1	small carrot, chopped
2	cloves garlic, minced
¼	teaspoon salt
⅛	teaspoon dried thyme leaves, crushed
1	small bay leaf
2	teaspoons dry sherry or ½ teaspoon sherry extract
	Freshly ground black pepper (to taste)

In a large saucepan, combine the water, broth, beans, ham, onions, carrots, garlic, salt, thyme and bay leaf. Bring to a boil, then reduce the heat. Cover and simmer for 1½ to 2 hours or until the beans are very tender. Remove and discard the bay leaf.

Transfer the bean mixture, in small batches, to a blender or food processor. Process until almost smooth. Stir in the sherry or sherry extract. Season to taste with the pepper. If desired, either reheat or chill the soup before serving.

TEST KITCHEN TIP: To add a finishing touch to this soup, top each serving with a spoonful of reduced-fat sour cream and a sprig of flat-leaf parsley or a sprinkle of thinly sliced green onion tops.

Makes 6 main-dish servings.

૨⅃ PER SERVING: 159 calories, 1.4 g. total fat, 0.4 g. saturated fat, 6 mg. cholesterol, 465 mg. sodium

Newport Clam Chowder

Adapted from *California Sizzles*
JUNIOR LEAGUE OF PASADENA

You can give skim milk a thicker, creamier body and extra flavor by mixing in nonfat dry milk powder. This trick was used here to cut fat, but not the characteristic goodness of this New England treat.

1   tablespoon reduced-calorie butter blend
1   small onion, chopped
½   cup bottled clam juice
2   cans (6½ ounces each) minced clams (with liquid)
2   large potatoes, peeled and diced
3   cups skim milk
¼   cup all-purpose flour
3   tablespoons nonfat dry milk powder
     Ground white pepper (to taste)

Melt the butter blend in a medium saucepan. Add the onions. Cook and stir over medium heat about 3 minutes or until the onions are tender.

Add the bottled clam juice plus the liquid from the clams. Then add the potatoes. Bring to a boil. Reduce the heat. Cover and simmer about 12 minutes or until the potatoes are nearly tender.

In a small bowl, use a wire whisk to stir together 1 cup of the skim milk, flour and milk powder. Slowly stir the milk mixture into the potato mixture. Then stir in the remaining 2 cups skim milk. Cook and stir over medium heat until the soup begins to thicken and just comes to a boil.

Add the clams, then cook and stir for 1 minute more. Season to taste with the pepper.

Makes 4 main-dish servings.

ð⊷ PER SERVING: 235 calories, 4.1 g. total fat, 1 g. saturated fat, 61 mg. cholesterol, 224 mg. sodium

Oven-Baked Beef Stew

Adapted from *Prairie Potpourri*

IMMANUEL MEDICAL CENTER AUXILIARY

What's labeled "stew meat" at the grocery store is usually bite-size pieces of beef cut from the chuck arm. For this oven-baked stew we used round steak. It's much leaner, and you won't be able to tell the difference.

1	can (16 ounces) tomatoes (with juice), cut up
1	tablespoon quick-cooking tapioca
1	teaspoon sugar
12	ounces beef top round steak, trimmed of all visible fat and cut into 1″ pieces
2	large potatoes, cut into ¾″ cubes
2	medium carrots, cut into 1″ chunks
½	small onion, sliced
½	cup sliced celery
½	teaspoon ground black pepper

Preheat the oven to 250°. Lightly coat a 2½-quart casserole with no-stick spray. In the casserole, stir together the tomatoes (with juice), tapioca and sugar. Then add the beef, potatoes, carrots, onions, celery and pepper. Toss until the meat and vegetables are coated.

Cover and bake for 5 to 6 hours or until the meat and vegetables are tender, stirring the mixture after 3 hours.

TEST KITCHEN TIP: For an herb-flavored tomato stew, stir ½ teaspoon crushed dried basil and ¼ teaspoon crushed dried thyme leaves into the tomato mixture. Or use 1 teaspoon garlic-and-herb salt-free seasoning.

Makes 4 main-dish servings.

&❧ PER SERVING: 247 calories, 3.4 g. total fat, 1.1 g. saturated fat, 53 mg. cholesterol, 241 mg. sodium

Greek Beef Stew

Adapted from *River Feast*
JUNIOR LEAGUE OF CINCINNATI

For a hearty, healthy meal, we teamed this slightly sweet-and-spicy stew with couscous. (You could also use rice.) For a simple, wholesome dessert, serve apple and orange wedges.

3½ pounds beef top round steak, cut ½″–¾″ thick and trimmed of all visible fat
    Pinch of salt
    Pinch of freshly ground black pepper
2½ pounds pearl onions, peeled
1   can (6 ounces) tomato paste
¾   cup dry red wine or nonalcoholic red wine
2   tablespoons red wine vinegar
2   tablespoons currants or raisins
1   tablespoon packed brown sugar
1   clove garlic, minced
¼   teaspoon ground cumin
⅛   teaspoon ground cloves
1   bay leaf
1   small cinnamon stick (2½″)
¼–½ cup dry red wine, nonalcoholic red wine or water (optional)
3   cups hot cooked couscous

Preheat the oven to 300°. Sprinkle the meat with the salt and pepper, then cut the meat into 1″ pieces. Transfer the meat to a Dutch oven or a 3- or 4-quart casserole. Place the onions on top.

In a small bowl, stir together the tomato paste, ¾ cup wine, vinegar, currants or raisins, brown sugar, garlic, cumin and cloves. Pour the mixture over the meat and onions. Add the bay leaf and cinnamon stick.

Cover and bake about 3 hours or until the meat is very tender. If necessary, add enough of the additional wine or water to prevent drying out. Remove and discard the bay leaf and cinnamon stick. Serve the meat mixture with the couscous.

Makes 6 main-dish servings.

ｱ PER SERVING: 591 calories, 9.8 g. total fat, 3.2 g. saturated fat, 163 mg. cholesterol, 113 mg. sodium

Brunswick Stew

Adapted from *Calico Cupboards*
JUNIOR AUXILIARY OF BENTON

In the 1800s this time-honored stew was often made with squirrel meat. Today, however, it's more commonly made with chicken. We modified this classic by removing the skin from the chicken and browning the meat in a small amount of reduced-calorie butter.

1	tablespoon reduced-calorie butter blend
1½–2	pounds meaty chicken pieces (breasts, thighs and drumsticks), skin removed
¼	teaspoon paprika
2	medium onions, sliced
1	medium green pepper, chopped
2	cans (14½ ounces each or about 3⅔ cups total) reduced-sodium chicken broth, defatted
1	can (16 ounces) tomatoes (with juice), cut up
2	tablespoons chopped fresh parsley
1	teaspoon Worcestershire sauce
½	teaspoon hot-pepper sauce
2	cups frozen whole kernel corn
1	package (10 ounces) frozen lima beans
2	tablespoons cornstarch

Lightly coat an unheated Dutch oven with no-stick spray. Add the butter blend and heat. Sprinkle the chicken with the paprika. Then add the chicken to the Dutch oven and brown it on all sides. Remove the chicken and set aside.

Add the onions and green peppers. Cook and stir over medium heat about 3 minutes or until the onions are tender. Stir in 3 cups of the broth, the tomatoes (with juice), parsley, Worcestershire sauce and hot-pepper sauce. Add the chicken. Bring to a boil, then reduce the heat. Cover and simmer for 30 minutes.

Add the corn and beans. Return to a boil, then reduce the heat. Cover and simmer about 10 minutes or until the chicken and vegetables are tender.

If desired, remove the chicken from its bones; discard the bones and return the meat to the stew. Use a wire whisk to stir the corn-

OUR CAUSE

Junior Auxiliary of Benton

From the Ozark Mountains to the flat Grand Prairie, the frontier women of Arkansas could quilt like no other women in our young country. Keeping warm was a necessity, of course. But as every woman knows, making the house pretty brings a special sort of warmth, too.

The feminine forebears of today's Arkansas women weren't about to sacrifice beauty to usefulness. For generations, they made an art of the ancient skill of quilting, passing their talent and skills on to their daughters and granddaughters.

The Junior Auxiliary of Benton, Arkansas, puts it nicely when they note in *Calico Cupboards* that every quilt was an act of love for a woman's family and a sign of her faith in the future. The auxiliary first published its pretty cookbook in 1980. Since then, the art of quilting has had a vibrant rebirth across the country, and the women of the Junior Auxiliary are proud to show off their heritage.

Sales of the cookbook are earmarked for projects of the auxiliary that benefit the children of Saline County, Arkansas.

starch into the remaining ⅔ cup chicken broth. Then slowly stir the cornstarch mixture into the vegetable mixture. Cook and stir until the mixture begins to thicken and just comes to a boil. Cook and stir for 2 minutes more.

Makes 6 main-dish servings.

PER SERVING: 251 calories, 4.1 g. total fat, 1 g. saturated fat, 46 mg. cholesterol, 497 mg. sodium

Log House Gumbo

Adapted from *Sensational Seasons*
JUNIOR LEAGUE OF FORT SMITH

Cajun dishes, like this traditional gumbo, often are made with a roux—a mixture of equal parts flour and fat that is slowly cooked over low heat. We made this step easier and lighter by omitting the fat and baking the flour until it's light brown in color.

3	tablespoons all-purpose flour
2	cups water
1	whole medium chicken breast (about 1½ pounds), skin removed
2	teaspoons canola oil
¾	cup chopped onions
½	cup chopped celery
¼	cup chopped green peppers
2	teaspoons reduced-calorie, reduced-sodium ketchup
2	teaspoons Worcestershire sauce
3	cloves garlic, minced (1½ teaspoons)
¼	teaspoon hot-pepper sauce
⅛	teaspoon ground red pepper
⅛–¼	teaspoon salt
	Pinch of ground black pepper
1	bay leaf
1	package (10 ounces) frozen cut okra
1	can (16 ounces) no-salt-added tomatoes (with juice), cut up
12	ounces medium shrimp, shelled and deveined
¾	teaspoon gumbo filé
3	cups hot cooked rice

Preheat the oven to 400°. Place the flour in a pie pan. Bake about 15 minutes or until the flour turns caramel in color, stirring every 5 minutes.

Meanwhile, in a medium skillet, bring the water to a boil. Add the chicken, then reduce the heat. Cover and simmer for 20 to 25 minutes or until the chicken is tender and no longer pink. Remove the chicken from the liquid. Set the cooking liquid aside. Cool the chicken slightly, then remove and discard the bones and shred the meat with a fork. Set the chicken aside.

Lightly coat an unheated large skillet with no-stick spray, then add the oil and heat. Add the onions, celery and green peppers. Cook and stir over medium heat about 3 minutes or until the onions are tender.

Sprinkle with the browned flour. Then stir in the cooking liquid from the chicken, ketchup, Worcestershire sauce, garlic, hot-pepper sauce, red pepper, salt, black pepper and bay leaf.

Add the okra and tomatoes (with juice). Bring to boil, then reduce the heat. Cover and simmer for 30 to 40 minutes or until the vegetables are tender, stirring occasionally. If necessary, add a small amount of water if the mixture becomes too thick.

Add the chicken and shrimp. Simmer about 5 minutes or until the shrimp turn pink. Stir in the filé. Remove and discard the bay leaf. Serve over the rice.

Makes 6 main-dish servings.

ò& PER SERVING: 338 calories, 4.6 g. total fat, 0.9 g. saturated fat, 133 mg. cholesterol, 242 mg. sodium

Light-Hearted Cincinnati Chili

Adapted from *River Feast*
JUNIOR LEAGUE OF CINCINNATI

The Junior League of Cincinnati contributed this good-for-you version of their area's signature chili. If you like a heartier meal, serve the chili in the traditional manner—over spaghetti.

½ cup chopped onions
1 pound ground turkey breast
1 can (15 ounces) spicy-style chili beans (with liquid)
1 can (8 ounces) no-salt-added tomato sauce
½ cup water
1 tablespoon chili powder
½ teaspoon sugar
½ teaspoon ground cumin
½ teaspoon ground cinnamon
¼ teaspoon ground allspice
  Freshly ground black pepper

Lightly coat an unheated large skillet with no-stick spray. Add the onions. Cook and stir over medium heat about 3 minutes or until the onions are tender.

Add the turkey. Cook until it is no longer pink, stirring occasionally. Drain the turkey mixture in a strainer or colander, then transfer it to a large plate lined with paper towels. Blot the top of the mixture with additional paper towels.

Wipe out the skillet with paper towels and return the turkey mixture to the skillet. Add the beans (with liquid), tomato sauce, water, chili powder, sugar, cumin, cinnamon, allspice and pepper. Bring to a boil, then reduce the heat. Cover and gently simmer for 20 minutes, stirring occasionally.

Makes 4 main-dish servings.

ど PER SERVING: 257 calories, 1.5 g. total fat, 0.2 g. saturated fat, 74 mg. cholesterol, 431 mg. sodium

Meats of
Every Variety

Popover Pizza

Adapted from *The Kitchen Connection*
NATIONAL COUNCIL OF JEWISH WOMEN, OMAHA SECTION

Reduced-fat products like spaghetti sauce, mozzarella cheese and skim milk lightened this upside-down pizza.

PIZZA FILLING

8	ounces ground beef (95% lean)
½	cup chopped onions
1¼	cups reduced-fat spaghetti sauce
2	tablespoons no-salt-added tomato paste
	Pinch of sugar
4	ounces reduced-fat mozzarella cheese, very thinly sliced (see tip)

POPOVER TOPPING

½	cup all-purpose flour
½	cup skim milk
¼	cup fat-free egg substitute
2	tablespoons grated Parmesan cheese
1	teaspoon canola oil
⅛	teaspoon salt

FOR THE PIZZA FILLING: Preheat the oven to 400°. Lightly coat an 8″ × 8″ baking pan with no-stick spray and set aside.

In a medium skillet, cook the beef and onions until the beef is browned and the onions are tender, stirring occasionally. Drain the beef mixture in a strainer or colander, then transfer it to a large plate lined with paper towels. Blot the top of the mixture with additional paper towels.

Wipe out the skillet and return the beef mixture to the skillet. Stir in the spaghetti sauce, tomato paste and sugar. Bring to a boil, then reduce the heat. Gently simmer, uncovered, for 5 minutes.

Transfer the meat mixture to the prepared pan. Place the mozzarella slices on top of the meat mixture, covering the entire surface.

FOR THE POPOVER TOPPING: Meanwhile, in a medium bowl, use a wire whisk to beat together the flour, milk, egg substitute, Parmesan, oil and salt until smooth.

Pour the topping over the cheese. Bake in the 400° oven for 30 to 35 minutes or until puffy and golden brown. Serve immediately while hot and puffy. Cut into squares to serve.

TEST KITCHEN TIP: You'll need very thin slices of cheese in order to cover the entire top of the meat mixture. So have the deli slice the cheese with their meat/cheese slicer. Packaged presliced cheese will be too thick for this dish.

Makes 4 servings.

🍴 PER SERVING: 331 calories, 13.2 g. total fat, 6.4 g. saturated fat, 38 mg. cholesterol, 632 mg. sodium

---

Jalapeño Cornbread and Ground Meat Casserole

Adapted from *The Gulf Gourmet*
WESTMINSTER ACADEMY PTA

To shave fat from the spicy meat filling, we used ground turkey breast instead of ground beef. But if your family still prefers the taste of beef, use 8 ounces of ground beef that's labeled 95% lean and 8 ounces of ground turkey breast. The filling will have a beefy flavor, but it'll be much lower in fat than if you used all beef.

FILLING

1	pound ground turkey breast
1	large onion, chopped
1	can (16 ounces) no-salt-added tomatoes (with juice), cut up
2–3	jalapeño chili peppers, seeded and finely chopped (wear disposable gloves when handling)

CORNBREAD

1	cup yellow cornmeal
1	teaspoon salt
¼	teaspoon baking soda
1	cup nonfat buttermilk
1	can (8½ ounces) reduced-sodium cream-style corn
¼	cup fat-free egg substitute
3	tablespoons canola oil
2	slices turkey bacon, finely cut up, cooked and drained

Westminster Academy PTA

Tucked among majestic oak trees that dot the Mississippi Gulf Coast is the Westminster Academy. This school for kindergartners through sixth graders puts emphasis on small classes and individual attention to its students. The school has slightly less than 300 children, but the 50,000 copies of *The Gulf Gourmet* that have been printed since the first edition came out in 1978 speak volumes about the dedication of the school's PTA.

Ever since the Spanish first laid claim to the territory along the Gulf Coast in the mid-1500s, all who come here revel in the tranquil breezes that ruffle the leaves of the moss-draped oak trees growing so close to the water's edge. Westminster Academy echoes the genteel atmosphere of Gulfport. This school has a simple but noble mission: It is devoted to awakening young minds to the excitement of learning and providing a solid educational foundation these youngsters can build upon.

FOR THE FILLING: Lightly coat an unheated large skillet with no-stick spray. Add the turkey and onions. Cook until the turkey is no longer pink, stirring occasionally. Then stir in the tomatoes (with juice) and peppers. Remove from the heat and set aside.

Preheat the oven to 375°. Coat an 11″ × 7″ baking dish with no-stick spray and set aside.

FOR THE CORNBREAD: In a medium bowl, stir together the cornmeal, salt and baking soda. In a small bowl, stir together the buttermilk, corn, egg substitute, oil and bacon. Add the buttermilk mixture to the cornmeal mixture and stir until smooth.

To assemble, spread about a third of the cornbread mixture in the prepared baking dish. Carefully spoon the filling evenly on top. Then carefully spread the remaining cornbread mixture on top.

Bake about 40 minutes or until golden and a toothpick inserted in the cornbread portion comes out clean.

Makes 4 servings.

ðã PER SERVING: 449 calories, 13.9 g. total fat, 1.6 g. saturated fat, 79 mg. cholesterol, 808 mg. sodium

Enchilada Casserole

Adapted from *The Golden Taste of South Carolina*
SOUTH CAROLINA FARM BUREAU FEDERATION

Many Mexican dishes call for softening the tortillas by dipping them in hot oil. This recipe, however, steams them in the oven instead.

8	ounces ground beef (95% lean)
1	can (8 ounces) no-salt-added tomato sauce
½	cup water
1½	teaspoons chili powder
¼	teaspoon salt
¼	teaspoon ground cumin
4	corn or flour tortillas (6″ in diameter)
¼	cup finely chopped onions
2	tablespoons finely chopped green peppers
1	cup (4 ounces) finely shredded reduced-fat sharp Cheddar cheese

Preheat the oven to 350°. In a medium no-stick skillet, cook the beef until browned, stirring occasionally. Drain the beef in a strainer or colander, then transfer it to a large plate lined with paper towels. Blot the top of the beef with additional paper towels.

Wipe out the skillet and return the beef to the skillet. Stir in the tomato sauce, water, chili powder, salt and cumin. Set the beef mixture aside.

Tightly wrap the stack of tortillas in foil and bake for 15 to 20 minutes or until soft and pliable. (Or, wrap the tortillas in paper towels and cook in a microwave oven on high power for 30 to 60 seconds or just until soft and pliable.)

Lightly coat a 1- or 1½-quart round casserole with no-stick spray. Place one of the tortillas in the casserole. Layer one-quarter each of the meat mixture, onions, peppers and Cheddar. Repeat the layers 3 more times with the remaining tortillas, meat mixture, onions, peppers and cheese. Cover and bake in the 350° oven for 15 minutes. Then uncover and bake for 5 to 10 minutes more or until heated through.

Makes 4 servings.

 PER SERVING: 277 calories, 12.3 g. total fat, 5.1 g. saturated fat, 47 mg. cholesterol, 646 mg. sodium

Cheese Meat Loaf

Adapted from *Cookbook 25 Years*
MADISON COUNTY FARM BUREAU WOMEN'S COMMITTEE

For this special meat loaf, we mixed extra-lean ground beef with a small amount of couscous rather than the standard cracker crumbs. The grains of couscous trap the water, keeping the meat loaf juicy and moist.

2　　tablespoons couscous
3　　tablespoons very hot water
¼　　cup finely chopped onions
3　　tablespoons + ⅓ cup reduced-fat spaghetti sauce
1　　egg white, lightly beaten
¼　　teaspoon dried oregano, crushed
¼　　teaspoon salt
　　　Pinch of ground black pepper
12　ounces ground beef (95% lean)
¾　　cup (3 ounces) finely shredded part-skim mozzarella cheese

Preheat the oven to 350°. In a medium bowl, stir together the couscous and water. Cover and let stand about 5 minutes or until the water is absorbed. Stir in the onions, 3 tablespoons of the spaghetti sauce, egg whites, oregano, salt and pepper. Add the beef and combine until well-mixed.

To assemble the meat loaf, on a piece of foil about 12″ long, form the meat mixture into a 6″ × 5″ rectangle. Spread the mozzarella on top of the meat rectangle, keeping the cheese within ½″ from the edges. Beginning from a short side, gently lift the foil to roll up the meat and cheese, jelly-roll fashion, into a tight roll. Press the ends together to seal the cheese inside the meat loaf.

Coat an 8″ × 8″ baking pan with no-stick spray. Carefully transfer the meat roll, seam side down, to the pan. Cover with foil and bake for 20 minutes.

Remove the foil. If necessary, pour off any excess fat. Then pour the remaining ⅓ cup spaghetti sauce over the meat loaf and bake for 15 to 20 minutes more or until the meat is no longer pink.

Makes 4 servings.

PER SERVING: 213 calories, 8.7 g. total fat, 4.2 g. saturated fat, 60 mg. cholesterol, 406 mg. sodium

Beef Burgundy Stroganoff

Adapted from *Land of Cotton*
JOHN T. MORGAN ACADEMY

Less is more, as in the case of this healthier version of beef Stroganoff. The amount of meat has been reduced and cut thinner than usual so that it looks like more. To make up the missing volume, more mushrooms were added.

1	beef round tip or top sirloin steak (12 ounces), trimmed of all visible fat
½	cup chopped onions
1	clove garlic, minced
12	ounces fresh mushrooms, sliced (about 4 cups)
1	can (13¾ ounces) reduced-sodium beef broth, defatted
3	tablespoons burgundy or nonalcoholic red wine
2	tablespoons fresh lemon juice
¼	teaspoon ground black pepper
2	tablespoons flour
1	container (8 ounces) fat-free sour cream
	Hot, cooked yolk-free egg noodles

Thinly slice the meat across the grain into bite-size strips. Coat an unheated large skillet with no-stick spray. Add the beef. Cook and stir over medium-high heat for 2 to 3 minutes or until browned. Use a slotted spoon to remove the beef from the skillet.

Add the onions and garlic. Cook and stir over medium heat for 2 minutes. Then add the mushrooms. Cook and stir about 2 minutes more or until the onions are tender.

Return the beef to the skillet. Add the broth, wine, lemon juice and pepper. Bring to a gentle boil, then reduce the heat. Cover and simmer for 15 minutes.

In a small bowl, stir the flour into the sour cream. Remove the skillet from the heat, then stir the sour cream mixture into the beef mixture. Serve over the noodles.

Makes 6 servings.

 PER SERVING (WITH ½ CUP YOLK-FREE EGG NOODLES):
209 calories, 2.6 g. total fat, 0.8 g. saturated fat, 32 mg. cholesterol, 214 mg. sodium

Sauerbraten with Gingersnap Gravy

Adapted from *Calico Cupboards*
JUNIOR AUXILIARY OF BENTON

In keeping with the recommendations of today's health experts, the serving size of meat in this dish is four ounces. To add filling carbohydrates—and soak up the delicious gravy—serve the sauerbraten over boiled potatoes or cooked yolk-free egg noodles.

SAUERBRATEN

½	teaspoon salt
¼	teaspoon ground black pepper
2–2½	pounds beef bottom round or boneless round rump roast
2	medium onions, sliced
1	small carrot, finely chopped
1	stalk celery, chopped
4	bay leaves
8	whole cloves
½	teaspoon black peppercorns
2½	cups water
1½	cups red wine vinegar

GINGERSNAP GRAVY

2	tablespoons sugar
10–12	gingersnaps, crushed
	Hot, cooked yolk-free egg noodles or boiled potatoes

FOR THE SAUERBRATEN: Using your fingers, rub the salt and pepper into the surface of the meat. Then place the meat in a deep earthenware crock or glass bowl. Add the onions, carrots, celery, bay leaves, cloves and peppercorns.

In a small saucepan, bring the water and vinegar to a boil. Pour the hot mixture over the meat. Cover and marinate the meat in the refrigerator for at least 48 hours, but no longer than 3 days.

Preheat the broiler. Remove the meat from the crock. Reserve the marinade. Discard the vegetables and spices.

Pat the meat dry with paper towels and transfer the meat to a rack in a broiling pan. Broil 4″ from the heat about 10 minutes or until the surface is browned, turning the meat over if necessary.

Transfer the meat to a large heavy saucepan or small Dutch oven. Strain the reserved marinade and pour it over the meat. Bring to a boil, then reduce the heat to medium-low. Cover and simmer for 2 to 2½ hours or until the meat is tender when pierced with a fork. Transfer the meat to a serving platter. Reserve the cooking liquid for the gravy. Cover the meat with foil to keep it warm while preparing the gravy.

FOR THE GINGERSNAP GRAVY: Measure the reserved cooking liquid from the meat. If necessary, add enough hot water to make 2 cups. Set the liquid aside.

In a small heavy saucepan, cook and stir the sugar over medium-high heat until it is melted and turns golden brown. Gradually stir in the hot liquid from the meat. Then stir in the gingersnaps.

To serve, slice the sauerbraten. Serve over the noodles and topped with the gravy.

Makes 8 servings.

PER SERVING (WITH ½ CUP YOLK-FREE EGG NOODLES): 332 calories, 8.9 g. total fat, 2.9 g. saturated fat, 77 mg. cholesterol, 250 mg. sodium

Cold Marinated Tenderloin

Adapted from *Cordonbluegrass*
JUNIOR LEAGUE OF LOUISVILLE

So full of flavor and so low in fat! This recipe uses red wine (or you can use beef broth) to replace oil in the marinade. Serve the meat thinly sliced in buffet buns for party sandwiches or on top of lettuce for a main-dish salad.

> 1   beef tenderloin roast (2–3 pounds)
> ¾   cup dry red wine, nonalcoholic red wine or defatted reduced-sodium beef broth
> ¼   cup reduced-sodium soy sauce
> 3   tablespoons honey
> 2   tablespoons red wine vinegar
> 1   green onion, chopped
> 8   cloves garlic, minced
> 1½ teaspoons ground ginger
>   Buffet rolls (optional)
>   Dijon or honey-Dijon mustard (optional)

Place the roast in a large resealable plastic bag. In a small bowl, stir together the wine or broth, soy sauce, honey, vinegar, onions, garlic and ginger. Pour the mixture over the roast. Seal the bag and marinate the meat in the refrigerator for 12 to 14 hours, turning the bag occasionally.

To prepare the grill for cooking, coat the unheated grill rack with no-stick spray. Then light the grill according to the manufacturer's directions. (If using a charcoal grill, place a foil pan in the center of the fire box to catch the drippings. Arrange the coals around the pan.) Check the temperature for grilling; the temperature should be "medium-hot" (see tip). Place the rack on the grill.

Remove the roast from the bag, reserving the marinade. If necessary, to make the roast a uniform size, fold the narrow ends under and tie. Or, if the roast is wide and flat, push it together crosswise and tie with string.

Place the roast on the grill rack. (If using a charcoal grill, make sure the roast is over the drip pan, not over the coals.) Insert a meat thermometer near the center of the roast. Cover (with the damper open) and grill for 45 to 60 minutes for medium-rare doneness, or until the thermometer registers 150°. Occasionally brush the roast with the marinade during the last 10 minutes of grilling. Discard the remaining marinade.

Cool the roast slightly. Then cover and chill in the refrigerator. To serve, thinly slice. If desired, serve with the rolls and mustard.

TEST KITCHEN TIP: When grilling, here's how to test the temperature of the coals: Place your hand 4" above the drip pan (if using a charcoal grill) or above the center coals (if using a gas grill). Count the number of seconds that the palm of your hand can withstand the heat before you have to remove your hand. For a *hot* temperature, that should be 2 seconds. For a *medium-hot* temperature, it should be 3 seconds. *Medium* heat would be 4 seconds, and *low* would be 5 seconds.

Makes 8 to 12 servings.

   PER SERVING: 207 calories, 7.1 g. total fat, 2.8 g. saturated fat, 64 mg. cholesterol, 314 mg. sodium

London Broil on the Grill

Adapted from *Cranbrook Reflections*
CRANBROOK HOUSE & GARDENS AUXILIARY

Fruit juice is a great substitute for oil in marinades. In this oriental marinade, we used orange juice, but you might also like the flavor of pineapple juice.

1   beef flank steak (1–1½ pounds)
½   cup reduced-sodium soy sauce
2   tablespoons packed brown sugar
2   tablespoons fresh lemon juice
2   tablespoons fresh orange juice
1   tablespoon dried minced onion or 2 tablespoons
    very finely chopped fresh onions
1   teaspoon ground ginger or ¼ teaspoon grated fresh ginger
1   clove garlic, minced
¼   teaspoon ground black pepper

Score both sides of the steak by making shallow cuts in a diamond pattern. Place the steak in a large resealable plastic bag. In a small bowl, stir together the soy sauce, brown sugar, lemon juice, orange juice, onions, ginger, garlic and pepper. Pour the mixture over the steak in the bag. Seal the bag and marinate the meat in the refrigerator for 8 to 12 hours, turning the bag occasionally.

To prepare the grill for cooking, coat the unheated grill rack with no-stick spray. Then light the grill according to the manufacturer's directions. Check the temperature for grilling; the temperature should be "medium," or 4 seconds that the palm of your hand can withstand the heat (see tip on page 131). Place the rack on the grill.

Remove the steak from the bag, reserving the marinade. Place the steak on the rack over the coals. Grill, uncovered, for 7 minutes. Brush with the marinade, then turn the steak over. Grill, uncovered, about 7 minutes more for medium doneness. Discard the remaining marinade.

If desired, let the meat stand for 5 minutes before slicing. To slice, cut the meat at an angle into ¼"-thick slices. Then overlap the slices on a platter to serve.

TEST KITCHEN TIP: To broil the steak instead of grilling it, place the meat on the rack of a broiling pan. Brush the steak with the marinade, then broil it 3″ from the heat for 7 minutes. Turn the steak over and brush it with more of the marinade. Broil about 7 minutes more for medium doneness.

Makes 4 to 6 servings.

   🕸 PER SERVING: 195 calories, 8 g. total fat, 3.5 g. saturated fat, 53 mg. cholesterol, 623 mg. sodium

---

Country Pot Roast

Adapted from *Southern Elegance*
JUNIOR LEAGUE OF GASTON COUNTY

A fat-free way to brown beef is to broil it, as we did here. By using this method, you'll eliminate at least 2 tablespoons of oil from standard pot roast recipes.

2	teaspoons paprika
¼	teaspoon salt
¼	teaspoon ground black pepper
1	boneless beef chuck pot roast (1½–2 pounds), trimmed of all visible fat
1	cup water
1	bay leaf
8–10	boiling onions, peeled
8–10	small carrots, bias-sliced into 3″ pieces
4–6	potatoes, quartered
1	can (16 ounces) no-salt-added tomato sauce
1	container (8 ounces) fat-free plain yogurt
1	tablespoon all-purpose flour
1	tablespoon chopped fresh parsley

Preheat the broiler. In a custard cup, stir together the paprika, salt and pepper. Sprinkle the mixture over the surface of the roast. Then rub the mixture into the meat with your fingers.

Coat the rack of a broiling pan with no-stick spray. Place the roast on the rack. Broil 4″ from the heat about 10 minutes or until

(continued)

the surface is browned. Drain the meat, then pat it with paper towels. Transfer the meat to a Dutch oven.

Add the water and bay leaf. Bring to a boil, then reduce the heat to medium-low. Cover and cook for 45 minutes. Add the onions, carrots and potatoes. Pour the tomato sauce over the meat and vegetables. Cover and cook for 50 to 60 minutes or until the meat and vegetables are tender. Remove and discard the bay leaf.

Transfer the meat and vegetables to a serving platter. In a small bowl, stir together the yogurt and flour. Then stir the yogurt mixture into the tomato mixture. Add the parsley. Cook and stir just until heated through. Serve the sauce with the roast and the vegetables.

TEST KITCHEN TIP: For smaller families, this makes a great "cook once, eat twice" meal. Prepare this pot roast meal on a weekend, when you have more time to cook. Then during the week, reheat the leftovers in the microwave for a quick, hearty meal.

Makes 6 to 8 servings.

 PER SERVING: 458 calories, 8.8 g. total fat, 3.3 g. saturated fat, 83 mg. cholesterol, 238 mg. sodium

Slow-Cooker Pepper Steak

Adapted from *The Golden Taste of South Carolina*
SOUTH CAROLINA FARM BUREAU FEDERATION

This recipe calls for a teaspoon of cracked pepper, which children might find too spicy for their taste. But you can easily decrease or increase the amount of pepper to suit your family's preferences.

    1   teaspoon cracked black pepper
    ¼   teaspoon salt
    1   boneless beef round steak (1¼ pounds), cut ¾" thick and
        trimmed of all visible fat
    1   can (4 ounces) diced green chili peppers, drained
    1   medium onion, sliced
    1   can (10¾ ounces) 99% fat-free condensed cream of
        tomato soup with ⅓ less salt
    1   cup water
    1   tablespoon fresh lemon juice
    1   clove garlic, minced
        Hot cooked yolk-free egg noodles or rice

Preheat the broiler. Sprinkle both sides of the steak with the black pepper and salt. Then rub the pepper and salt into the meat surface with your fingers.

Place the steak on the rack in a broiling pan. Broil 4" from the heat for 2 to 3 minutes on each side or until the surface is browned.

Cut the steak into 6 pieces. Place 3 of the pieces in a 4- or 6-quart Crock-Pot. Then layer on top half each of the chili peppers and onions. Repeat layers using the remaining steak, chili peppers and onions.

In a small bowl, stir together the soup, water, lemon juice and garlic. Then pour the soup mixture over the steak and vegetables. Cover and cook on the low heat setting for 5 to 7 hours or until the meat is tender.

Makes 6 servings.

& PER SERVING (WITH ½ CUP COOKED YOLK-FREE EGG
    NOODLES): 318 calories, 8.4 g. total fat, 2.7 g. saturated fat,
    61 mg. cholesterol, 492 mg. sodium

Country Pork Ribs

Adapted from *Among Friends*
JUNIOR AUXILIARY OF RUSSELLVILLE

*Occasionally, you can still have barbecued ribs and eat healthy,
too. Just follow a few healthful tips: Use country-style ribs—
they're the meatiest ribs on the market. And prebake them so that
you can drain off much of the fat before adding the sauce.*

PORK RIBS

3   pounds pork country-style ribs, trimmed of all visible fat

BARBECUE SAUCE

1   can (10¾ ounces) 99% fat-free condensed tomato soup
      with ⅓ less salt
¾   cup water
¼   cup reduced-calorie, reduced-sodium ketchup
3   tablespoons packed brown sugar
2   tablespoons finely chopped onions
2   tablespoon cider vinegar
1   tablespoon reduced-sodium Worcestershire sauce
¼   teaspoon ground black pepper
1–2 dashes of hot-pepper sauce

FOR THE PORK RIBS: Preheat the oven to 350°. Place the ribs
on a wire rack in a shallow pan. Tightly cover with foil. Prebake the
ribs for 1 hour.

Transfer the ribs to a large plate or platter lined with paper towels. Blot the ribs with additional paper towels. Then transfer the ribs
to a Dutch oven or small, deep roasting pan. Set the ribs aside.

FOR THE BARBECUE SAUCE: Place half the can of soup (⅔ cup)
into a medium bowl. (To reserve the remaining soup for another use,
transfer the soup to a plastic or glass container. Cover tightly and refrigerate for up to 3 days or freeze for up to 1 month.)

To the soup in the bowl, add the water, ketchup, brown sugar,
onions, vinegar, Worcestershire sauce, black pepper and hot-pepper
sauce.

Pour the sauce mixture over the ribs. Cover and bake for 45 to
60 minutes or until very tender, spooning sauce over the ribs occasionally.

TEST KITCHEN TIP: Almost 70% of the calories in pork ribs come from fat. To reduce the fat calories to about 37%, you can make "mock ribs." Use 1½ pounds pork loin, cut into 1" cubes. Thread the cubes onto 6 bamboo skewers, leaving a small space between the pieces. Do not prebake the mock ribs. Instead, just place them in a Dutch oven or roasting pan, add the sauce mixture and bake as directed. (Per serving of mock ribs with ⅓ cup sauce: 190 calories, 7.8 g. total fat, 2.6 g. saturated fat, 51 mg. cholesterol, 217 mg. sodium.)

Makes 6 servings.

❧ PER SERVING OF RIBS (WITH ⅓ CUP SAUCE): 479 calories, 30.2 g. total fat, 10.7 g. saturated fat, 124 mg. cholesterol, 341 mg. sodium

---

Mexican Pork Chops

Adapted from *Some Like It Hot*
JUNIOR LEAGUE OF MCALLEN

Chili powder and cumin are the prime ingredients in many high-sodium taco seasoning mixes that are often used to flavor dishes like this. So by using the individual spices, you'll cut way back on the sodium content.

6	pork center loin chops (2½ pounds total), cut ¾"–1" thick and trimmed of all visible fat
¾	cup long-grain white rice
1	can (16 ounces) no-salt added tomato sauce or 1 can (14 ounces) recipe-style stewed tomatoes (with juice)
1½	cups water
1	tablespoon chili powder
¼	teaspoon ground cumin
¼	teaspoon salt
1	cup (4 ounces) finely shredded reduced-fat sharp Cheddar cheese

Preheat the oven to 350°. Coat an 11" × 7" baking dish with no-stick spray and set aside.

Coat an unheated large skillet with no-stick spray. Heat over medium-high heat. Add the chops and brown on both sides. Transfer the chops to the prepared baking dish. Top with the rice.

(continued)

In a small bowl, stir together the tomato sauce or tomatoes (with juice), water, chili powder, cumin and salt. Carefully pour the mixture over the rice and chops.

Cover with foil and bake for 1 hour. Uncover and sprinkle with the Cheddar. Bake for 5 to 10 minutes more or until the cheese is melted.

Makes 6 servings.

&▲ PER SERVING: 293 calories, 10 g. total fat, 4 g. saturated fat, 56 mg. cholesterol, 430 mg. sodium

---

Chinese Oven-Fried Pork Chops

Adapted from *Gracious Goodness... Charleston!*
BISHOP ENGLAND HIGH SCHOOL

Pork cuts labeled "loin" or "leg" are your best choices in terms of leanness. This healthy breaded pork chop recipe from the Bishop England High School uses center loin chops.

¼ cup fat-free egg substitute or egg whites
3 tablespoons water
½ teaspoon garlic powder
¼ teaspoon ground ginger
4 pork center loin chops (4–5 ounces each), cut ½"–¾" thick and trimmed of all visible fat
1 cup fine, dry plain bread crumbs

Preheat the oven to 350°. Lightly coat a baking sheet with no-stick spray, then set aside.

In a shallow bowl, beat together the egg substitute or egg whites, water, garlic powder and ginger until combined.

To coat the chops, dip them in the egg mixture. Then dip the chops in the bread crumbs to evenly cover all sides. If necessary, press the crumbs onto the chops to stick.

Place the chops on the prepared baking sheet. Bake for 10 minutes. Turn the chops over and bake for 8 to 10 minutes more or until the pork has just a hint of pink in the center.

Makes 4 servings.

&▲ PER SERVING: 241 calories, 8.6 g. total fat, 2.8 g. saturated fat, 51 mg. cholesterol, 244 mg. sodium

Spinach–Mushroom Stuffed Pork Tenderloin

Adapted from *Uptown Down South*
JUNIOR LEAGUE OF GREENVILLE

This variation on old-fashioned stuffed pork chops uses the very leanest cut of pork, making this recipe lower in fat than pork chops.

STUFFING

- ¾ cup chopped fresh mushrooms
- ½ cup chopped onions
- ¼ teaspoon salt
- ¼ teaspoon ground nutmeg
- ⅛ teaspoon ground black pepper
- 1 package (10 ounces) frozen chopped spinach, thawed and well-drained

PORK TENDERLOIN

- 1 pork tenderloin (1–1½ pounds), trimmed of all visible fat

WINE SAUCE

- 1 tablespoon butter
- 1 cup + 2 tablespoons dry white wine or nonalcoholic white wine
- 2 teaspoons cornstarch

FOR THE STUFFING: Lightly coat an unheated medium skillet with no-stick spray. Add the mushrooms and onions. Cook and stir over medium heat about 5 minutes or until the vegetables are tender. If necessary, drain off any cooking juices.

Stir in the salt, nutmeg and pepper. Then stir in the spinach. Set the stuffing aside.

FOR THE PORK TENDERLOIN: Preheat the oven to 400°. Cut a pocket in the side of the tenderloin by cutting a lengthwise slit from one side to almost the other side and stopping about ½" from each of the tapered ends.

Spoon the stuffing mixture into the pocket of the tenderloin. Secure it closed with wooden toothpicks. Place the tenderloin on a rack in a shallow roasting pan. Roast, uncovered, for 20 to 25 minutes or until the pork has just a hint of pink in the center. Loosely cover with foil and let stand for 10 minutes before slicing.

(continued)

FOR THE WINE SAUCE: Meanwhile, in an 8″ skillet, cook and stir the butter over medium-high heat just until golden brown. (Be careful not to burn the butter.)

Stir in 1 cup of the wine. Cook, uncovered, over high heat about 4 minutes or until the wine reduces to ½ cup. Reduce the heat to medium.

In a custard cup, stir together the cornstarch and the remaining 2 tablespoons wine until smooth. Using a wire whisk, slowly stir the cornstarch mixture into the reduced wine. Cook and stir until the mixture begins to thicken and just comes to a boil. Then remove from the heat.

To serve, cut the stuffed tenderloin into 8 slices. Drizzle the sauce over the slices.

Makes 4 servings.

&⬥ PER SERVING: 158 calories, 4.7 g. total fat, 2 g. saturated fat,
64 mg. cholesterol, 148 mg. sodium

Marinated Pork Tenderloin

Adapted from *Savannah Style*
JUNIOR LEAGUE OF SAVANNAH

When you want a slightly different marinade, try this one from the Junior League of Savannah. It's a little sweet, a little salty and accented with cinnamon. Serve the pork with sautéed apple slices or baked acorn squash.

1	pork tenderloin (¾–1 pound), trimmed of all visible fat
2	tablespoons reduced-sodium soy sauce
1	tablespoon dry red wine or nonalcoholic red wine
1	green onion, very finely chopped
2	teaspoons packed brown sugar
1	teaspoon honey
1	small clove garlic, minced
¼	teaspoon ground cinnamon

Place the tenderloin in a large resealable plastic bag. In a small bowl, stir together the soy sauce, wine, onions, brown sugar, honey, garlic and cinnamon. Pour the soy sauce mixture over the tenderloin.

Seal the bag and marinate the meat in the refrigerator for 12 to 24 hours, turning the bag occasionally.

Meanwhile, prepare the grill for cooking. Coat the unheated grill rack with no-stick spray. Then light the grill according to the manufacturer's directions. (If using a charcoal grill, place a foil pan in the center of the fire box to catch the drippings. Arrange the coals around the pan.) Check the temperature for grilling; the temperature should be "low" or 5 seconds that the palm of your hand can withstand the heat (see tip on page 131). Place the rack on the grill.

Remove the tenderloin from the bag, reserving the marinade. If necessary, to make the tenderloin a uniform size, fold the narrow ends under and tie with string. Place the tenderloin on the rack. (If using a charcoal grill, make sure the tenderloin is over the drip pan, not over the coals.) Insert a meat thermometer near the center of the roast. Cover (with the damper open) and grill the tenderloin for 30 to 45 minutes or until the thermometer registers 160°. Brush the tenderloin with the reserved marinade during the last 15 minutes of grilling. Discard the remaining marinade.

To serve, cut the tenderloin into very thin slices.

Makes 4 servings.

꒛ PER SERVING: 131 calories, 3.1 g. total fat, 1.1 g. saturated fat, 60 mg. cholesterol, 309 mg. sodium

Pork Loin Roast with Orange Barbecue Sauce

Adapted from *Desert Treasures*
JUNIOR LEAGUE OF PHOENIX

The sweet and tangy barbecue sauce used on this pork roast is also great on grilled poultry.

PORK ROAST

½ teaspoon garlic salt

1 boneless pork top loin roast (single loin, 2–3 pounds), trimmed of all visible fat

BARBECUE SAUCE

1 can (6 ounces) frozen orange juice concentrate, thawed

¼ cup wine vinegar

2 tablespoons packed brown sugar

2 tablespoons honey

2 teaspoons prepared mustard

2 teaspoons reduced-sodium soy sauce

FOR THE PORK ROAST: About 30 minutes before grilling, rub the garlic salt into the surface of the roast. Cover with plastic wrap and refrigerate.

FOR THE BARBECUE SAUCE: In a small saucepan, stir together the orange juice concentrate, vinegar, brown sugar, honey, mustard and soy sauce. Cook and stir over low heat until the brown sugar is melted and the mixture is blended. Remove from the heat and set aside.

To prepare the grill for cooking, coat the unheated grill rack with no-stick spray. Then light the grill according to the manufacturer's directions. (If using a charcoal grill, place a foil pan in the center of the fire box to catch the drippings. Arrange the coals around the pan.) Check the temperature for grilling; the temperature should be "low" or 5 seconds that the palm of your hand can withstand the heat (see tip on page 131). Place the rack on the grill.

Unwrap the pork and place the roast on the rack, fat side up. (If using a charcoal grill, make sure the roast is over the drip pan, not over the coals.) Insert a meat thermometer near the center of the roast. Cover (with the damper open) and grill for 1 to 1¼ hours or until the thermometer registers 160°, brushing the roast occasionally with the sauce during the last 15 minutes of grilling.

Remove the roast from the grill. Loosely cover it with foil and let it stand for 10 minutes before slicing. Serve with the remaining sauce.

TEST KITCHEN TIP: To roast the pork loin instead of grilling it, place the meat, fat side up, on a rack in a shallow roasting pan. Roast, uncovered, in a 325° oven for 25 to 35 minutes or until the thermometer registers 160°; brush occasionally with the sauce during roasting.

Makes 8 to 12 servings.

> PER SERVING: 201 calories, 7.4 g. total fat, 2.5 g. saturated fat, 51 mg. cholesterol, 229 mg. sodium

---

Holiday Stuffed Ham

Adapted from *Among Friends*
JUNIOR AUXILIARY OF RUSSELLVILLE

A pork leg roast is also sometimes called a fresh ham. The advantage of this "ham" is that it's a lot lower in sodium than regular ham. Serve this herb-and-onion stuffed pork roast when you have a large gathering or a party. Or make it for the family and enjoy the leftovers for quick dinners later in the week.

⅔ cup finely chopped sweet white onions
3 green onions, finely chopped
⅓ cup chopped fresh parsley
2 small cloves garlic, minced
½ teaspoon salt
½ teaspoon dried basil leaves, crushed
½ teaspoon dried marjoram leaves, crushed
1 boneless pork leg roast (2–3 pounds), butterflied and trimmed of all visible fat (see tip on page 144)
1 can (14½ ounces) reduced-sodium vegetable or beef broth, defatted

Preheat the oven to 325°. In a small bowl, combine the white onions, green onions, parsley, garlic, salt, basil and marjoram. Set the onion mixture aside.

(continued)

On a flat work surface, open the roast and spread it flat, fat side down. Using a meat mallet, pound the roast to a ¾" thickness. Spread the onion mixture on top of the roast. Then tightly roll the roast up, jelly-roll fashion, beginning from one of its short sides. Tie with string to hold the roll together.

Coat a shallow roasting pan with no-stick spray. Place the meat roll in the pan, seam side down. Pour the broth over the roll. Insert a meat thermometer near the center of the roast. Roast, uncovered, for 2 to 2¾ hours or until the thermometer registers 160° to 170°.

Transfer the roast to a cutting board. Loosely cover it with foil and let it stand for 10 minutes before slicing. Meanwhile, skim the fat from the broth.

Slice the meat roll and transfer the slices to a meat platter. Serve the broth over the meat slices.

TEST KITCHEN TIP: You may need to special-order a boneless pork leg roast. When you do, make sure to ask that it be butterflied so you can just open it up and flatten it to an even thickness.

Makes 12 servings.

ﮬ PER SERVING: 98 calories, 4.9 g. total fat, 1.7 g. saturated fat, 34 mg. cholesterol, 187 mg. sodium

Smoked Sausage and Pasta Jambalaya

Adapted from *Southern Elegance*
JUNIOR LEAGUE OF GASTON COUNTY

Using turkey sausages yields a big fat savings in this twist on jambalaya. Two ounces of pork sausage has about 15 grams of fat, but the same amount of turkey sausage has only about 5 grams.

1	cup corkscrew pasta (rotini), tiny shell pasta or yolk-free wide egg noodles
12	ounces fully cooked smoked turkey sausages or turkey kielbasa, diagonally sliced
½	cup chopped onions
½	cup chopped green peppers
½	cup chopped celery
2	cloves garlic, minced
2	cans (16 ounces each) no-salt-added tomatoes (with juice), cut up
½	teaspoon thyme leaves, crushed
⅛	teaspoon ground red pepper

Cook the pasta or noodles according to the package directions, but without adding salt. Drain, rinse with hot water and drain again. If necessary, cover to keep warm.

Lightly coat an unheated large skillet with no-stick spray. Add the sausages, onions, green peppers, celery and garlic. Cook and stir over medium heat about 5 minutes or until the vegetables are tender and the sausages are heated through.

Add the tomatoes (with juice), thyme and red pepper. Bring to a boil, then reduce the heat. Cover and gently simmer for 10 minutes. Stir in the pasta or noodles. If necessary, heat through. Serve immediately.

Makes 6 servings.

ॐ PER SERVING: 191 calories, 4.7 g. total fat, 1.3 g. saturated fat, 36 mg. cholesterol, 508 mg. sodium

Moussaka

Adapted from *A Taste of New England*
JUNIOR LEAGUE OF WORCESTER

Substituting ground turkey breast for some of the lamb reduces the fat in this classic Greek dish without changing the flavor.

FILLING

- ½ cup chopped onions
- 1 clove garlic, minced
- 6 ounces ground turkey breast
- 6 ounces ground lean lamb
- 1 can (8 ounces) no-salt-added tomato sauce
- 1 tablespoon no-salt-added tomato paste
- 2 tablespoons chopped fresh parsley
- ½ teaspoon dried oregano leaves, crushed
- ½ teaspoon ground cinnamon
- ¼ teaspoon salt (optional)

EGGPLANT

- 1 medium eggplant (1–1¼ pounds), peeled and cut into ½" slices

SAUCE

- 1 cup skim milk
- 1 tablespoon cornstarch
- ¼ cup egg substitute
- ½ cup reduced-fat ricotta cheese
  Pinch of ground nutmeg
- ¼ cup fine, dry plain bread crumbs
- 2 tablespoons grated Parmesan cheese

FOR THE FILLING: Lightly coat an unheated large skillet with no-stick spray. Add the onions and garlic. Cook and stir over medium heat about 3 minutes or until the onions are tender. Then add the turkey and lamb. Cook until the turkey is no longer pink and the lamb is browned, stirring occasionally. Drain the meat mixture in a strainer or colander, then transfer it to a large plate lined with paper towels. Blot the top of the mixture with additional paper towels.

Wipe out the skillet with paper towels and return the mixture to the skillet. Stir in the tomato sauce, tomato paste, parsley, oregano, cinnamon and salt, if desired. Bring to a boil, then reduce the heat. Gently simmer for 10 minutes. Remove from the heat.

FOR THE EGGPLANT: Meanwhile, preheat the broiler. Place the eggplant in a single layer on a baking sheet. Coat the eggplant with olive oil no-stick spray. Broil 4″ from the heat for 5 minutes. Remove the baking sheet from the oven. Then turn the slices over and coat with the olive oil no-stick spray. Return the baking sheet to the oven and broil about 5 minutes more or until tender.

FOR THE SAUCE: In a small saucepan, use a wire whisk to stir together the milk and cornstarch until smooth. Cook and stir over medium heat until the mixture begins to thicken and just comes to a boil. Cook and stir for 1 minute more. Remove from the heat and cool slightly.

In a small bowl, slowly stir some of the milk mixture into the egg substitute to warm it. Then slowly stir the egg mixture into the remaining milk mixture. Stir in the ricotta and nutmeg.

Preheat the oven to 350°. Coat an 11″ × 7″ baking dish with the no-stick spray. Lightly sprinkle the baking dish with some of the bread crumbs. Then layer half each of the eggplant and bread crumbs. Top with all of the meat mixture and the remaining eggplant and bread crumbs. Carefully pour the sauce on top and sprinkle with the Parmesan.

Bake for 35 to 40 minutes or until set. Let stand for 15 minutes before cutting. Cut into squares to serve.

Makes 6 servings.

   PER SERVING: 170 calories, 3.5 g. total fat, 1.2 g. saturated fat, 32 mg. cholesterol, 143 mg. sodium

Lamb Pilaf with Apricots

Adapted from *Savoring the Southwest*
ROSWELL SYMPHONY GUILD

A pleasant blend of cinnamon, allspice and nutmeg adds a Middle Eastern flavor to this lean one-dish meal from the Roswell Symphony Guild. If you like, you can increase the rice to stretch the meat even further.

1　medium onion, chopped
1　clove garlic, minced
1　pound boneless leg of lamb, trimmed of all visible fat and cut into 1″ cubes
1　can (14¾ ounces) reduced-sodium chicken broth, defatted
2　tablespoons raisins or dried currants
¼　teaspoon ground cinnamon
⅛　teaspoon ground allspice
⅛　teaspoon grated fresh nutmeg or pinch of ground nutmeg
¼　teaspoon salt
⅛　teaspoon ground black pepper
½　cup dried apricots, quartered
2　cups cooked long-grain white rice

Lightly coat an unheated large skillet with no-stick spray. Add the onions and garlic. Cook and stir over medium heat for 3 minutes.

Add the lamb. Cook and stir over medium-high heat until tender. Add the broth, raisins or currants, cinnamon, allspice, nutmeg, salt and pepper. Bring to a boil, then reduce the heat to low. Cover and cook for 30 minutes.

Add the apricots. Cover and cook for 30 minutes more. Stir in the rice and serve.

Makes 4 servings.

ஐ　PER SERVING: 329 calories, 5.5 g. total fat, 1.9 g. saturated fat, 57 mg. cholesterol, 399 mg. sodium

Moroccan Lamb

Adapted from *The Philadelphia Orchestra Cookbook*

WEST PHILADELPHIA COMMITTEE FOR THE PHILADELPHIA ORCHESTRA

A blend of spices gives this colorful dish its unique flavor.
Serve the lamb with whole-wheat pita breads.

1	small onion, chopped
1	clove garlic, minced
1	pound boneless leg of lamb or lamb loin, trimmed of all visible fat and cut into ¾" cubes
2	large ripe tomatoes, chopped
¼	teaspoon salt
¼	teaspoon ground ginger
¼	teaspoon saffron threads, crushed (optional)
¼	teaspoon ground black pepper
1	bay leaf
1	whole clove
½	cup water (optional)
1	large yellow onion, cut into 8 wedges
½	cup light raisins
	Hot cooked rice or couscous
2	tablespoons slivered almonds, toasted

Lightly coat an unheated large skillet with no-stick spray. Add the chopped onions and garlic. Cook and stir over medium heat about 3 minutes or until the onions are tender.

Add the lamb. Cook and stir over medium-high heat until browned. Stir in the tomatoes, salt, ginger, saffron (if desired), pepper, bay leaf and clove. Cook for 2 minutes, stirring occasionally.

If the mixture seems dry, stir in the water. Bring to a boil, then reduce the heat. Cover and gently simmer for 45 minutes, stirring occasionally.

Add the yellow onions and raisins. Cover and gently simmer about 30 minutes more or until both the meat and yellow onions are tender.

To serve, remove and discard the bay leaf and clove. Serve over the rice or couscous and sprinkle with the almonds.

Makes 5 servings.

PER SERVING (WITH ½ CUP COOKED RICE): 305 calories, 4.6 g. total fat, 1.6 g. saturated fat, 46 mg. cholesterol, 152 mg. sodium

Lamb Chops en Papillote

Adapted from *Virginia Seasons*
JUNIOR LEAGUE OF RICHMOND

"En papillote" is a fancy term for cooking food in packets of either parchment or foil. It is also an elegant, easy and healthful method of cooking. For this dish, each lamb chop is wrapped with potatoes, carrots and zucchini and baked to perfection in the oven.

4	lamb loin or sirloin chops (4 ounces each), cut ½" thick and trimmed of all visible fat
1	teaspoon finely chopped fresh chervil or ¼ teaspoon dried chervil, crushed
½	teaspoon celery salt
2	small onions, sliced ¼" thick and separated into rings
2	small zucchini, cut into 2"-long julienne strips
2	medium carrots, cut into 2"-long julienne strips
4	new potatoes, sliced
	Freshly ground black pepper (to taste)

Preheat the oven to 350°. Cut four 20" squares of parchment paper or heavy foil. Fold each square on the diagonal to form a triangle, then open the triangles.

Place a chop on each piece of paper near the folded line. Sprinkle each chop with equal amounts of the chervil and celery salt. Then top each with equal amounts of the onions, zucchini, carrots and potatoes. Sprinkle each to taste with the pepper.

For each packet, fold the paper over the chop and vegetables and align the edges. To seal, fold the edges of each side of the triangle together in a triple fold. Then twist the three corners to close the package.

Place the packets on a large baking sheet. Bake for 1 hour. Carefully cut a large X in the top of each packet and fold back the points. Check to see if the chops are of desired doneness and the vegetables are crisp-tender. If not, close the packets and bake about 5 minutes more.

To serve, transfer the packets to dinner plates. Or remove the chops and vegetables from the packets and transfer to dinner plates.

Makes 4 servings.

🍃 PER SERVING: 346 calories, 7.6 g. total fat, 2.7 g. saturated fat, 70 mg. cholesterol, 342 mg. sodium

America
Loves Poultry

Chicken à l'Orange

Adapted from *Savoring the Southwest*
ROSWELL SYMPHONY GUILD

This oven-baked chicken is great for entertaining. You can assemble the dish in the morning, then refrigerate it until you're ready to bake it.

CHICKEN

1¾   pounds skinless chicken breasts, halved, or 2 pounds chicken pieces, skin removed
1   medium onion, thinly sliced and separated into rings
1   cup quartered fresh mushrooms
1   cup chopped green peppers

SAUCE

1   cup water
1   tablespoon cornstarch
2   teaspoons finely shredded orange peel
1½   cups fresh orange juice
3   tablespoons dry sherry or nonalcoholic wine
1½   tablespoons finely chopped fresh parsley
1   tablespoon packed brown sugar
¼   teaspoon salt
¼   teaspoon freshly ground black pepper
     Paprika (optional)
     Orange slices (optional)

FOR THE CHICKEN: Preheat the oven to 375°. Place the chicken, bone side down, in a 13″ × 9″ baking dish. Top with the onions, mushrooms and peppers.

FOR THE SAUCE: In a small saucepan, use a wire whisk to stir together the water and cornstarch until well-combined. Then stir in the orange peel, orange juice, sherry or wine, parsley, brown sugar, salt and pepper. Cook and stir over medium heat until the mixture begins to thicken and just comes to a boil. (If assembling the dish ahead, let the sauce cool.)

Pour the sauce over the chicken. Bake, uncovered, about 30 minutes for the chicken breasts or 1 hour for the chicken pieces, basting

Roswell Symphony Guild

The town of Roswell, New Mexico, has a population of 50,000 and is a good 200 miles from the nearest major city. To have a symphony orchestra is unusual enough, but to have one that's as good, and as acclaimed, as the Roswell Symphony is really extraordinary.

The Roswell Symphony Guild formed in 1961 to support the brand-new orchestra. That first year, the volunteer musicians played a scant three performances. Now the ensemble has professional musicians who play under the direction of the esteemed conductor John Farrer. The orchestra performs five subscription concerts a year, plus a free outdoor summer concert and a handful of free performances for schoolchildren.

Members of the Symphony Guild do much more than raise money for the orchestra—although they have obviously done a good job of that. They also conduct the season-ticket drive, provide housing for visiting musicians, act as ushers at the performances, provide refreshments at rehearsals and help out in the orchestra's offices. *Savoring the Southwest* helps the guild continue its good work.

occasionally. The chicken should be tender when done. If desired, sprinkle the chicken with the paprika and garnish with the orange slices.

Makes 6 servings.

✍ PER SERVING: 169 calories, 2.5 g. total fat, 0.7 g. saturated fat, 53 mg. cholesterol, 138 mg. sodium

Indonesian Grilled Chicken Breasts

Adapted from *Hospitality*
NORTH SHORE MEDICAL CENTER AUXILIARY

You'll go nuts over the peanut sauce on this chicken, especially knowing that the dish gets only 28 percent of its calories from fat. By using reduced-fat peanut butter and removing the skin from the chicken, we kept this dish within healthy standards.

CHICKEN
4 skinless, boneless chicken breast halves (1 pound total)

PASTA
4 ounces spaghettini or linguine

INDONESIAN SAUCE
⅓ cup water
¼ cup reduced-fat creamy peanut butter
4 teaspoons reduced-sodium soy sauce
4 teaspoons fresh lemon juice
2 teaspoons packed brown sugar
3 cloves garlic, minced
1 teaspoon oriental sesame oil
¼ teaspoon hot-pepper sauce
1 tablespoon dry sherry, nonalcoholic wine or orange juice
4 green onions, slivered lengthwise

FOR THE CHICKEN: To prepare the grill for cooking, coat the unheated grill rack with no-stick spray. Then light the grill according to the manufacturer's directions. Check the temperature for grilling; the temperature should be "medium-hot" or 3 seconds that the palm of your hand can withstand the heat (see tip on page 131). Place the rack on the grill.

Place the chicken on the rack. Grill, uncovered, for 8 minutes. Turn the chicken over and grill for 7 to 10 minutes more or until the chicken is tender and the juices run clear when the thickest part of the chicken is pierced with a fork.

FOR THE PASTA: While the chicken is grilling, cook the pasta according to the package directions, but without adding salt. Drain, rinse with hot water and drain again. Transfer the pasta to a medium bowl. If desired, to prevent the pasta from sticking together, lightly coat it with no-stick spray and toss. Cover to keep warm until serving time.

FOR THE INDONESIAN SAUCE: In a small heavy saucepan, combine the water, peanut butter, soy sauce, lemon juice, brown sugar, garlic, oil and hot-pepper sauce. Stir in the sherry, wine or orange juice. Cook and stir over medium heat until smooth.

To serve, place the chicken on individual beds of the pasta. Drizzle each with the sauce and garnish with the onions.

TEST KITCHEN TIP: To broil the chicken instead of grilling it, coat the unheated rack of a broiling pan with no-stick spray. Place the chicken on the rack. Broil 4" from the heat for 5 minutes. Turn the chicken over and broil for 4 to 6 minutes more or until cooked through.

Makes 4 servings.

&. PER SERVING: 314 calories, 9.9 g. total fat, 2 g. saturated fat, 70 mg. cholesterol, 323 mg. sodium

---

Chicken Cordon Bleu

Adapted from *Our Country Cookin'*
JUNIOR SOCIAL WORKERS OF CHICKASHA

Two simple changes easily shaved fat and calories from this classic entrée: switching to low-fat ingredients and using cornflakes instead of potato chips for the coating.

CHICKEN

4 skinless, boneless chicken breast halves (1 pound total)
4 very thin slices (½ ounce each) low-sodium, 96% fat-free cooked ham
4 slices (1 ounce each) fat-free processed Swiss cheese
¼ cup skim milk
1 cup fine corn flake crumbs

(continued)

SAUCE

1 can (10¾ ounces) condensed cream of mushroom soup
   with ⅓ less salt and 99% fat free
1 can (4 ounces) sliced mushrooms, drained
¼ cup fat-free plain yogurt or fat-free sour cream
¼ cup cooking sherry
   Hot cooked rice

FOR THE CHICKEN: Preheat the oven to 350°. Lightly coat a
baking sheet with no-stick spray. Set the baking sheet aside.

Place each chicken breast half between two pieces of plastic
wrap. Working from the center to the edges, lightly pound the
chicken with the flat side of a meat mallet to ¼" thickness. Remove
and discard the plastic wrap.

To assemble, place one slice of the ham on top of each breast
half. Then place a slice of the cheese on top. Fold in the short sides
of the chicken breast, then roll up to enclose the ham and cheese. Secure with wooden toothpicks.

Dip the breasts in the milk, then roll in the corn flake crumbs.
Place on the prepared baking sheet and bake about 40 minutes or
until the chicken is tender and the juices run clear when the thickest
part of the chicken is pierced with a fork.

FOR THE SAUCE: In a small saucepan, stir together the soup,
mushrooms, yogurt or sour cream and sherry. Cook over medium
heat until heated through, stirring occasionally.

To serve, arrange the chicken breasts in a shallow dish. Remove
the toothpicks and pour the sauce over the chicken. Serve with the
rice.

Makes 4 servings.

ૐ PER SERVING (WITH ½ CUP COOKED RICE): 458 calories, 4.4 g.
   total fat, 0.9 g. saturated fat, 53 mg. cholesterol, 1,337 mg. sodium

Chicken Breasts Parmesan

Adapted from *Cane River Cuisine*
SERVICE LEAGUE OF NATCHITOCHES

To get a crispy coating without the fat, you oven-fry these breaded chicken steaks instead of panfrying them. The paprika in the coating mixture helps give the chicken color that you'd associate with frying.

⅓ cup fine, dry seasoned bread crumbs
½ cup grated Parmesan cheese
½ teaspoon paprika
4 skinless, boneless chicken breast halves (1 pound total)
⅛ teaspoon salt
⅛ teaspoon ground black pepper
½ cup all-purpose flour
2 tablespoons tub-style reduced-calorie margarine, melted

Preheat the oven to 400°. Lightly coat a baking sheet with no-stick spray, then set aside. In a shallow dish, combine the bread crumbs, Parmesan and paprika.

Using the flat side of a meat mallet or the palm of your hand, slightly flatten the chicken to about ½″ thickness. Sprinkle the chicken with the salt and pepper.

To coat the chicken, first roll the pieces in the flour to evenly cover all sides. Then dip the chicken in the margarine and, finally, roll it in the bread crumb mixture.

Place the coated chicken pieces on the prepared baking sheet. Bake for 15 to 20 minutes or until the chicken is tender and the juices run clear when the thickest part of the chicken is pierced with a fork.

Makes 4 servings.

PER SERVING: 281 calories, 11.2 g. total fat, 3.5 g. saturated fat, 56 mg. cholesterol, 460 mg. sodium

Walnut Chicken

Adapted from A *Touch of Atlanta*
MARIST PARENTS' CLUB

This oriental stir-fry is much lower in fat than restaurant versions of the dish. That's because we use no-stick spray instead of oil to cook the ingredients. For double insurance against sticking, use a no-stick skillet or wok.

2	tablespoons unsweetened pineapple or orange juice or water
5	teaspoons reduced-sodium soy sauce
3	teaspoons cornstarch
1	pound skinless, boneless chicken breasts, cut into thin 1"-long strips
½	cup defatted reduced-sodium chicken broth
½	teaspoon ground ginger
½	teaspoon crushed red pepper
8	ounces small broccoli florets
1	medium onion, cut into 1" pieces
1	clove garlic, minced
1	sweet red pepper, cut into thin 1"-long strips
⅓	cup broken walnuts, toasted
	Hot cooked rice

In a medium bowl, stir together the juice or water, 2 teaspoons of the soy sauce and 1 teaspoon of the cornstarch. Add the chicken. Stir until coated. Cover and refrigerate for 30 minutes.

In a small bowl, stir together the broth, ginger and the remaining 3 teaspoons soy sauce and 2 teaspoons cornstarch. Set the broth mixture aside.

Lightly coat an unheated wok or large skillet with no-stick spray. Heat over medium-high heat. Add the chicken mixture. Sprinkle with the crushed red pepper. Stir-fry about 4 minutes or until the chicken is tender. Using a slotted spoon, remove the chicken from the wok.

Add the broccoli, onions and garlic to the wok. Stir-fry for 2 minutes. Then add the sweet red peppers and stir-fry for 1 minute more.

Add the chicken and broth mixtures. Bring to a boil, then reduce the heat. Cook and stir for 2 minutes more.

To serve, transfer the mixture to a shallow serving dish and sprinkle with the walnuts. Serve with the rice.

Makes 4 servings.

ஃ PER SERVING (WITH ½ CUP COOKED RICE): 369 calories, 11.3 g. total fat, 1.2 g. saturated fat, 46 mg. cholesterol, 338 mg. sodium

---

Crispy Baked Chicken

Adapted from *A Taste of New England*
JUNIOR LEAGUE OF WORCESTER

This crispy chicken from the Junior League of Worcester is sure to win approval at your next picnic or Sunday dinner. Serve it with Sour Cream Potato Salad (page 40) and corn on the cob.

1   cup fine corn flake crumbs
1   teaspoon dried rosemary, crushed
⅛   teaspoon freshly ground black pepper
2½–3   pounds chicken pieces, skin removed, or 6 skinless, boneless chicken breast halves
1   cup skim milk

Preheat the oven to 400°. Lightly coat a baking sheet with no-stick spray. Set the baking sheet aside.

In a shallow dish or pie plate, stir together the corn flake crumbs, rosemary and pepper.

To coat the chicken, dip it in the milk. Then roll the pieces in the crumb mixture. If necessary for the crumbs to adhere, let the pieces stand a few seconds, then roll them in the crumbs again.

Place the coated chicken pieces on the prepared baking sheet. Bake about 45 minutes for the chicken pieces or about 20 minutes for the boneless breast halves, or until the chicken is tender and the juices run clear when the thickest part of the chicken is pierced with a fork.

Makes 6 servings.

ஃ PER SERVING: 300 calories, 5.6 g. total fat, 1.6 g. saturated fat, 106 mg. cholesterol, 281 mg. sodium

Patio Cassoulet

Adapted from *Bay Leaves*
JUNIOR SERVICE LEAGUE OF PANAMA CITY

Beans, chicken and sausage are the hallmarks of this classic one-dish meal. Increasing the amount of beans and decreasing the amount of sausage increases fiber and reduces fat.

1	medium onion, chopped
8	ounces fresh turkey Italian sausages or fully cooked turkey kielbasa, cut into ½" slices
1	tablespoon olive oil
2½–3	pounds chicken pieces, skin removed
1	can (16 ounces) plum tomatoes (with juice)
1	green pepper, cut into thin rings
¼	teaspoon salt
2	cans (15 ounces each) Great Northern beans, rinsed and drained
1	teaspoon Worcestershire sauce
¼	teaspoon hot-pepper sauce

Preheat the oven to 350°. Lightly coat an unheated large skillet with no-stick spray. Add the onions and sausages. Cook and stir over medium heat about 5 minutes or until the sausages are lightly browned. Push the mixture to one side of the skillet.

Add the oil to the skillet. Then add the chicken and cook about 15 minutes or until lightly browned, turning the pieces to brown evenly. Remove the chicken and set it aside.

To the sausages and onions, add the tomatoes (with juice), green peppers and salt. Bring to a boil, then reduce the heat. Gently simmer, uncovered, for 5 minutes.

Transfer the tomato mixture to a 13" × 9" baking dish or shallow casserole. Stir in the beans, Worcestershire sauce and hot-pepper sauce. Arrange the chicken pieces on top in a single layer. Cover with foil and bake for 45 to 60 minutes or until the chicken is tender.

Makes 6 servings.

֍ PER SERVING: 444 calories, 12.9 g. total fat, 1.4 g. saturated fat, 76 mg. cholesterol, 294 mg. sodium

Roast Chicken Stuffed with Mushrooms

Adapted from *Settings*
JUNIOR LEAGUE OF PHILADELPHIA

This wonderful juicy chicken is stuffed with mushrooms instead of a fatty bread stuffing. Keep the skin on the bird during roasting so that the meat doesn't dry out. Before serving, however, be sure to remove it because the skin contains a lot of fat.

1	roasting or broiler-fryer chicken (2½–3 pounds)
1	medium clove garlic, halved
	Pinch of ground black pepper
8	ounces fresh mushrooms, cut into quarters
½	cup chopped fresh parsley
2	sprigs fresh thyme, chopped, or ¾ teaspoon dried thyme leaves, crushed
2	cups pearl onions (optional)

Preheat the oven to 375°. Pour ¼″ of water into a roasting pan. Coat the unheated rack from the roasting pan with no-stick spray, then place it in the pan. Set the pan aside.

Rub the outside of the chicken and inside the cavity with the garlic. Then sprinkle the pepper inside the cavity.

In a medium bowl, toss together the mushrooms, parsley and thyme. Loosely stuff the chicken with about a third of the mixture.

Skewer the neck skin to the back of the chicken and tie the legs to the tail. Place the chicken, breast side up, on the rack in the pan. Insert a meat thermometer into the thickest part of a thigh.

Roast, uncovered, for 30 minutes. Baste the chicken with the liquid in the pan. Then place the remaining mushroom mixture and, if desired, onions on the rack around the chicken. Roast, uncovered, about 45 to 60 minutes more or until the thermometer registers 180° to 185° and the juices from the chicken run clear, basting the chicken every 30 minutes.

Transfer the vegetables from the pan to a serving dish and cover to keep warm. Loosely cover the chicken with foil and let stand for 10 minutes before carving. Remove and discard the skin before serving. If desired, remove the meat from the bones before serving.

Makes 6 servings.

❧ PER SERVING: 170 calories, 6.2 g. total fat, 1.7 g. saturated fat, 73 mg. cholesterol, 66 mg. sodium

Herb-Basted Cornish Hens

Adapted from *Thymes Remembered*
JUNIOR LEAGUE OF TALLAHASSEE

To get butter flavor without the fat, this recipe uses a commercial butter-flavor mix. Look for this product in the cooking-oil or spice section of your supermarket.

½   teaspoon grated lime peel
2   tablespoons fresh lime juice
2   tablespoons prepared butter-flavor mix
4   teaspoons olive oil
1   clove garlic, minced
½   teaspoon dried thyme leaves, crushed
¼   teaspoon freshly ground black pepper
⅛   teaspoon salt
2   Cornish hens (1–1½ pounds each), halved and skin removed

Preheat the broiler. In a small bowl, stir together the lime peel, lime juice, butter-flavor mix, oil, garlic, thyme, pepper and salt.

Coat the rack of a broiling pan with no-stick spray. Place the hens on the rack, bone side up. Brush with the lime mixture. Broil 5" to 6" from the heat for 15 minutes. Turn the pieces over. Brush with the lime mixture again and broil about 15 minutes more or until the hens are tender and the juices run clear when the thickest part of the chicken is pierced with a fork.

To serve, brush with the remaining lime mixture.

TEST KITCHEN TIP: These Cornish hens are also delicious served cold, making them a great choice for a picnic or bag lunch.

Makes 4 servings.

PER SERVING: 235 calories, 11.6 g. total fat, 2.6 g. saturated fat, 88 mg. cholesterol, 141 mg. sodium

OUR CAUSE

Junior League of Tallahassee

For a century and a half, the rolling hills, fragrant flowers and abundant trees of Tallahassee have lent the city a beauty that has charmed thousands into making it their home. Like so many southern cities, Tallahassee is noted for its hospitality as well.

Thymes Remembered, from the Junior League of Tallahassee, offers a sampling of classic special-occasion menus and recipes enjoyed through the years in Tallahassee homes. The League has been a visible presence in the city since 1949 and provides an example of the impact that dedicated volunteers can make to a community.

Over the years, the group has aided dozens of causes with an array of purposes. The women in this active group contribute their time and talent for everything from organizing cultural programs to supporting the city's wildlife museum and from developing education programs to assisting the elderly. Care, support and shelter for the homeless and abused is another favorite project of the group.

Turkey Quiche with Stuffing Crust

Adapted from *Necessities and Temptations*
JUNIOR LEAGUE OF AUSTIN

Here's an innovative way to use up leftover Thanksgiving turkey. The Junior League of Austin recommends making a hearty quiche that uses stuffing for an easy, low-fat crust.

CRUST

2½ cups prepared cornbread stuffing mix or chicken-flavored stuffing mix

FILLING

1 cup (4 ounces) finely shredded reduced-fat Swiss cheese
2 teaspoons cornstarch
1 cup cooked and chopped turkey breast
1 cup fat-free egg substitute
1 can (5 ounces or ⅔ cup) evaporated skim milk
⅛ teaspoon ground white pepper
Paprika (optional)
Tomato wedges (optional)

FOR THE CRUST: Preheat the oven to 400°. Coat a 9″ pie plate with no-stick spray. Then press the stuffing onto the bottom and up the sides to form an even crust. Bake about 10 minutes or until golden. Remove the crust from the oven, then reduce the oven temperature to 350°.

FOR THE FILLING: In a medium bowl, toss together the cheese and cornstarch. Add the turkey and toss until combined. Transfer the turkey mixture to the hot crust and set aside.

In the bowl, stir together the egg substitute, milk and pepper. Pour the egg mixture evenly over the turkey mixture.

Bake in the 350° oven for 25 to 30 minutes or until a knife inserted near the center comes out clean. Let stand for 10 minutes before serving.

If desired, sprinkle with the paprika and garnish with the tomatoes and serve. Cut into wedges and serve.

Makes 6 servings.

❧ PER SERVING: 286 calories, 11.2 g. total fat, 3.5 g. saturated fat, 28 mg. cholesterol, 639 mg. sodium

Turkey Piccata

Adapted from *A Touch of Atlanta*
MARIST PARENTS' CLUB

This recipe uses just enough tub-style margarine when cooking the turkey to add a buttery flavor without an excess of fat.

4   turkey breast slices or cutlets (3 ounces each), cut ⅜" thick
⅛   teaspoon salt
       Pinch of ground black pepper
2   lightly beaten egg whites
1   tablespoon skim milk
1½ cups fresh bread crumbs (3 – 4 slices)
2   tablespoons tub-style reduced-calorie margarine
1   cup defatted reduced-sodium chicken broth
2   tablespoons fresh lemon juice
       Lemon slices
       Fresh chopped parsley

Sprinkle the turkey with the salt and pepper. In a shallow dish, stir together the egg whites and milk. Dip the turkey in the egg white mixture, then roll the turkey in the bread crumbs.

Lightly coat an unheated large skillet with no-stick spray. Add the margarine and heat. Then add the turkey and brown both sides. Remove the turkey from the skillet.

Add the broth and lemon juice to the skillet. Bring to a boil, then reduce the heat to low. Return the turkey to the skillet. Simmer, uncovered, for 5 to 10 minutes or until the turkey is tender. Transfer to a platter and garnish with the lemon slices and parsley.

Makes 4 servings.

   PER SERVING: 196 calories, 6.1 g. total fat, 0.8 g. saturated fat, 59 mg. cholesterol, 395 mg. sodium

Turkey with Raspberry Sauce

Adapted from *Desert Treasures*
JUNIOR LEAGUE OF PHOENIX

This raspberry sauce, with a hint of orange, is also fantastic over chicken or lean pork. For best results, serve the sauce on the side. If it stands too long on the meat, the raspberries discolor the meat.

TURKEY
- 1½ pounds turkey tenderloins
- 1 tablespoon water
- 1 tablespoon fresh lemon juice
- 2 teaspoons reduced-sodium soy sauce

RASPBERRY SAUCE
- ½ cup orange juice
- 1 tablespoon arrowroot
- 1 package (10 ounces) frozen unsweetened red raspberries, thawed
- 2 tablespoons finely shredded orange peel
- 1 tablespoon raspberry vinegar
- ½ teaspoon sugar (optional)
- 1 cup fresh raspberries (optional)
- 4-6 orange slices (optional)

FOR THE TURKEY: Pierce both sides of the turkey with a fork, then place the turkey in a large resealable plastic bag. In a custard cup, stir together the water, lemon juice and soy sauce. Pour the mixture over the turkey in the bag. Seal the bag and marinate the turkey in the refrigerator for at least 2 hours, turning the bag occasionally.

Remove the turkey from the bag, reserving the marinade. Lightly coat an unheated large skillet with no-stick spray. Add the turkey and brown it on both sides over medium-high heat. Brush the turkey with the reserved marinade. Reduce the heat to medium. Cover and cook for 5 minutes. Turn the tenderloins over and cook, covered, about 5 minutes more or until the turkey is tender and no longer pink. Discard the remaining marinade.

FOR THE RASPBERRY SAUCE: Meanwhile, in a small saucepan, mix the orange juice and arrowroot until well-combined. Add the frozen raspberries, orange peel, vinegar and sugar, if desired.

Junior League of Phoenix

If Phoenix can be considered a desert city, then the Junior League of Phoenix might best be described as an oasis of help and comfort to the city's residents. Since its founding in 1935, the League has organized, funded or volunteered for projects that affect all the citizens of this sunny city.

The environment, the arts and community members from children to the elderly have benefited from the good works of this active and devoted group. Past projects have been wide-ranging and include housing programs for the homeless, adult literacy projects, the renovation of a landmark local theater and helping run an education center at the Phoenix zoo.

The money raised from *Desert Treasures*, an ambitious collection of recipes from group members as well as professional chefs in the Phoenix area, will go toward the League's Healthy Touch program. This project helps elementary school children avoid abuse by learning how to recognize the difference between "good touching" and "bad touching" by grown-ups.

Cook over low heat until slightly thickened, stirring occasionally. (Do not boil.) Cook and stir for 2 minutes more. If desired, sieve the sauce to remove the seeds.

To serve, cut the turkey at an angle into ¼"-thick slices. Arrange the slices, overlapping them slightly, on a serving platter. If desired, garnish with the fresh raspberries and orange slices. Serve with the sauce.

TEST KITCHEN TIP: In the summertime, enjoy these marinated turkey tenderloins hot off the grill. Just grill them over medium-hot coals for 15 to 20 minutes or until cooked through.

Makes 8 servings.

> PER SERVING: 113 calories, 1.9 g. total fat, 0.6 g. saturated fat, 37 mg. cholesterol, 78 mg. sodium

Roast Turkey Breast

Adapted from *A Cook's Tour of the Azalea Coast*
THE AUXILIARY TO THE NEW HANOVER–
PENDER COUNTY MEDICAL SOCIETY

To keep this turkey healthful, the New Hanover–Pender County Medical Society suggests removing the skin from the turkey breast before baking it. Cooking the turkey in an oven roasting bag helps keep it moist. To make sure that the herb rub adheres to the meat, lightly coat the turkey with no-stick spray before adding the seasonings.

1	fresh or frozen bone-in turkey breast (5–6 pounds)
1	medium onion, cut into quarters
2	stalks celery, cut in half
1½	tablespoons lemon-pepper seasoning
1½	teaspoons garlic powder
1½	teaspoons onion powder
1	teaspoon poultry seasoning
½	teaspoon paprika
1	tablespoon all-purpose flour

If using frozen turkey, thaw it. Remove and discard the skin from the turkey. Place the onions and celery in the breast cavity.

Preheat the oven to 325°. In a custard cup, stir together the lemon-pepper seasoning, garlic powder, onion powder, poultry seasoning and paprika. Lightly coat the turkey breast with no-stick spray. Then sprinkle it with the seasoning mixture. Rub the seasonings into the meat with your fingers.

Add the flour to an oven roasting bag, then shake. (Leave the flour in the bag to prevent the bag from bursting.) Then place the turkey in the bag. Close the bag with the nylon tie provided. Place the turkey in a shallow roasting pan, about 2" deep. Roast the turkey for 1 hour. Cut six ½" slits in the top of the bag; roast for 25 to 45 minutes more or until a meat thermometer inserted in the thickest part of the breast registers 170° to 175°.

Remove the turkey from the bag. Let it stand for 15 minutes before carving. Remove and discard the onions and celery.

Makes 12 servings.

᠗ PER SERVING (3 OUNCES COOKED MEAT): 123 calories,
0.7 g. total fat, 0.2 g. saturated fat, 71 mg. cholesterol, 51 mg. sodium

*Fisherman's
Catch*

Jazzy Orange Roughy

Adapted from *Heart and Soul*
JUNIOR LEAGUE OF MEMPHIS

Yellow, red and green peppers along with fresh basil and oregano turn plain fish into a dish with pizzazz.

2	skinless orange roughy fillets (about 4 ounces each and ½″ thick)
⅛	teaspoon ground black pepper
	Pinch of salt
2	teaspoons finely chopped fresh basil or ½ teaspoon dried basil, crushed
1	teaspoon finely chopped fresh oregano or ¼ teaspoon dried oregano, crushed
1	clove garlic, minced
2	teaspoons olive oil
1	small onion, thinly sliced and separated into rings
½	green pepper, cut into thin strips
½	sweet yellow pepper, cut into thin strips
½	sweet red pepper, cut into thin strips
	Orange or lemon wedges

Preheat the oven to 275° (see tip). Coat an 8″ × 8″ baking dish with no-stick spray. Place the fish in the dish, folding under any thin edges. Sprinkle with the black pepper and salt. Then sprinkle with the basil, oregano and garlic. Cover with foil and bake about 35 minutes or until the fish flakes easily with a fork.

Meanwhile, lightly coat an unheated medium skillet with olive oil no-stick spray. Add the oil and heat. Then add the onions. Cook and stir over medium-high heat for 2 minutes. Add the green, yellow and red peppers. Cook and stir for 2 to 3 minutes more or until the vegetables are crisp-tender.

OUR CAUSE

Junior League of Memphis

More than anything else, Memphis is a music city—from rockabilly to opera, from country to jazz—and the city is home to many renowned musicians. The Junior League of Memphis capitalizes on that worthy claim to fame in *Heart and Soul*, a collection of recipes, photographs and personal reminiscences that celebrate the joy of music, Memphis-style.

It's a creative idea, to be sure, to show off the very best of Southern recipes alongside mini-biographies of acclaimed area musicians. But then the 1,700 women of the League, which was formed in the early 1920s, have always approached their causes with a special energy and creative spirit.

The League does things in a big way, too: The release party for *Heart and Soul* was held at Graceland, Elvis Presley's famous home. What's more, the book took first prize in the 1993 National Tabasco Community Awards Cookbook competition, a feat that brought national attention. The League is devoted to helping children and families in need. Currently in the works is a day care center for HIV-infected children and children of parents living with HIV or AIDS.

To serve, transfer the fish to a serving platter and top with the vegetable mixture. Garnish with the orange or lemon wedges.

TEST KITCHEN TIP: Baking the fish at this low oven temperature allows you time to cut up and cook the peppers and onions at an easy pace. But if you're in a hurry, you can bake the fish, uncovered, in a 450° oven about 5 minutes.

Makes 2 servings.

&❧ PER SERVING: 154 calories, 5.5 g. total fat, 0.7 g. saturated fat, 23 mg. cholesterol, 76 mg. sodium

Grilled Catfish with Dijon Sauce

Adapted from *Impressions*
AUXILIARY TO THE MEMPHIS DENTAL SOCIETY

Sour cream and Dijon mustard blend together to create a simple yet delicious sauce for the catfish. By using reduced-fat sour cream instead of the regular type, we saved 16 grams of fat.

CATFISH

4 skinless catfish fillets (about 4 ounces each and ½" thick)
1 tablespoon tub-style reduced-calorie margarine, melted
1 teaspoon Worcestershire sauce
1 teaspoon lemon-pepper seasoning

DIJON SAUCE

½ cup reduced-fat sour cream
2 tablespoons Dijon mustard
2 – 3 teaspoons skim milk (optional)
Small sprigs of fresh herb (optional)
Lemon twists (optional)

FOR THE CATFISH: Light the grill according to the manufacturer's directions. Check the temperature for grilling; the temperature should be "medium-hot" or 3 seconds that the palm of your hand can withstand the heat (see tip on page 131).

Meanwhile, coat a grill basket or a piece of heavy foil with no-stick spray. Then place the fish in the basket or on the foil. In a custard cup, stir together the margarine, Worcestershire sauce and lemon-pepper seasoning until well-combined. Brush both sides of the fillets with the mixture.

Grill, uncovered, over the coals for 5 minutes. Turn the fish over and grill about 5 minutes more or until the fish flakes easily when tested with a fork.

FOR THE DIJON SAUCE: Meanwhile, in a small microwave-safe bowl, stir together the sour cream and mustard. Cook in a microwave oven on high power about 45 seconds or until heated through, stirring after 25 seconds. If necessary, stir in enough of the milk to make a desired consistency.

Auxiliary to the Memphis Dental Society

For more than 50 years, the Auxiliary to the Memphis Dental Society has been bringing smiles to the people in their community. Hundreds of thousands of free toothbrush kits have been distributed to children and the elderly, and many volunteer hours have been spent teaching good dental health habits in schools and nursing homes.

The auxiliary has provided funding for countless projects, including hospital dental clinics and community treatment centers. The auxiliary contributed to the Health Science Wing of the Memphis Pink Palace Museum's special exhibit commemorating the history of dentistry in the South.

The auxiliary's main focus—and the cause to which sales of *Impressions* are devoted—is the Dr. Mike Overbey Dental Health Exhibit at the Children's Museum of Memphis. This exhibit helps youngsters get an early start in understanding the importance of good dental health.

To serve, spoon 2 tablespoons of the sauce over each of the fillets. If desired, garnish with the herb sprigs and lemon twists.

TEST KITCHEN TIP: To broil the fish, preheat the broiler. Coat the rack of a broiling pan with no-stick spray. Place the fish on the rack, then brush with half the margarine mixture. Broil 4" from the heat for 5 minutes. Turn the fish over and brush with the remaining margarine mixture. Broil about 5 minutes or until the fish is cooked through.

Makes 4 servings.

æ **PER SERVING:** 193 calories, 7.8 g. total fat, 1.4 g. saturated fat, 65 mg. cholesterol, 257 mg. sodium

Rolled Fillets of Flounder with Lemon Sauce

Adapted from *Fast and Fancy*
SADDLE RIVER DAY SCHOOL PARENTS' GUILD

This creamy lemon sauce is so thick, rich and flavorful that you won't believe it's made with low-fat milk instead of heavy cream.

VEGETABLE STOCK

3	cups water
1½	cups dry white wine or nonalcoholic white wine
5	slices yellow onion
1	small carrot, cut up
½	teaspoon salt
7	white peppercorns
3	whole allspice berries
2	bay leaves

FLOUNDER ROLLS

6	skinless flounder fillets (4 ounces each and ¼"–½" thick)

LEMON SAUCE

½	cup 1% or 2% low-fat milk
4	teaspoons cornstarch
2	tablespoons nonfat dry milk
1	tablespoon reduced-calorie butter blend
⅛	teaspoon ground white pepper
2	teaspoons fresh lemon peel

FOR THE VEGETABLE STOCK: In a medium saucepan, combine the water, wine, onions, carrots, salt, peppercorns, allspice and bay leaves. Bring to a boil, then reduce the heat. Cover and gently boil for 20 minutes. Strain and discard the vegetables and spices from the broth. Set ¾ cup of the broth aside for the sauce.

FOR THE FLOUNDER ROLLS: Loosely roll up each fillet, jelly-roll fashion, starting from the tapered end. Secure with wooden toothpicks.

Place the fish rolls in a large skillet. Add enough of the remaining vegetable stock to partially cover the fish. Bring to a boil, then reduce the heat. Cover and gently simmer for 8 to 10 minutes or just until the fish flakes easily in the center when tested with a fork. (Do not overcook.)

Using a slotted spatula, transfer the fish rolls to a serving platter. If necessary, cover to keep warm while preparing the sauce. Discard the cooking liquid.

FOR THE LEMON SAUCE: In a small saucepan, use a wire whisk to stir together the low-fat milk and cornstarch.

Stir in the ¾ cup vegetable stock. Then stir in the dry milk, butter blend and pepper.

Cook and stir over medium heat until the mixture begins to thicken and just comes to a boil. Cook and stir for 2 minutes more. Remove from the heat and stir in the lemon peel. Serve over the fish rolls.

Makes 6 servings.

&. PER SERVING: 169 calories, 3.6 g. total fat, 0.9 g. saturated fat, 78 mg. cholesterol, 154 mg. sodium

Trout Almondine

Adapted from *Cane River Cuisine*
SERVICE LEAGUE OF NATCHITOCHES

Light butter (also known as reduced-calorie butter blend) gives these fillets a rich flavor with far less fat than regular butter.

TROUT

6   trout fillets (about 4 ounces each and ¼"–½" thick)
1   cup skim milk
½   cup all-purpose flour
   Pinch of salt
   Pinch of ground black pepper
4   teaspoons canola oil

ALMOND TOPPING

⅓   cup sliced almonds
¼   cup prepared butter-flavor mix
2   tablespoons reduced-calorie butter blend

FOR THE TROUT: Place the fish, in a single layer, in a 13" × 9" baking dish. Pour the milk over the fish. Cover and marinate in the refrigerator for 2 hours, turning the fish over after 1 hour.

In a shallow dish, combine the flour, salt and pepper. Drain the fish and discard the milk. Roll the fish in the flour mixture to evenly coat.

Lightly coat an unheated large skillet with no-stick spray. Add 2 teaspoons of the oil and heat. Then add half the fish in a single layer. Cook over medium heat for 3 to 6 minutes, turning the fish over halfway through cooking. The fish will be done when it flakes easily when tested with a fork and is golden. Transfer the fish to a platter and loosely cover to keep warm. Repeat cooking with the remaining 2 teaspoons oil and fillets.

FOR THE ALMOND TOPPING: Use paper towels to wipe out the skillet. Add the almonds. Cook and stir for 1 to 2 minutes or until lightly golden. Stir in the butter-flavor mix and butter blend and heat until melted. Pour the mixture over the fish. Serve immediately.

Makes 6 servings.

   PER SERVING: 276 calories, 3.6 g. total fat, 2 g. saturated fat, 65 mg. cholesterol, 70 mg. sodium

Crispy Oven-Fried Fish Fingers

Adapted from *The Black Family Dinner Quilt Cookbook*

NATIONAL COUNCIL OF NEGRO WOMEN

Just a squirt of fresh lemon gives these homemade fish sticks tang without using a fatty tartar sauce.

½ cup fine, dry seasoned bread crumbs
1 tablespoon grated Parmesan cheese
2 teaspoons finely shredded lemon peel
¾ teaspoon dried marjoram leaves, crushed
½ teaspoon paprika
¼ teaspoon dried thyme leaves, crushed
⅛ teaspoon garlic powder
3 tablespoons fresh lemon juice
2 tablespoons dry white wine, nonalcoholic white wine
    or water
1 pound skinless cod fillets (about ½" thick)
1 tablespoon canola or olive oil

Preheat the oven to 425°. Lightly coat a baking sheet with no-stick spray and set aside.

In a shallow dish, combine the bread crumbs, Parmesan, lemon peel, marjoram, paprika, thyme and garlic powder. In another shallow dish, combine the lemon juice and wine or water.

Cut the fillets crosswise into ¾"-wide sticks. Dip the sticks into the lemon juice mixture, then roll them in the bread crumb mixture to coat well.

Place the coated fish in a single layer on the prepared baking sheet. Drizzle with the oil. Bake for 10 to 12 minutes or until the fish flakes easily when tested with a fork.

Makes 4 servings.

PER SERVING: 215 calories, 5.5 g. total fat, 0.8 g. saturated fat, 64 mg. cholesterol, 210 mg. sodium

Skewered Fish Mediterranean

Adapted from *Savannah Style*
JUNIOR LEAGUE OF SAVANNAH

Orange juice replaces the oil in this savory marinade, making this dish very low in fat.

1½	pounds skinless sea bass, swordfish or cod fillets or steaks (1″ thick)
¼	cup fresh lemon juice
¼	cup fresh lime juice
¼	cup fresh orange juice
1	teaspoon dried basil, crushed
1	teaspoon dried oregano, crushed
¼	teaspoon freshly ground black pepper
⅛	teaspoon salt
3	medium oranges, cut into chunks
2	medium green peppers, cut into 1″ pieces

Cut the fish into 1″ chunks. Place the fish in a large resealable plastic bag. In a small bowl, stir together the lemon juice, lime juice, orange juice, basil, oregano, black pepper and salt. Pour the juice mixture over the fish in the bag. Seal the bag and marinate the fish in the refrigerator for 1 hour, turning the bag occasionally.

Preheat the broiler. Coat the rack of a broiling pan with no-stick spray. Remove the fish from the bag. Reserve the marinade.

Thread the fish, oranges and green peppers onto metal skewers, leaving a small space between the pieces. Place the skewers on the prepared rack.

Broil 4″ from the heat for a total of 8 to 10 minutes, brushing with the marinade and turning the skewers a quarter-turn three times during broiling. The fish will be done when it flakes easily when tested with a fork.

To serve the marinade with the kabobs, transfer it to a small saucepan and bring to a boil.

Makes 6 servings.

 PER SERVING: 159 calories, 2.5 g. total fat, 0.6 g. saturated fat, 47 mg. cholesterol, 123 mg. sodium

Swordfish with Mushroom and Tomato Sauce

Adapted from *Cultivated Palate*

THE ARBORETUM FOUNDATION, WASHINGTON PARK ARBORETUM

Chock-full of mushrooms in a rich tomato mixture, this sauce is also delicious on halibut, as suggested by the University of Washington Arboretum Foundation.

2	teaspoons tub-style reduced-calorie margarine
4	swordfish steaks (4 ounces each), cut ¾" thick
2	cups coarsely chopped fresh shiitake mushrooms
½	cup seeded and chopped tomatoes
¼	cup chopped green onions
¼	cup dry white wine or nonalcoholic white wine
¼	cup clam juice or additional wine
2	tablespoons no-salt-added tomato paste
4	cloves garlic, minced (2 teaspoons)
1	teaspoon finely chopped fresh thyme
¼	teaspoon ground cumin
1	tablespoon fresh lemon juice

Lightly coat an unheated large no-stick skillet with butter-flavored no-stick spray. Add the margarine, then heat over medium heat until hot. Add the swordfish and cook about 3 minutes on each side or just until the fish flakes easily when tested with a fork. Transfer the fish to a plate and cover to keep warm.

Wipe out the skillet with paper towels, then lightly coat it again with no-stick spray. Add the mushrooms. Cook and stir over medium heat for 1 minute.

Add the tomatoes, onions, wine, clam juice or additional wine, tomato paste, garlic, thyme and cumin. Bring to a boil, then reduce the heat to medium. Cover and cook for 2 minutes. Place the fish on top, then cover and continue cooking about 1 minute more or just until the fish is heated through.

To serve, transfer the fish to a serving platter. Stir the lemon juice into the tomato mixture, then spoon the tomato mixture over the fish. Serve immediately.

Makes 4 servings.

&. **PER SERVING:** 222 calories, 6.6 g. total fat, 1.5 g. saturated fat, 45 mg. cholesterol, 152 mg. sodium

Salmon in Parchment

Adapted from *Holy Cow, Chicago's Cooking*
WOMEN OF THE CHURCH OF THE HOLY COMFORTER

Fat-free and reduced-fat Swiss cheeses combine to create a rich, smooth sauce for salmon fillets. Serve this elegant entrée with boiled, tiny new potatoes for a simple meal accompaniment.

MORNAY SAUCE

2	ounces (1½ slices) fat-free processed Swiss cheese, finely cut up
½	cup (2 ounces) finely shredded reduced-fat Swiss cheese
1	teaspoon + ¼ cup all-purpose flour
2	cups skim milk
2	tablespoons nonfat dry milk
⅛	teaspoon ground nutmeg
	Ground white pepper (to taste)

SALMON

6	skinless salmon fillets (about 4 ounces each and ¼″ thick)
2	medium carrots, cut into 1½″-long julienne strips
2	medium stalks celery, cut into 1½″-long julienne strips
18	medium shrimp, shelled and deveined (optional)
6	tablespoons chopped fresh dill

FOR THE MORNAY SAUCE: In a small bowl, combine the fat-free Swiss and reduced-fat Swiss. Sprinkle with 1 teaspoon of the flour and toss until coated. Set the cheese mixture aside.

In a small saucepan, use a wire whisk to stir the remaining ¼ cup flour into the skim milk. Then stir in the dry milk and nutmeg. Cook and stir over medium heat until the mixture begins to thicken and just comes to a boil. Then stir in the cheese mixture. Continue to cook and stir about 1 minute more or just until the cheese has melted. Remove from the heat and season to taste with the pepper. Cover and chill in the refrigerator at least 1 hour or until thickened.

FOR THE SALMON: Preheat the oven to 350°. Cut parchment paper into six 12″ squares. Fold each square on the diagonal to form a triangle, then open the triangles.

Place a fillet on half of each paper triangle near the folded line. Top each piece of fish with equal amounts of the carrots and celery. If desired, arrange three shrimp on top of each fillet. Sprinkle each fillet with 1 tablespoon of the dill. Spoon ¼ cup of the sauce on top of each fillet. Refrigerate the remaining sauce until serving time.

For each packet, fold the paper over the salmon and vegetables and align the edges. To seal, fold the edges of each side of the triangle together in a triple fold. Then twist the three corners to close the package.

Place the packets on a large baking sheet. If desired, refrigerate for up to 6 hours before baking.

Bake for 25 to 30 minutes or until the paper is browned and puffed. Carefully cut a large X in the top of each packet and fold back the points. Check to see if the salmon flakes easily when tested with a fork and the vegetables are crisp-tender. If not, close the packets and bake about 3 minutes more. Meanwhile, heat the remaining sauce to serve with the salmon and vegetables.

To serve, transfer the packets to dinner plates. Open the packets and serve with the remaining sauce.

Makes 6 servings.

   PER SERVING: 218 calories, 5.8 g. total fat, 2 g. saturated fat, 27.6 mg. cholesterol, 910 mg. sodium

Salmon Tart

Adapted from *Cultivated Palate*

THE ARBORETUM FOUNDATION, WASHINGTON PARK ARBORETUM

Cultivated Palate is filled with many healthy recipes like this. Serve this quichelike tart warm as an entrée for brunch or a light meal. Or cut the tart into smaller pieces and serve it chilled as an appetizer.

PARMESAN CRUST

- 1½ cups unbleached flour
- ½ cup (2 ounces) finely shredded fresh Asiago, Romano or Parmesan cheese
- ⅓ cup canola oil
- ¼ cup skim milk

FILLING

- 1 tablespoon tub-style reduced-calorie margarine
- 1 cup chopped onions
- 2–3 cloves garlic, minced
- 4 egg whites, lightly beaten
- 1 egg, lightly beaten
- 1 container (16 ounces) fat-free plain yogurt
- 1 teaspoon dillweed
- ⅛ teaspoon salt
- 1 pound cooked salmon, skin and bones removed and flaked
- 1 cup (4 ounces) finely shredded reduced-fat Swiss cheese

FOR THE PARMESAN CRUST: Preheat the oven to 375°. In a medium bowl, stir together the flour and Asiago, Romano or Parmesan. In a small bowl, stir together the oil and milk.

Add the milk mixture to the flour mixture. Using a fork, stir just until moistened.

Transfer the mixture to a 10″ quiche plate or 9″ × 2″ (deep-dish) pie plate. Pat the dough on the bottom and up the sides to form an even crust. Bake for 10 minutes.

FOR THE FILLING: Melt the margarine in a medium skillet. Add the onions and garlic. Cook and stir over medium heat about 3 minutes or until the onions are tender. Remove from the heat.

The Arboretum Foundation, Washington Park Arboretum

In the beautiful Puget Sound area of the state of Washington, the Washington Park Arboretum could be Eden itself, with its 200 rolling acres of trees, shrubs and plants from all over the world. Back in the 1930s, a small group of garden enthusiasts had the imagination and wisdom to envision the Arboretum. With the help of the well-known Olmsted Brothers landscapers of Boston, they created this paradise that sits in a narrow valley next to Lake Washington.

Today, more than 3,000 Arboretum Foundation supporters tend to the ever-growing park and its programs. Thousands of schoolchildren visit the Arboretum every year as part of the Saplings Program. They learn not only how to recognize trees and shrubs but also the importance of caring for the environment. Five hundred volunteers work all year long to plan the foundation's biggest fund-raiser, a spring plant sale that nets some $25,000 for the Arboretum. The *Cultivated Palate*, the foundation's cookbook, provides a beautiful—and tasteful—introduction to the Washington Park Arboretum.

In a large bowl, stir together the egg whites, eggs, yogurt, dillweed and salt until well-combined. Add the onion mixture, salmon and Swiss. Gently stir until combined.

Transfer the filling to the partially baked crust. Bake in the 375° oven for 45 to 50 minutes or until a knife inserted in the center comes out clean. Cool on a wire rack for 15 minutes before cutting to serve.

Makes 6 servings.

 PER SERVING: 549 calories, 26.6 g. total fat, 4.4 g. saturated fat, 94 mg. cholesterol, 390 mg. sodium

Simply Delicious Scallops

Adapted from *Thymes Remembered*
JUNIOR LEAGUE OF TALLAHASSEE

For a sensational low-fat pasta dish, we sautéed these scallops in a mixture of chicken broth, wine and butter blend. Serve the scallops, as suggested by the Junior League of Tallahassee, on a colorful bed of mixed carrot linguine and plain linguine. Look for the carrot variety, as well as other vegetable pastas, in specialty food shops.

1	pound fresh plain linguine or 8 ounces fresh plain linguine + 8 ounces fresh carrot linguine
1½	pounds bay scallops
4	tablespoons defatted chicken broth
3	tablespoons white wine or nonalcoholic white wine
2	tablespoons reduced-calorie butter blend
1	clove garlic, minced
1	teaspoon finely chopped fresh dill or basil (optional)
½	teaspoon freshly ground black pepper
	Pinch of salt
6	sprigs fresh dill or basil

Cook the pasta according to the package directions, but without adding salt. Drain, rinse with hot water and drain again. Transfer the pasta to a large bowl. If necessary, cover to keep warm.

In a large skillet, combine the scallops, 2 tablespoons of the broth and 1 tablespoon of the wine. Cook and stir over medium heat about 1 minute or until the scallops are opaque. Using a slotted spoon, transfer the scallops to a plate. Discard the liquid.

Melt the butter blend in the skillet. Add the garlic. Cook and stir over medium heat for 30 seconds. Stir in the remaining 2 tablespoons each of the broth and wine, the chopped dill or basil (if desired), pepper and salt. Add the scallops and heat through.

Add the scallop mixture to the pasta. Toss until the pasta is coated and the scallops are combined.

To serve, transfer the pasta mixture to dinner plates and garnish each serving with a sprig of dill or basil. Serve immediately.

Makes 6 servings.

PER SERVING: 537 calories, 7.1 g. total fat, 1 g. saturated fat, 114 mg. cholesterol, 321 mg. sodium

Shrimp Creole

Adapted from *Prairie Potpourri*
IMMANUEL MEDICAL CENTER AUXILIARY

Adding just a modest amount of salt to salt-free canned tomatoes gives them plenty of flavor, with much less sodium than you'd get from regular canned tomatoes.

½	cup chopped onions
½	cup chopped celery
½	cup chopped green peppers
1	clove garlic, minced
1	can (16 ounces) salt-free tomatoes (with juice), cut up
¼	cup + 1 tablespoon water
1	teaspoon paprika
½	teaspoon dried thyme leaves, crushed
¼	teaspoon sugar
¼	teaspoon salt
¼	teaspoon hot-pepper sauce
1	bay leaf
1½	teaspoons tapioca flour (see tip)
12	ounces cooked and deveined shrimp
	Hot cooked rice

Lightly coat an unheated medium saucepan with no-stick spray. Add the onions, celery, green peppers and garlic. Cook and stir over medium heat about 9 minutes or until the celery is tender.

Stir in the tomatoes (with juice), ¼ cup of the water, paprika, thyme, sugar, salt, hot-pepper sauce and bay leaf. Bring to a boil, then reduce the heat. Cover and simmer for 15 minutes.

In a custard cup, stir together the flour and remaining 1 tablespoon water. Stir the mixture into the tomato mixture. Bring to a boil, then reduce the heat. Add the shrimp. Cook and stir for 2 minutes more. Remove and discard the bay leaf. Serve over the rice.

TEST KITCHEN TIP: Tapioca flour is a finely ground form of tapioca. Look for it in specialty food markets. Or make your own by pulverizing quick-cooking tapioca with a mortar and pestle.

Makes 4 servings.

PER SERVING (WITH ½ CUP COOKED RICE): 242 calories, 1.4 g. total fat, 0.3 g. saturated fat, 131 mg. cholesterol, 315 mg. sodium

Low Country Shrimp Boil

Adapted from *Savannah Style*
JUNIOR LEAGUE OF SAVANNAH

Extra corn on the cob makes this finger-licking, down-home meal quite filling and less fatty than traditional recipes.

SHRIMP SAUCE

1	cup reduced-calorie, reduced-sodium ketchup
¼ – ½	teaspoon prepared horseradish
	Dash of Worcestershire sauce (optional)
	Fresh lemon juice (to taste)

SHRIMP BOIL

10	cups water
¼	teaspoon salt
3	teaspoons hot-pepper sauce
8	ears corn, husks and silks removed and broken in half
1	pound medium shrimp, unshelled
8	ounces cooked smoked turkey sausages, cut into 2″ pieces
¼	cup reduced-calorie butter blend, melted

FOR THE SHRIMP SAUCE: In a small bowl, stir together the ketchup, horseradish and Worcestershire sauce, if desired. Flavor to taste with the lemon juice. Cover and refrigerate the sauce until serving time.

FOR THE SHRIMP BOIL: In a Dutch oven, bring the water, salt and hot-pepper sauce to a boil. Then add the corn and gently boil for 5 minutes.

Add the shrimp and sausages. Gently boil about 2 minutes or until the shrimp turn pink and the sausages are heated through. Drain well.

Junior League of Savannah

Savannah has been renowned for its hospitality since it was founded as Georgia's first outpost in 1733. In those early days, Savannah was a favorite place for all-day parties and all-night dances. Today, the city is still a charmer, with its elegantly restored houses on tree-lined squares. *Savannah Style*, from the Junior League of Savannah, celebrates the city's legendary style with recipes from well-known cooks in the city.

Since its founding in 1926, the League has contributed countless volunteer hours and dollars to community organizations. The group, which currently numbers about 700 active and sustaining members, was involved in the founding of several important city institutions, including the Community Children's Theatre and the Savannah Speech and Hearing Center.

Proceeds from *Savannah Style* help the League with its current projects, such as organizing conferences and seminars to prevent child abuse and funding and volunteering time to establish a parenting coalition.

To serve, transfer the mixture to a large bowl and serve with the sauce for the shrimp and the butter blend for the corn.

TEST KITCHEN TIP: Most recipes for shrimp boil serve a crowd. We scaled this recipe down for a family or a small get-together. But if you're having a Savannah-style party, you can easily double or triple the ingredients. Be sure to serve the dish as they do in the Low Country—outdoors, with the shrimp poured in a heap on top of paper-covered tables.

Makes 4 servings.

PER SERVING: 401 calories, 12.7 g. total fat, 2.7 g. saturated fat, 167 mg. cholesterol, 1,181 mg. sodium

Crab Cakes

Adapted from *Two and Company*
ST. THOMAS CHURCH

*Often, removing fat and salt from a recipe takes away flavor, too.
But these crab cakes contain plenty of seasonings that more than
compensate for what was removed.*

2	egg whites, lightly beaten
1	egg, lightly beaten
3	tablespoons reduced-fat mayonnaise
1	teaspoon Worcestershire sauce
½	teaspoon ground red pepper
½	teaspoon fresh lemon juice
1	pound lump crab meat, flaked
20	low-sodium saltine crackers

In a medium bowl, combine the egg whites, eggs, mayonnaise,
Worcestershire sauce, pepper and lemon juice until well-combined.
Then stir in the crab.

Break (do not roll) the crackers into very small pieces, then add
the crackers to the crab mixture. Mix well.

Using about ½ cup of the crab mixture for each, shape into six
½"-thick patties.

Coat an unheated large skillet with no-stick spray. Add the patties. Cook over medium heat about 3 minutes or until the patties are
golden brown. Turn the patties over and cook about 3 minutes more
or until golden brown.

Makes 6.

PER CRAB CAKE: 163 calories, 4.1 g. total fat, 0.9 g. saturated fat,
107 mg. cholesterol, 344 mg. sodium

Amber Waves
of Grain...
and More

Golden Rice

Adapted from *Deep in the Heart*
DALLAS JUNIOR FORUM

Apples give this curried rice dish a crunchiness usually gotten from nuts. The apples also add a touch of sweetness that blends well with the other seasonings.

1	teaspoon tub-style reduced-calorie margarine
¼	cup thinly sliced green onions
¼	cup coarsely shredded carrots
½	cup long-grain white rice
½	cup water
½	cup apple or orange juice
¼	cup light raisins
1	teaspoon packed brown sugar
¼	teaspoon curry powder
⅛	teaspoon salt
⅛	teaspoon ground ginger
⅛	teaspoon ground cinnamon
⅛	teaspoon ground black pepper
¼	cup peeled and finely chopped apple

Lightly coat an unheated small saucepan with no-stick spray. Add the margarine and heat. Then add the onions and carrots. Cook and stir over medium heat about 2 minutes or until the onions are crisp-tender.

Stir in the rice, water, apple or orange juice, raisins, brown sugar, curry powder, salt, ginger, cinnamon and pepper. Bring to a boil, then reduce the heat. Cover and simmer about 20 minutes or until the rice is tender and the liquid is absorbed.

To serve, add the apples and toss with a fork.

Makes 4 side-dish servings.

    PER SERVING: 152 calories, 1.1 g. total fat, 0.1 g. saturated fat, 0 mg. cholesterol, 83 mg. sodium

Spanish Rice

Adapted from *Calico Cupboards*
JUNIOR AUXILIARY OF BENTON

Here's a low-sodium rice dish that's packed with flavor. Serve it as an accompaniment to beef, pork or poultry. Or serve larger portions and make it your main dish.

2   slices turkey bacon, finely cut up
½   cup chopped onions
2   tablespoons finely chopped green peppers
1   can (8 ounces) reduced-sodium tomatoes (with juice),
     cut up
1   cup water
½   cup long-grain white rice
1   teaspoon sugar
     Pinch of ground black pepper
2   tablespoons finely shredded reduced-fat Cheddar cheese
     (optional)

Lightly coat an unheated medium skillet with no-stick spray. Add the bacon, onions and green peppers. Cook and stir over medium heat about 5 minutes or until the bacon is lightly browned and the onions are tender.

Add the tomatoes (with juice), water, rice, sugar and black pepper. Bring to a boil, then reduce the heat. Cover and simmer for 20 to 25 minutes, or until the rice is tender and the liquid is absorbed. Fluff with a fork and transfer the mixture to a serving bowl. If desired, sprinkle with the Cheddar to garnish.

Makes 4 side-dish servings.

& PER SERVING: 125 calories, 1.6 g. total fat, 0.4 g. saturated fat,
    4 mg. cholesterol, 10 mg. sodium

Arroz con Salsa Verde

Adapted from *Lone Star Legacy*
AUSTIN JUNIOR FORUM

In this Mexican rice dish, we suggest using the fat-free version of sour cream. If you like, you can use fat-free yogurt, but expect the rice to be less creamy.

1	container (8 ounces) fat-free sour cream
1	can (4 ounces) salsa verde (see tip) or diced green chili peppers, drained
2	cups cooked long-grain rice
1	cup (4 ounces) finely shredded reduced-fat Monterey Jack cheese
¼	cup (2 ounces) finely shredded reduced-fat Cheddar cheese

Preheat the oven to 350°. In a small bowl, stir together the sour cream and salsa or chili peppers.

Coat a 1½-quart casserole with no-stick spray. To assemble, layer a third of the rice and half each of the Monterey Jack and sour cream mixture. Repeat the layers with the rice, Monterey Jack and sour cream mixture. Top with the remaining rice. Loosely cover with foil.

Bake for 10 to 15 minutes or until heated through. Sprinkle with the Cheddar and bake, uncovered, about 5 minutes more or until the cheese melts.

TEST KITCHEN TIP: There are many types of salsa available on the market. The type called salsa verde is green and is a mixture of tomatillos, chili peppers and cilantro. Look for it in the Mexican food section of your supermarket or at a specialty food store.

Makes 8 side-dish servings.

PER SERVING: 159 calories, 4.8 g. total fat, 2.1 g. saturated fat, 13 mg. cholesterol, 283 mg. sodium

Saffron Risotto

Adapted from *Family and Company*
JUNIOR LEAGUE OF BINGHAMTON

The Junior League of Binghamton calls this "a nouveau taste for an heirloom dish." We've taken it one tiny step further—we used olive oil no-stick spray along with a small amount of olive oil to lower the fat and still keep the flavor.

2½ cups defatted reduced-sodium chicken broth
⅛ teaspoon ground saffron
½ cup chopped onions
¾ cup Arborio rice (see tip)
½ teaspoon olive oil
2 teaspoons grated Romano cheese

In a small saucepan, bring the broth to a boil. Stir in the saffron and set aside.

Meanwhile, lightly coat an unheated large skillet with olive oil no-stick spray. Add the onions. Cook and stir over medium heat about 3 minutes or until the onions are tender.

Meanwhile, place the rice in a strainer and rinse under cold running water. Then drain well.

Stir the oil into the onions, then add the rice. Using a wooden spoon, cook and stir the rice over medium heat for 2 minutes.

Stir 1 cup of the broth into the rice mixture. Then cook and stir about 10 minutes or until almost all of the liquid has been absorbed. Repeat the cooking and stirring process 2 more times, using ¾ cup of broth each time. Transfer the rice mixture to a serving dish and sprinkle with the Romano.

TEST KITCHEN TIP: Arborio rice is a special variety of rice that has a high starch content. It's ideal for achieving the creamy texture that's characteristic of this Italian rice dish. Look for it in large supermarkets and specialty shops.

Makes 8 side-dish servings.

❧ PER SERVING: 78 calories, 0.6 g. total fat, 0.2 g. saturated fat, 1 mg. cholesterol, 155 mg. sodium

Wild Rice Pecan Casserole

Adapted from *Sea Island Seasons*
BEAUFORT COUNTY OPEN LAND TRUST

Chopped water chestnuts replace some of the pecans in this dish. They contribute the crunch that you associate with nuts, but have no fat. (Carrots have the same effect, so you can use them if you don't have water chestnuts.)

1	tablespoon tub-style reduced-calorie margarine
6	ounces fresh mushrooms, sliced
2	tablespoons finely chopped onions
2	tablespoons finely chopped green peppers
1	small clove garlic, minced (optional)
⅓	cup chopped water chestnuts or carrots
⅔	cup wild rice
1⅓	cups defatted reduced-sodium chicken broth
	Ground black pepper (to taste)
¼	cup pecans, toasted and coarsely chopped

Preheat the oven to 325°. Heat the margarine in a medium skillet. Add the mushrooms, onions, green peppers and garlic, if desired. Cook and stir over medium heat about 4 minutes or until the mushrooms are tender. Remove from the heat. Stir in the water chestnuts or carrots.

Place the rice in a strainer and rinse under cold running water. Then drain well. Coat a 1-quart casserole with no-stick spray. In the casserole, stir together the rice, mushroom mixture and broth. Cover and bake about 1 hour or until the rice is tender and the liquid is absorbed.

To serve, fluff the rice mixture with a fork. Season to taste with the black pepper. Sprinkle the pecans on top.

Makes 4 side-dish servings.

ð PER SERVING: 214 calories, 7.7 g. total fat, 0.7 g. saturated fat, 0 mg. cholesterol, 191 mg. sodium

Citrus Couscous with Basil and Apricots

Adapted from *Holy Cow, Chicago's Cooking*

WOMEN OF THE CHURCH OF THE HOLY COMFORTER

Couscous is a granulated pasta that's not only free of fat and cholesterol but also quick-cooking.

1	can (14½ ounces) reduced-sodium chicken broth, defatted
1–2	teaspoons finely shredded orange peel
1	teaspoon finely shredded lemon peel
1	teaspoon finely shredded lime peel
1	cup couscous
½	cup chopped dried apricots
¼	cup chopped and loosely packed fresh basil

In a medium saucepan, combine the broth and orange, lemon and lime peels. Bring to a boil.

Stir in the couscous and apricots. Cover and remove from the heat. Let stand for 5 to 8 minutes or until the liquid is absorbed. Add the basil and toss with a fork.

Makes 4 side-dish servings.

PER SERVING: 220 calories, 0.4 g. total fat, 0.1 g. saturated fat, 0 mg. cholesterol, 219 mg. sodium

Barley and Pine Nut Casserole

Adapted from *The Fine Art of Cooking*
THE WOMEN'S COMMITTEE OF THE PHILADELPHIA MUSEUM OF ART

Barley, because of its pleasant nutty flavor, made it easy to reduce the amount of pine nuts—and fat—in this side dish. We sprinkled the nuts on top to give it a nutty look and stirred water chestnuts into the barley mixture to give it a crunchy texture.

2   tablespoons pine nuts
1   teaspoon tub-style reduced-calorie margarine
½   cup pearl barley
½   cup chopped white onions
¼   cup chopped water chestnuts or finely chopped celery
2   tablespoons finely chopped fresh parsley
2   tablespoons finely chopped fresh chives or green onions
⅛   teaspoon salt
     Freshly ground black pepper (to taste)
1   can (14½ ounces) reduced-sodium beef or
     chicken broth, defatted

Preheat the oven to 350°. Coat a 1-quart casserole with no-stick spray and set aside.

Lightly coat an unheated medium skillet with no-stick spray. Add the pine nuts. Cook and stir over medium heat about 2 minutes or until lightly golden. Remove the nuts from the skillet and set aside.

Heat the margarine in the skillet. Add the barley and white onions. Cook and stir over medium heat about 3 minutes or until the onions are tender and the barley is golden.

Remove the skillet from the heat and stir in the water chestnuts or celery, parsley, chives or green onions and salt. Season to taste with the pepper. Set the barley mixture aside.

Bring the broth to a boil, then stir it into the barley mixture. Transfer the mixture to the prepared casserole. Bake about 45 minutes or until the barley is tender and the liquid is absorbed.

To serve, fluff with a fork. Top with the pine nuts.

TEST KITCHEN TIP: To save a little time at dinnertime or to take this to a covered-dish party, you can make the casserole ahead.

The Women's Committee of the Philadelphia Museum of Art

Who can argue about the connection between art and food? Art is sustenance for the soul, and food, we all know, nourishes both body and spirit. The Women's Committee knows this— that's why they combined the two in *The Fine Art of Cooking,* a book that juxtaposes creative recipes with pictures of and information about many of the museum's most important works.

Picture this: You're just about to dive into a recipe for, say, kiwi sorbet, when suddenly you find yourself gazing at a vivid reprint of Henri Matisse's *Lady in Blue.* Could education get any more palatable?

The Women's Committee was founded in 1875 and has long been an important source of support for the museum. Its goal is unpretentious enough: to encourage, support and increase public interest in the museum. But its methods are as stimulating as the art that inspires them. Earnings from this first cookbook go directly to the Philadelphia Museum of Art.

Store it, covered, in the refrigerator for up to 24 hours. Then reheat it, covered, at 350° about 20 minutes.

Makes 4 side-dish servings.

ð• PER SERVING: 159 calories, 3.6 g. total fat, 0.2 g. saturated fat, 0 mg. cholesterol, 296 mg. sodium

Red Pepper Sauce for Pasta

Adapted from *Holy Cow, Chicago's Cooking*
WOMEN OF THE CHURCH OF THE HOLY COMFORTER

Red peppers add sweetness to this pasta sauce. The women of the Church of the Holy Comforter suggest serving the sauce over pasta, but it's also great over grilled chicken or fish.

2	teaspoons olive oil
2	cups coarsely chopped sweet red peppers
1	tablespoon + 1 cup defatted reduced-sodium chicken broth
2	cups chopped onions
1½	teaspoons (3 cloves) minced garlic
¼	teaspoon crushed red pepper
1½	tablespoons tomato paste
	Pinch of salt
	Freshly ground black pepper (to taste)
2	tablespoons finely chopped fresh basil
	Hot cooked spaghetti or no-yolk linguine
2	tablespoons finely shredded fresh Parmesan cheese (optional)

Heat the oil in a large skillet or medium saucepan. Add the sweet red peppers and 1 tablespoon of the broth. Cook and stir over medium heat for 5 minutes.

Add the onions, garlic and crushed red pepper. Cook and stir for 2 minutes. Add the remaining 1 cup broth, tomato paste and salt. Season to taste with the black pepper. Bring to a boil, then reduce the heat. Cover and gently simmer for 10 minutes.

Transfer the mixture to a blender or food processor. Process until nearly smooth (the vegetables will be in tiny pieces).

Return the mixture to the skillet. Bring to a boil, then reduce the heat. Cover and gently simmer for 2 minutes. Stir in the basil. Serve over the pasta and, if desired, sprinkle with the Parmesan.

Makes 2 cups; 8 side-dish servings.

෨ PER ¼ CUP (WITH ½ CUP COOKED PASTA): 132 calories, 1.7 g. total fat, 0.2 g. saturated fat, 0 mg. cholesterol, 89 mg. sodium

Pasta with Lemon Cream Sauce

Adapted from *Cranbrook Reflections*
CRANBROOK HOUSE & GARDENS AUXILIARY

This rich, creamy sauce is made with milk rather than a mixture of heavy cream and half-and-half. Serve the sauce over spaghetti as an accompaniment to pork, veal, fish or shrimp.

5 ounces spaghetti or yolk-free egg noodles
1 can (5 ounces or ⅔ cup) evaporated skim milk
⅓ cup skim milk
1 teaspoon cornstarch
1 teaspoon finely shredded lemon peel
⅛ teaspoon salt
   Pinch of crushed red pepper
3 tablespoons finely shredded fresh Parmesan cheese
   Freshly ground black pepper (to taste)
1 tablespoon finely chopped fresh parsley

Cook the pasta according to the package directions, but without adding salt. Drain, rinse with hot water and drain again. Transfer the pasta to a serving bowl.

Meanwhile, for the sauce, in a small saucepan, use a wire whisk to stir together the evaporated milk, skim milk, cornstarch, lemon peel, salt and red pepper.

Cook and stir over medium heat until the mixture begins to thicken and just comes to a boil. Cook and stir for 2 minutes more. Stir in the Parmesan.

Add the sauce mixture to the pasta. Toss until combined. Season to taste with the black pepper. Sprinkle with the parsley to garnish. Serve immediately.

Makes 6 side-dish servings.

& PER SERVING: 133 calories, 1.5 g. total fat, 0.7 g. saturated fat, 4 mg. cholesterol, 138 mg. sodium

Parmesan Primavera

Adapted from *The Shadows-on-the-Teche Cookbook*
THE SHADOWS SERVICE LEAGUE

This very easy recipe pairs spaghetti with vegetables and herbs.

7   ounces spaghetti or narrow yolk-free egg noodles
1   cup broccoli florets cut into 1" pieces
½   cup sliced fresh mushrooms
1   tablespoon extra-virgin olive oil
1   teaspoon finely chopped fresh oregano or ¼ teaspoon
    dried oregano leaves, crushed
2   teaspoons finely chopped fresh basil or ½ teaspoon basil,
    crushed
2   cups seeded and chopped tomatoes
3   tablespoons + 6 teaspoons grated Parmesan cheese

Cook the pasta according to the package directions, but without adding salt. Drain, rinse with hot water and drain again. Transfer the pasta to a medium serving bowl. If necessary, cover to keep warm.

While the pasta is cooking, lightly coat an unheated medium skillet with no-stick spray. Add the broccoli. Cook and stir over medium-high heat for 1 minute. Add the mushrooms. Cook and stir for 1 to 2 minutes more or until the broccoli is crisp-tender and the mushrooms are tender. Using a slotted spoon, remove the vegetables from the skillet and transfer to a small bowl. Cover to keep warm.

Add the oil, oregano and basil to the skillet. Cook and stir for 30 seconds. Drizzle the oil mixture over the pasta, then toss until coated. Add the broccoli mixture and tomatoes. Toss until combined. Sprinkle with 3 tablespoons of the Parmesan and toss again.

To serve, sprinkle each serving with 1 teaspoon of the remaining Parmesan.

Makes 6 side-dish servings.

⋇ PER SERVING: 193 calories, 4.7 g. total fat, 1.4 g. saturated fat,
   4 mg. cholesterol, 107 mg. sodium

The Shadows Service League

The Shadows-on-the-Teche is a historic house museum set among moss-draped tall oak trees in southern Louisiana. It was built in 1834 for David Weeks, a sugar planter. David and his wife, Mary, looked forward to moving into their new columned brick house on its 160 acres near the Bayou Teche. Sadly, David died without ever living in the home, and Mary was left to raise the couple's six children on her own.

For more than a century, Shadows-on-the-Teche was home to four generations of the Weeks family. In the 1940s, Weeks Hall, the great-grandson of David and Mary, began to grow concerned about the future of the home that he so loved. Upon his death in 1958, Hall's will indicated that the Shadows was to become a museum property of the National Trust for Historic Preservation.

The *Shadows-on-the-Teche* cookbook is the product of the Shadows Service League, a group of about 100 dedicated volunteers. Money raised from the book and other League projects is used to fund education programs, care for the collections and maintain and preserve this national historic landmark.

Low-Fat Noodle Kugel

Adapted from *Still Fiddling in the Kitchen*
NATIONAL COUNCIL OF JEWISH WOMEN

The National Council of Jewish Women took the fat out of this
traditional favorite. Serve it as a side dish at your next holiday
meal or as a hearty dessert after a light supper.

8   ounces yolk-free egg noodles
3   tablespoons tub-style reduced-calorie margarine
⅓   cup sugar
¼   cup light raisins
1   cup orange juice
¼   cup fat-free small curd cottage cheese (optional)
¼   teaspoon ground cinnamon (optional)
3   egg whites
1   egg
2   medium apples, peeled and finely shredded

Cook the noodles according to the package directions, but without adding salt. Drain, rinse with hot water and drain again.

Transfer the noodles to a large bowl. Stir in the margarine until melted. Then stir in the sugar and raisins. Pour the orange juice over the noodle mixture. Cover and refrigerate for 1 hour.

Preheat the oven to 350°. Coat an 11" × 7" baking dish with no-stick spray and set aside.

If desired, stir the cottage cheese and cinnamon into the noodle mixture.

In a small bowl, beat together the egg whites and egg until combined. Fold the eggs into the noodle mixture, then fold in the apples. Transfer the noodle mixture to the prepared baking dish. Bake, uncovered, for 45 to 60 minutes or until a knife inserted near the center comes out clean. Cut into pieces to serve.

TEST KITCHEN TIP: Store leftover kugel, covered, in the refrigerator. To reheat it, place one piece on a microwave-safe plate. Loosely cover with wax paper. Microwave on high power about 1 minute, rotating the plate a quarter turn after 30 seconds.

Makes 6 side-dish servings.

❧ PER SERVING: 262 calories, 6.5 g. total fat, 0.9 g. saturated fat,
35 mg. cholesterol, 105 mg. sodium

Exceptional Macaroni and Cheese

Adapted from *Among Friends*
JUNIOR AUXILIARY OF RUSSELLVILLE

What makes this version of macaroni and cheese exceptional is the addition of chopped tomatoes. Fresh tomatoes are best, but you could also use canned ones that have no added salt.

   1   package (8 ounces or 2 cups) elbow macaroni
   1   cup (4 ounces) reduced-fat sharp Cheddar cheese
   1   cup (4 ounces) fat-free sharp Cheddar cheese
   1   teaspoon + 1 tablespoon all-purpose flour
   1   medium onion, chopped
 1¼   cups skim milk
   2   tablespoons nonfat dry milk
   2   cups peeled, seeded and chopped tomatoes or 1 can
       (24 ounces) no-salt-added tomatoes, drained and cut up
   1   cup fat-free small curd cottage cheese
       Pinch of ground black pepper
   ¼   cup herb-seasoned stuffing mix or toasted fresh
       bread crumbs
   2   tablespoons Parmesan cheese

Preheat the oven to 350°. Coat a 2½-quart casserole with no-stick spray and set aside.

Cook the macaroni according to the package directions, but without adding salt. Drain, rinse with cold water and drain again. Set the macaroni aside.

Meanwhile, in a medium bowl, combine the reduced-fat Cheddar and fat-free Cheddar. Sprinkle with 1 teaspoon of the flour and toss until coated. Set the cheese mixture aside.

Coat the saucepan from the macaroni with no-stick spray. Add the onions. Cook and stir over medium heat about 3 minutes or until the onions are tender.

In a small bowl, use a wire whisk to stir together ½ cup of the skim milk, dry milk and the remaining 1 tablespoon flour until smooth. Stir the mixture into the onions. Add the remaining ¾ cup skim milk. Cook and stir until the mixture begins to thicken and just comes to a boil. Add the Cheddar mixture. Cook and stir until melted. Remove the saucepan from the heat.

(continued)

Stir in the tomatoes, cottage cheese and pepper. Add the macaroni and gently stir until coated. Transfer the mixture to the prepared casserole. Top with the stuffing mix or bread crumbs and sprinkle with the Parmesan. Bake for 35 to 40 minutes or until heated through.

TEST KITCHEN TIP: Leftovers are great. Reheat them, loosely covered, in a microwave oven on high power for 30 to 40 seconds for a ½-cup portion (do 1 cup for 1 to 1½ minutes).

Makes 8 side-dish servings.

> ₴ PER SERVING: 228 calories, 3.2 g. total fat, 1.6 g. saturated fat, 8 mg. cholesterol, 484 mg. sodium

---

Blintz Soufflé

Adapted from *Vintage Vicksburg*
VICKSBURG JUNIOR AUXILIARY

This wonderful Sunday brunch dish was made light with the use of lower-fat dairy products. Top it with fresh fruit and serve it with bran muffins for a simple, healthful meal.

FILLING

1	cup fat-free small curd cottage cheese
4	ounces light cream cheese, softened
2	egg whites
1½	teaspoons sugar
½	teaspoon vanilla

BATTER

2	tablespoons margarine or butter (not reduced-calorie), softened
1	ounce (2 tablespoons) light cream cheese, softened
3	tablespoons sugar
4	egg whites
1	egg
¾	cup reduced-fat sour cream
½	cup all-purpose flour
¼	cup fresh orange juice
1	teaspoon baking powder

TOPPINGS

> 1   cup fat-free, sugar-free vanilla-flavored yogurt
> 1   cup sliced fresh strawberries or blueberries

Preheat the oven to 350°. Then coat an 8″ × 8″ baking dish or a 1½-quart casserole with no-stick spray and set aside.

FOR THE FILLING: In a small bowl, use an electric mixer to beat together the cottage cheese, cream cheese, egg whites, sugar and vanilla until well-combined.

FOR THE BATTER: In a medium bowl, use the electric mixer to beat together the margarine or butter, cream cheese, sugar, egg whites and egg until combined. Then beat in the sour cream, flour, orange juice and baking powder until well-combined.

To assemble, pour half the batter into the prepared baking dish. Drop the filling by small spoonfuls on top of the batter. Then spoon on the remaining batter and carefully spread it over the filling. Bake about 40 minutes or until puffy.

FOR THE TOPPINGS: Serve the soufflé immediately, topped with the yogurt and strawberries or blueberries.

Makes 4 main-dish servings.

☙ PER SERVING: 429 calories, 15.6 g. total fat, 6.8 g. saturated fat, 66 mg. cholesterol, 536 mg. sodium

Spinach Ricotta Tart

Adapted from *The Kitchen Connection*
NATIONAL COUNCIL OF JEWISH WOMEN, OMAHA SECTION

Spinach is a rich source of vitamins A and C. Even people who think they don't like spinach will relish this tart. The spinach is combined with ricotta and Parmesan cheeses and flavored with a hint of nutmeg.

CRUST

1¼	cups all-purpose flour
	Pinch of salt
2	tablespoons stick margarine (not reduced-calorie)
2	tablespoons canola oil
2–3	tablespoons skim milk

FILLING

1	small onion, finely chopped
2	packages (10 ounces each) frozen chopped spinach, thawed and well-drained
¼	teaspoon ground nutmeg
	Pinch of ground black pepper
6	egg whites, lightly beaten
1	container (15 ounces) reduced-fat ricotta cheese
1	cup evaporated skim milk
⅓	cup finely shredded Parmesan cheese
	Cherry tomatoes (optional)
	Fresh parsley (optional)

FOR THE CRUST: Preheat the oven to 450°. In a medium bowl, stir together the flour and salt. Using a pastry blender, cut in the margarine. In a custard cup, stir together the oil and 2 tablespoons of the milk. Drizzle the oil mixture over the flour mixture. Using a fork, toss and stir lightly until the dry ingredients are moistened. If necessary, add enough of the remaining 1 tablespoon milk to moisten. Then use your hands to gently shape the mixture into a ball.

Place the ball of dough between two 12"-square pieces of wax paper. Gently roll out the dough to a 12" circle. Remove the top piece of wax paper. Then invert the dough onto a 9" pie plate. Remove the remaining piece of wax paper and gently fit the dough into the pan. Fold the edges of pastry under and flute. Do not prick the pastry.

Line the pastry shell with a double thickness of heavy foil. Bake for 5 minutes, then remove the foil and bake for 5 to 7 minutes more or until the pastry is almost golden. Remove from the oven and reduce the oven temperature to 350°.

FOR THE FILLING: Lightly coat an unheated medium skillet with no-stick spray. Add the onions. Cook and stir over medium heat about 3 minutes or until the onions are tender. Remove from the heat.

If necessary, squeeze the spinach to remove excess moisture. Stir the spinach, nutmeg and pepper into the onions.

In a large bowl, beat together the egg whites, ricotta, milk and Parmesan until well-combined. Stir in the spinach mixture.

Transfer the mixture to the pastry shell. Bake in the 350° oven about 50 minutes or until a knife inserted in the center comes out clean. Let stand at least 5 minutes before cutting.

If desired, garnish with the cherry tomatoes and parsley.

Makes 8 side-dish servings.

ða PER SERVING: 247 calories, 9.4 g. total fat, 1.7 g. saturated fat, 12 mg. cholesterol, 232 mg. sodium

Breakfast Pizza

Adapted from *Come and Get It*
JUNIOR WELFARE LEAGUE OF TALLADEGA

This pizza is an unusual egg-and-sausage variety. It uses refrigerated pizza dough that you top with turkey sausage, egg substitute and reduced-fat cheese.

SAUSAGE FILLING
1   package (14 ounces) turkey breakfast sausage patties

EGG FILLING
¾   cup fat-free egg substitute or 6 egg whites
3   eggs
½   cup skim milk
¾   teaspoon dried oregano leaves, crushed
⅛   teaspoon ground black pepper

CRUST
1   can (10 ounces) refrigerated pizza dough
1   cup (4 ounces) finely shredded reduced-fat sharp Cheddar cheese
1   cup (4 ounces) finely shredded reduced-fat mozzarella cheese

FOR THE SAUSAGE FILLING: Crumble the sausage patties into a large skillet. Cook until the sausage is no longer pink, stirring occasionally. Drain the sausage in a strainer or colander, then transfer it to a large plate lined with paper towels. Blot the top of the sausage with additional paper towels. Set the sausage aside.

FOR THE EGG FILLING: Meanwhile, in a medium bowl, lightly beat together the egg substitute or egg whites, eggs, milk, oregano and pepper. Set aside.

FOR THE CRUST: Preheat the oven to 375°. Coat a 12" round pizza pan or a 13" × 9" baking pan with no-stick spray.

On a piece of wax paper, unroll the pizza dough. Lightly roll the dough to a 13" circle or a 14" × 10" rectangle. Transfer the dough to the pan. Pinch the edges to form a ½" high lip. Bake for 5 minutes. (The crust will be puffy when removed from the oven.) Reduce the oven temperature to 350°.

Spoon the sausage on the crust. Sprinkle with the Cheddar and mozzarella. Then pour the egg mixture over all.

Bake in the 350° oven for 30 to 35 minutes or until a knife inserted in the center comes out clean.

Makes 8 main-dish servings.

> PER SERVING: 331 calories, 16.5 g. total fat, 6.3 g. saturated fat, 120 mg. cholesterol, 786 mg. sodium

---

Baked Chili Rellenos

Adapted from *Simply Simpático*
JUNIOR LEAGUE OF ALBUQUERQUE

Surprise—this egg dish looks like it contains egg yolks, but it doesn't. The golden yellow color comes from turmeric. It's a trick that you can use with other egg dishes, such as frittatas, omelets and quiches.

8	canned whole green chili peppers
1½	cups (6 ounces) finely shredded reduced-fat Monterey Jack cheese
¾	cup (3 ounces) finely shredded reduced-fat Cheddar cheese
6	egg whites
1	can (5 ounces or ⅔ cup) evaporated skim milk
¼	cup all-purpose flour
¼	teaspoon ground black pepper
	Pinch of turmeric
	Dash of hot-pepper sauce
	Salsa (optional)

Preheat the oven to 350°. Coat an 8″ × 8″ baking dish with no-stick spray and set aside.

Wearing disposable gloves, cut the chili peppers in half lengthwise. Remove and discard most of the seeds for medium-hot rellenos; remove all of the seeds for mild rellenos. Lay the peppers flat on paper towels and pat dry.

Divide the Monterey Jack evenly among the chili peppers, plac-

(continued)

Junior League of Albuquerque

The Junior League of Albuquerque dedicates its cookbook, *Simply Simpático*, to the vibrant and unique culture of New Mexico. The state's nickname, "the Land of Enchantment," is not just good public relations. It is a motto that speaks succinctly of the mystery and beauty of New Mexico.

Over four centuries, four cultures—the Indians, the Spanish, the Mexicans and the English—have allowed their customs and cuisines to blend into an intriguing whole. As a result, New Mexican cooking is as colorful as the state from which it comes, incorporating both indigenous foods such as squash, beans, corn, vanilla and cinnamon with the new foods—rice, garlic, citrus fruits, pork and chili peppers—introduced by the Spanish.

The proceeds from this intriguing and good-looking cookbook help the group with its many community projects that support women and children in need—endeavors that are as diverse as the recipes in the cookbook and as vibrant as the state of New Mexico.

---

ing the cheese lengthwise on one half of each pepper. Fold the other half of the pepper over the cheese to enclose the cheese. Then place the peppers, in a single layer, in the prepared baking dish. Sprinkle with the Cheddar.

In a medium bowl, beat together the egg whites, milk, flour, black pepper, turmeric and hot-pepper sauce until smooth. Carefully pour the egg mixture over the chili peppers and Cheddar. Bake, uncovered, about 45 minutes or until a knife inserted in the center in the egg custard portion comes out clean. If desired, serve with the salsa.

Makes 4 main-dish servings.

> PER SERVING: 264 calories, 12.2 g. total fat, 6.3 g. saturated fat, 40 mg. cholesterol, 967 mg. sodium

Simply
Salads

Assorted Fruit
with Banana Poppy Seed Dressing

Adapted from *Tropical Seasons*

BEAUX ARTS OF THE LOWE ART MUSEUM OF THE UNIVERSITY OF MIAMI

Asian pears look like green or yellow apples. They're crunchy like apples and juicy-sweet like pears. These pears are wonderful with this creamy lime dressing. If Asian pears are unavailable at your market, substitute an apple or another pear variety.

DRESSING

4	ounces light cream cheese, softened
½	ripe medium banana
1–2	tablespoons honey
1½	teaspoons Key lime juice or fresh lime juice
1	tablespoon poppy seeds
1	tablespoon skim milk (optional)

FRUIT

¼	cup water
2	tablespoons Key lime juice or fresh lime or lemon juice
1	ripe Asian pear or other pear or apple, cored and cut into thin wedges
1	ripe banana sliced
2	cups small strawberries
	Fresh mint sprigs (optional)

FOR THE DRESSING: In a blender or small food processor, process the cream cheese, banana, honey and lime juice until smooth. Stir in the poppy seeds. If desired, stir in the milk to make a pouring consistency. Transfer the dressing to a serving bowl or small pitcher. Cover and refrigerate until ready to serve.

FOR THE FRUIT: In a small bowl, stir together the water and lime juice or lemon juice. Dip the pears or apples in the juice mixture. Then remove, drain and set aside.

Dip the bananas in the juice mixture, then remove and drain.

To serve, place the bowl or pitcher of dressing near the edge of a serving plate. Arrange the pears or apples, bananas and strawberries

OUR CAUSE

Beaux Arts of the Lowe Art Museum of the University of Miami

Coral Gables, Florida, is so lovely that it hardly needs art to add to its beauty. Still, it's good to know that art flourishes, thanks to the Lowe Art Museum on the campus of the University of Miami and to Beaux Arts, a group of 100 young women dedicated to promoting art appreciation in the Miami area.

The Lowe Art Museum was founded in 1948 and is the oldest art museum in Dade County. It isn't a large museum, but among its collection of more than 7,000 works are some of the finest Native American textiles in the world as well as an extensive range of pre-Columbian, Asian and African art. The Lowe runs six major exhibitions each year, featuring works from the collection as well as art borrowed from institutions nationwide and worldwide.

The museum also offers art lectures, classes for children and adults and other educational outreach programs for the community. *Tropical Seasons*, the second book from Beaux Arts, will enable the museum to continue its programs and expand its acquisitions.

on the serving plate around the bowl or pitcher. If desired, garnish with the mint.

Makes 4 side-dish servings.

> ❧ PER SERVING: 182 calories, 6.7 g. total fat, 3.2 g. saturated fat, 10 mg. cholesterol, 164 mg. sodium

Fresh Broccoli-Cauliflower Salad

Adapted from *Impressions*
AUXILIARY TO THE MEMPHIS DENTAL SOCIETY

This recipe uses turkey bacon in place of pork bacon, which cuts back on fat without affecting flavor.

DRESSING

⅓ cup fat-free mayonnaise
4 teaspoons sugar
2 teaspoons cider vinegar

SALAD

2 cups small cauliflower florets
1½ cups small broccoli florets
½ cup light raisins
¼ cup chopped red onions
6 slices turkey bacon, finely cut up, cooked and drained

FOR THE DRESSING: In a medium bowl, stir together the mayonnaise, sugar and vinegar.

FOR THE SALAD: If desired, cut the cauliflower and broccoli florets in half. Add the cauliflower, broccoli, raisins, onions and bacon to the dressing. Stir until coated. Cover and chill in the refrigerator for at least 4 hours to blend the flavors.

Makes 6 side-dish servings.

& PER SERVING: 113 calories, 2.7 g. total fat, 0.7 g. saturated fat, 9 mg. cholesterol, 184 mg. sodium

Fresh Tomato Salad

Adapted from *Preserving Our Italian Heritage*
SONS OF ITALY FLORIDA FOUNDATION

Salad dressings, like this balsamic vinaigrette, should just lightly coat the vegetables for the best flavor. So by just using a minimum amount of this dressing, you'll keep the fat grams to a minimum, too.

2 tablespoons balsamic vinegar
1 tablespoon unsweetened white grape juice or defatted reduced-sodium chicken broth
1 tablespoon extra-virgin olive oil
2 teaspoons finely chopped fresh basil leaves
1 small clove garlic, minced
⅛ teaspoon salt
⅛ teaspoon dried oregano leaves, crushed
2 large tomatoes, cut into thin wedges
¼ cup finely chopped red or white onions
   Freshly ground or cracked black pepper (to taste)
   Italian bread, sliced (optional)

In a medium bowl, use a wire whisk to stir together the vinegar, grape juice or broth, oil, basil, garlic, salt and oregano.

Add the tomatoes and onions. Gently toss until coated. Season to taste with the pepper. If desired, cover and chill in the refrigerator about 2 hours to blend the flavors.

If desired, serve with the bread to soak up the juices from the salad.

TEST KITCHEN TIP: Here's a salad that you can easily scale up when you have a bumper crop of tomatoes in your garden. For 8 servings, just double the amount of each ingredient.

Makes 4 side-dish servings.

❧ PER SERVING: 58 calories, 3.6 g. total fat, 0.5 g. saturated fat, 0 mg. cholesterol, 74 mg. sodium

Spinach Salad

Adapted from *Necessities and Temptations*

JUNIOR LEAGUE OF AUSTIN

Fruit juice and chicken broth are nifty substitutes for oil when trimming fat and calories from salad dressings. We used apple juice in this creamy dressing because the fruitiness enhances the dressing's sweet character.

DRESSING

3	tablespoons apple juice
2	tablespoons fat-free sour cream
2	tablespoons red wine vinegar
1	tablespoon finely chopped fresh parsley
1	tablespoon canola oil
1	teaspoon sugar
1	clove garlic, minced
¼	teaspoon dry mustard
	Pinch of salt
	Freshly ground black pepper (to taste)

SALAD

5	cups loosely packed torn spinach
½	cup sliced fresh mushrooms
¼	small red onion, thinly sliced and separated into rings
3	slices turkey bacon, finely cut up, cooked and drained
2	hard-cooked egg whites (discard yolks), finely chopped

FOR THE DRESSING: In a small bowl, use a wire whisk to stir together the apple juice, sour cream, vinegar, parsley, oil, sugar, garlic, mustard and salt. Season to taste with the pepper. Cover and chill in the refrigerator for at least 4 hours to blend the flavors.

FOR THE SALAD: In a large bowl, combine the spinach, mushrooms, onions, bacon and egg whites. Pour the dressing over the spinach mixture and gently toss until coated.

Makes 4 side-dish servings.

 PER SERVING: 105 calories, 5.7 g. total fat, 0.8 g. saturated fat, 7 mg. cholesterol, 130 mg. sodium

Junior League of Austin

They say that everything is bigger in Texas. If the Junior League of Austin is any measure, the generosity of the people who live there is as large as the state they call home. For more than 60 years, the League has raised money for and provided volunteer assistance to an impressive number of community projects and agencies. They raise more than $300,000 a year, and their 500-plus members devote 16,000 volunteer hours annually to causes that help virtually every segment of the population.

The League chooses a number of worthy causes annually to focus on. Causes run the gamut from preserving the culture, heritage and environment of Texas to helping needy Austin residents. In recent years, the League has endowed the AIDS Services of Austin Food Bank, the Ronald McDonald House, shelters for abused children and runaway teens, a mentoring program for Hispanic mothers and daughters and an assistance program for the elderly. Proceeds from *Necessities and Temptations* enable this generous group to continue its work.

Tabbouleh

Adapted from *A Touch of Atlanta*
MARIST PARENTS' CLUB

There are many variations of this popular Middle Eastern salad. This version has a generous amount of bulgur, so its fiber content is higher than that of some other tabboulehs.

BULGUR

1 cup boiling water
½ cup bulgur

DRESSING

¼ cup lemon juice
2 tablespoons defatted reduced-sodium chicken broth
1 tablespoon olive or canola oil
1 small clove garlic, minced
½ teaspoon ground black pepper
Pinch of salt

SALAD

1 cup finely chopped and loosely packed fresh parsley
1 large tomato, chopped
½ cup thinly sliced green onions
2 tablespoons finely chopped fresh mint

FOR THE BULGUR: In a medium bowl, combine the water and bulgur, then set aside for 30 to 40 minutes. Drain the bulgur well.

FOR THE DRESSING: Meanwhile, in a small bowl, use a wire whisk to stir together the lemon juice, broth, oil, garlic, pepper and salt.

FOR THE SALAD: Stir the parsley, tomatoes, onions and mint into the bulgur. Then add the dressing and gently stir until combined. If desired, cover and chill in the refrigerator for at least 2 hours to blend the flavors.

Makes 4 side-dish servings.

ða PER SERVING: 111 calories, 3.9 g. total fat, 0.5 g. saturated fat, 0 mg. cholesterol, 28 mg. sodium

Hearts of Palm with Tangy Lemon Dressing

Adapted from *Desert Treasures*
JUNIOR LEAGUE OF PHOENIX

Here's a creamy fat-free dressing that you can make yourself.
Serve it over mild-flavored or baby greens. It's also wonderful as
a fresh vegetable dip for asparagus and green beans.

DRESSING

3 tablespoons fat-free sour cream
3 tablespoons fresh lemon juice
1 teaspoon sugar
1 teaspoon finely shredded lemon peel
1 clove garlic, crushed
¼ teaspoon seasoned salt
¼ teaspoon cracked black pepper
⅛ teaspoon paprika

SALAD

1–2 small heads (5 ounces each) Boston or Bibb lettuce,
torn into bite-size pieces
¾ cup sliced hearts of palm (see tip)
3 green onions, sliced (no tops)

FOR THE DRESSING: In a small bowl, use a wire whisk to stir together the sour cream, lemon juice, sugar, lemon peel, garlic, salt, pepper and paprika.

FOR THE SALAD: In a large bowl, combine the lettuce, hearts of palm and onions. Pour the dressing over the lettuce mixture and gently toss until coated.

TEST KITCHEN TIP: Hearts of palm resemble the stalks of white asparagus, and their delicate flavor is similar to that of artichokes. Look for hearts of palm at your supermarket in the gourmet and canned vegetable sections.

Makes 6 side-dish servings.

➽ PER SERVING: 46 calories, 0.2 g. total fat, 0 g. saturated fat,
0 mg. cholesterol, 71 mg. sodium

Black Bean Salad

Adapted from *California Sizzles*

JUNIOR LEAGUE OF PASADENA

This salad is also good as a tangy Southwestern-style topping for grilled chicken or fish.

SALAD

¾ cup dried black beans, sorted and rinsed
⅔ cup frozen whole kernel corn, thawed
⅔ cup seeded and chopped tomatoes
¼ cup thinly sliced green onions
1–2 tablespoons finely chopped cilantro

DRESSING

3 tablespoons fresh lime juice
2 tablespoons defatted reduced-sodium chicken broth
1 tablespoon olive oil
Pinch of salt

FOR THE SALAD: Place the beans in a medium saucepan and add enough cold water to cover them by 2″. Cover and let stand at room temperature for 12 hours or overnight.

Drain and rinse the beans. In the saucepan, combine the beans and add enough fresh cold water to cover them again by 2″. Bring to a boil, then reduce the heat. Cover and simmer for 1 to 1½ hours or until tender but firm.

Drain the beans, then transfer them to a medium bowl. Add the corn, tomatoes, onions and cilantro.

FOR THE DRESSING: In a small bowl, use a wire whisk to stir together the lime juice, broth, oil and salt.

While the beans are still warm, pour the dressing mixture over the salad mixture. Gently stir until combined. Then cool to room temperature, stirring occasionally.

Stir the mixture again before serving. Serve at room temperature or slightly chilled. Store any leftover salad in the refrigerator for up to 3 days.

Makes 8 side-dish servings.

& PER SERVING: 80 calories, 1.9 g. total fat, 0.3 g. saturated fat, 0 mg. cholesterol, 9 mg. sodium

Cold Beef Salad

Adapted from *Pow Wow Chow*
THE FIVE CIVILIZED TRIBES MUSEUM

For a lovely summertime evening meal, serve this marinated steak salad. It's an ideal way to use up leftover cooked beef.

MARINATED BEEF

¼ cup water
¼ cup red wine vinegar
2 tablespoons sugar
2 tablespoons fresh lemon juice
¼ teaspoon dillweed
⅛ teaspoon salt
⅛ teaspoon freshly ground black pepper
1 pound boneless cooked beef sirloin, tenderloin or round, thinly sliced and cut into bite-size strips

SALAD

1 medium head (1 pound) romaine lettuce, torn into bite-size pieces
1 package (9 ounces) frozen artichoke hearts, thawed
2 small tomatoes, cut into wedges
1 small red onion, thinly sliced and separated into rings
1 cup fat-free sour cream

FOR THE MARINATED BEEF: In a small saucepan, combine the water, vinegar, sugar, lemon juice, dillweed, salt and pepper. Bring to a simmer. Cover and simmer for 5 minutes. Cool to room temperature.

Place the beef in a large resealable plastic bag. Pour the vinegar mixture over the beef. Seal the bag and marinate the beef in the refrigerator for 6 to 12 hours, turning the bag occasionally.

Remove the beef from the bag, reserving the marinade.

FOR THE SALAD: In a large bowl, combine the beef, lettuce, artichokes, tomatoes and onions. Then transfer to plates.

In a small bowl, stir together the reserved marinade and sour cream, then drizzle the mixture over each salad.

Makes 6 main-dish servings.

&. PER SERVING: 261 calories, 7.1 g. total fat, 2.7 g. saturated fat, 67 mg. cholesterol, 199 mg. sodium

Grilled Chicken Salads with Corn, Peppers and Tortilla Chips

Adapted from *Sensational Seasons*
JUNIOR LEAGUE OF FORT SMITH

The tortilla chips used for these individual salads are baked rather than fried, which saves you fat, calories and a messy clean up.

CHICKEN

4 skinless, boneless chicken breast halves (1 pound total)
½ cup fresh lime juice
1 tablespoon finely chopped fresh oregano or 1 teaspoon dried oregano leaves, crushed

TORTILLA CHIPS

4 white corn tortillas
Pinch of salt (optional)

CORN RELISH

1–2 tablespoons fresh lime juice
4 teaspoons defatted reduced-sodium chicken broth
2 teaspoons finely chopped fresh oregano or ¼ teaspoon dried oregano leaves, crushed
1½ teaspoons olive oil
¼ teaspoon ground cumin
1 package (10 ounces) whole kernel corn, thawed
½ large sweet red pepper, chopped
2 small green onions, thinly sliced

SALADS

6 cups torn mixed salad greens
Freshly ground or cracked black pepper (to taste)

FOR THE CHICKEN: Place the chicken in a large resealable plastic bag. Pour the lime juice over the chicken, then sprinkle with the oregano. Seal the bag and marinate the chicken in the refrigerator for 30 minutes, turning the bag occasionally.

FOR THE TORTILLA CHIPS: Preheat the oven to 400°. Coat a large baking sheet with no-stick spray. Stack the tortillas, then cut the stack into 6 wedges. Place the tortilla wedges on the baking sheet in a single layer. Lightly coat them with no-stick spray. If desired, lightly sprinkle with the salt. Bake for 10 to 12 minutes or until lightly browned and crisp.

FOR THE CORN RELISH: In a medium bowl, use a wire whisk to stir together 1 tablespoon of the lime juice, broth, oregano, oil and cumin until well-blended.

Add the corn, peppers and onions. Toss until combined. If desired, add enough of the remaining 1 tablespoon lime juice to taste. Toss until well-mixed and set aside.

To grill the chicken, prepare the grill for cooking by coating the unheated grill rack with no-stick spray. Then light the grill according to the manufacturer's directions. Check the temperature for grilling; the temperature should be "medium-hot" or 3 seconds that the palm of your hand can withstand the heat (see tip on page 131). Place the rack on the grill.

Remove the chicken from the bag. Discard the marinade. Place the chicken on the rack. Grill, uncovered, for 8 minutes. Turn the chicken over and grill for 7 to 10 minutes more or until the chicken is tender and the juices run clear when the thickest part of the chicken is pierced with a fork.

Transfer the chicken to a cutting board. Cut it lengthwise into thin slices.

FOR THE SALADS: Divide the greens among 4 dinner plates. On top of each plate of greens, arrange the chicken, a mound of the corn relish and 6 tortilla chips. Season to taste with the pepper.

Make 4 main-dish servings.

๛ PER SERVING: 251 calories, 5.1 g. total fat, 0.8 g. saturated fat, 46 mg. cholesterol, 134 mg. sodium

Smoked Sausage Salad Medley

Adapted from *Peachtree Bouquet*
JUNIOR LEAGUE OF DEKALB COUNTY

*When cooking healthy, look for ways to sneak extra nutrients into
your dishes. In this salad, combining yogurt with mayonnaise in
the dressing adds a little extra calcium.*

SAUSAGE MEDLEY

7   ounces fully cooked smoked turkey sausages,
    diced (1½ cups)
1   cup cooked long-grain white or brown rice, cooled
    (see tip on page 226)
1   cup chopped celery
1   cup thinly bias-sliced carrots
1   cup frozen green peas, thawed

DRESSING

½   cup fat-free plain yogurt
¼   cup fat-free mayonnaise
¼   cup finely chopped onions
¼   cup very finely chopped green peppers
1   tablespoon chopped fresh parsley
½   teaspoon garlic powder
1   teaspoon prepared mustard
1   teaspoon finely shredded lemon peel
¼   teaspoon salt
⅛   teaspoon ground red pepper
    Leaf lettuce leaves

FOR THE SAUSAGE MEDLEY: In a medium bowl, combine
the sausages, rice, celery, carrots and peas. Cover and chill in the refrigerator for several hours or overnight.

FOR THE DRESSING: One hour before serving, in small bowl,
stir together the yogurt, mayonnaise, onions, green peppers, parsley,
garlic powder, mustard, lemon peel, salt and red pepper. Then add
the mayonnaise mixture to the sausage mixture. Stir until well-
combined. Cover and chill in the refrigerator to blend the flavors.

To serve, line 4 large salad plates with the lettuce leaves. Spoon
the sausage mixture on top.

OUR CAUSE

Junior League of DeKalb County

In springtime, Atlanta is radiant with the color and perfume of thousands of blossoms—from delicate dogwood to fragrant magnolia, from blazing azaleas to lovely roses in a magnificent array of colors. If you put them all together, you'd have a bouquet as unique and appealing as the culture and heritage of Atlanta itself.

That's what the Junior League of DeKalb County had in mind when it created *Peachtree Bouquet*, a culinary arrangement of Atlanta cuisine that reflects a city growing in sophistication while still savoring its oldest traditions. The cookbook includes specialties from area restaurants and caterers, mixing international cuisines and old Southern favorites.

This active Junior League is involved in a number of community projects that benefit from sales of its pretty cookbook. Most especially, though, the group plans to donate funds from the book to help the DeKalb County Rape Crisis Center.

TEST KITCHEN TIP: This salad is particularly attractive when made with yellow rice. Most yellow rice mixes contain monosodium glutamate (MSG), however. You can get the same vibrant color by adding a little turmeric to long-grain white rice as it cooks.

Makes 4 main-dish servings.

> PER SERVING: 225 calories, 4 g. total fat, 1.2 g. saturated fat, 32 mg. cholesterol, 851 mg. sodium

Florida Chicken Salad

Adapted from *Tropical Seasons*
BEAUX ARTS OF THE LOWE ART MUSEUM OF THE UNIVERSITY OF MIAMI

You can use most any greens for this salad, but a mixture of arugula, leaf lettuce, spinach or watercress and radicchio is especially appealing. These greens are not only pretty but also higher in vitamins and minerals than pale varieties like iceberg lettuce.

DRESSING

- ¼ cup defatted reduced-sodium chicken broth
- 3 tablespoons balsamic vinegar
- 1 teaspoon walnut or olive oil
- 1 teaspoon Dijon mustard
- ¼ teaspoon dried marjoram leaves, crushed

SALAD

- 6 cups torn mixed salad greens
- 12 ounces skinless, boneless chicken breasts, cooked and cut into bite-size strips
- 1 cup peeled and cubed papaya
- 1 cup peeled and cubed mango
- 1 cup red raspberries
- 4 tablespoons broken walnuts, toasted
- 1 tablespoon finely chopped fresh mint

FOR THE DRESSING: In a small bowl, use a wire whisk to stir together the broth, vinegar, oil, mustard and marjoram until well-blended.

FOR THE SALAD: Place the greens in a medium bowl. Add a small amount of the dressing. Gently toss until coated, then spoon the greens onto dinner plates.

In the medium bowl, combine the chicken, papaya, mango and raspberries. Add the remaining dressing. Gently toss until coated. Spoon and arrange the chicken mixture on top of each plate of greens. Sprinkle each salad with some of the walnuts and mint.

Makes 4 main-dish servings.

PER SERVING: 203 calories, 7.5 g. total fat, 0.9 g. saturated fat, 34 mg. cholesterol, 88 mg. sodium

Shrimp Mélange

Adapted from *Fast and Fancy*
SADDLE RIVER DAY SCHOOL PARENTS' GUILD

This salad makes a perfect entrée when you want a light meal.
Serve it with French bread and iced tea.

2	tablespoons fat-free mayonnaise
2	tablespoons fat-free plain yogurt
1	tablespoon fresh lemon juice
1	tablespoon chili sauce
1	tablespoon finely chopped fresh dill or
	1 teaspoon dillweed
¼	teaspoon Worcestershire sauce
	Pinch of freshly ground black pepper
12	ounces cooked tiny shrimp (about 1½ cups)
1	cup orange sections or halved grapefruit sections
1	small head Boston or Bibb lettuce

In a medium bowl, stir together the mayonnaise, yogurt, lemon juice, chili sauce, dill, Worcestershire sauce and pepper.

Add the shrimp and orange or grapefruit sections. Gently toss until coated. Cover and chill in the refrigerator for 1 hour to blend the flavors.

To serve, line large salad plates with the lettuce. Then mound the shrimp mixture on top of each.

Makes 4 main-dish servings.

🍃 PER SERVING: 121 calories, 1 g. total fat, 0.2 g. saturated fat, 131 mg. cholesterol, 316 mg. sodium

Slenderized Roquefort Dressing

Adapted from *Simply Simpático*
JUNIOR LEAGUE OF ALBUQUERQUE

For a thick, creamy dressing that's also low in fat, the Junior League of Albuquerque used pureed cottage cheese instead of mayonnaise.

½ cup 1% fat cottage cheese
2–3 tablespoons nonfat buttermilk
1 tablespoon white wine vinegar
3 tablespoons crumbled Roquefort or blue cheese
Freshly ground black pepper (to taste)

In a blender or a small food processor, process the cottage cheese, 2 tablespoons of the buttermilk and vinegar until nearly smooth.

Transfer the mixture to a small bowl. Stir in the Roquefort or blue cheese. If necessary, stir in enough of the remaining 1 tablespoon buttermilk to make a desired consistency. Season to taste with the pepper. To store, cover and refrigerate for up to 2 weeks. Stir before serving.

Makes 1 cup; 8 servings.

 PER 2 TABLESPOONS: 22 calories, 1 g. total fat, 0.6 g. saturated fat, 3 mg. cholesterol, 109 mg. sodium

*Vegetable
Harvest*

Asparagus Eleganté

Adapted from *Rave Reviews*
JUNIOR LEAGUE OF NORTH LITTLE ROCK

To create a rich, creamlike sauce without using cream, add a small amount of dry milk powder to skim milk, as we do in this Swiss cheese and ham sauce.

ASPARAGUS

1   pound asparagus

SAUCE

1½   teaspoons all-purpose flour
½   cup skim milk
1   tablespoon nonfat dry milk
2   tablespoons (½ ounce) grated reduced-fat Swiss cheese
½   cup diced low-sodium, 96% fat-free fully cooked ham
½   teaspoon fresh lemon juice
Pinch of salt
Pinch of ground nutmeg

FOR THE ASPARAGUS: Snap off the woody ends of the asparagus where they naturally break. Or, if you want to use more of the stalk, use a vegetable peeler to remove the tough skin.

In a large saucepan with a tight-fitting lid, bring 1″ of water to a boil. Place the asparagus in a steamer basket and set the basket in the saucepan, making sure the basket sits above the water. Cover the saucepan and steam for 10 to 15 minutes or until the asparagus is crisp-tender.

FOR THE SAUCE: Meanwhile, in a small saucepan, use a wire whisk to stir the flour into the skim milk until combined. Then stir in the dry milk. Cook and stir over medium heat until the mixture begins to thicken and just comes to a boil. Reduce the heat to low. Stir in the Swiss. Cook and stir until melted. Then stir in the ham, lemon juice, salt and nutmeg.

To serve, transfer the asparagus to a serving platter. Pour the sauce over the asparagus.

Makes 4 servings.

&   PER SERVING: 79 calories, 1.9 g. total fat, 0.8 g. saturated fat, 8 mg. cholesterol, 232 mg. sodium

Green Beans with Basil

Adapted from *The Maine Collection*
PORTLAND MUSEUM OF ART GUILD

This fresh basil and rosemary topping is also great on baby carrots or peas.

1   pound green beans, ends and strings removed and
    cut into 1″ pieces
1   tablespoon reduced-calorie butter blend
½   cup chopped onions
¼   cup chopped celery
1   clove garlic, minced
1   tablespoon defatted reduced-sodium chicken broth
1   teaspoon finely chopped fresh basil or ¼ teaspoon
    dried basil, crushed
¼   teaspoon dried rosemary, crushed

In a large saucepan with a tight-fitting lid, bring 1″ of water to a boil. Place the beans in a steamer basket and set the basket in the saucepan, making sure the basket sits above the water. Cover the saucepan and steam for 5 to 8 minutes or until the beans are crisp-tender.

Meanwhile, melt the butter blend in a small skillet. Add the onions, celery and garlic. Cook and stir over medium heat for 4 minutes. Add the broth, basil and rosemary. Cook and stir about 1 minute more or until the celery is tender.

To serve, transfer the beans to a bowl. Add the onion mixture and toss until combined.

Makes 6 servings.

ঌ PER SERVING: 50 calories, 2 g. total fat, 0.4 g. saturated fat,
0 mg. cholesterol, 28 mg. sodium

Harvard Beets

Adapted from *Between Greene Leaves*
GREENE COUNTY HOMEMAKERS EXTENSION ASSOCIATION

Here's a popular low-fat alternative to buttered beets.

BEETS

4	medium beets (about 1 pound total)

SAUCE

⅓	cup sugar
2	teaspoons cornstarch
¼	teaspoon salt
⅓	cup vinegar
2	teaspoons reduced-calorie margarine

FOR THE BEETS: Cut the roots from the beets. Then cut the tops from the beets, leaving 2″ of the stems. In a large saucepan, cover the beets with water. Bring to a boil, then reduce the heat. Simmer about 35 minutes or until tender.

Drain the beets. Holding the hot beets with a fork, use a sharp knife to remove their skin. Cut the beets into thin slices or small cubes. Transfer to a medium bowl.

FOR THE SAUCE: In a small saucepan, stir together the sugar, cornstarch and salt. Then stir in the vinegar. Bring to a boil, then reduce the heat. Simmer and stir for 5 minutes.

Add the margarine and stir until the margarine melts. Pour the sauce over the beets and gently toss until coated. Let stand for 5 minutes so the beets can absorb the flavor of the sauce. Gently toss again before serving.

Makes 4 servings.

&❧ PER SERVING: 100 calories, 1 g. total fat, 0.2 g. saturated fat, 0 mg. cholesterol, 181 mg. sodium

Gingered Carrots

Adapted from *A Taste of Aloha*
JUNIOR LEAGUE OF HONOLULU

The Junior League of Honolulu used ginger, cinnamon and brown sugar to add a special touch to these low-fat carrots.

4	medium carrots, cut into julienne strips ¼"-thick slices
¼	cup water
1	cinnamon stick (2½")
⅛	teaspoon salt
1	tablespoon packed brown sugar
2	teaspoons tub-style reduced-calorie margarine
½	teaspoon chopped fresh parsley
¼	teaspoon ground ginger

In a small saucepan, combine the carrots, water, cinnamon stick and salt. Bring to a boil, then reduced the heat. Cover and simmer for 5 to 8 minutes or until the carrots are crisp-tender. Drain the carrots and discard the cinnamon stick.

Transfer the carrots to a serving bowl. In the saucepan, heat together the brown sugar, margarine, parsley and ginger until the margarine and brown sugar are melted. Drizzle the mixture over the carrots and gently toss until coated.

TEST KITCHEN TIP: You could also prepare the carrots in the microwave. Reduce the water to 2 tablespoons. Place the carrots and water in a microwave-safe casserole and cook on high power for a total of 5 to 9 minutes or until the carrots are crisp-tender; stir the carrots and rotate the casserole a quarter turn every 3 minutes.

Makes 4 servings.

PER SERVING: 59 calories, 1.8 g. total fat, 0.2 g. saturated fat, 0 mg. cholesterol, 113 mg. sodium

Cheese-Sauced Cauliflower

Adapted from *Cordonbluegrass*
JUNIOR LEAGUE OF LOUISVILLE

A Cheddar sauce turns plain cauliflower into a company-special side dish. The sauce is also good over broccoli and other vegetables. For best results, make sure the cheese is finely shredded so that it melts evenly.

CAULIFLOWER
    4–5   cups small cauliflower florets

CHEESE SAUCE
    ½   cup (2 ounces) finely shredded reduced-fat sharp Cheddar cheese
    3   teaspoons all-purpose flour
    ½   cup skim milk
    1   tablespoon nonfat dry milk

TOPPINGS
    ¼   cup toasted fresh bread crumbs (see tip) or fat-free cracked pepper crackers crushed into coarse crumbs
    1   hard-cooked egg white (discard yolk), finely chopped
        Finely chopped fresh parsley or paprika

FOR THE CAULIFLOWER: In a large saucepan with a tight-fitting lid, bring 1″ of water to a boil. Place the cauliflower in a steamer basket and set the basket in the saucepan, making sure that the basket sits above the water.

Cover the saucepan and steam for 10 to 15 minutes or until the cauliflower is crisp-tender.

FOR THE CHEESE SAUCE: Meanwhile, place the Cheddar in a small bowl. Sprinkle with 1 teaspoon of the flour and toss until coated. Set the cheese mixture aside.

In a small saucepan, use a wire whisk to stir together the remaining 2 teaspoons flour, skim milk and dry milk until well-combined. Cook and stir over medium heat until slightly thickened and bubbly. Add the cheese mixture. Cook and stir just until the cheese is melted. Pour the sauce over the cauliflower and gently toss until coated.

Junior League of Louisville

Kentucky still has the aura of the pioneer about it. Perhaps that's because it is, in so many places, as beautiful and unspoiled now as it was when explorers first blazed the Cumberland Gap more than 200 years ago. Kentucky is host to much natural beauty, from the mountains rising out of the blue fog in the east to the endless pastures of bright green in the Bluegrass region.

Typical of the early pioneers, today's Kentuckians have an abundance of fellowship. The pride they take in working together for common goals shows in the devotion of the Junior League of Louisville to its community. Since 1921, the League has initiated, funded and volunteered to run many projects to help the city's residents.

Among the group's favorite projects are health care, education, assisting the elderly and substance-abuse prevention. *Cordonbluegrass* was published to raise money for all the League's projects, but especially for the group's Sister-to-Sister program.

FOR THE TOPPINGS: Transfer the mixture to a serving dish and top with the bread or cracker crumbs and egg whites. Sprinkle with the parsley or paprika.

TEST KITCHEN TIP: For butter-flavored bread crumbs without added fat, place the fresh bread crumbs in a thin layer in a shallow baking pan. Coat with butter-flavored no-stick spray. Bake in a 400° oven about 3 minutes or until crispy and golden.

Makes 4 servings.

PER SERVING: 94 calories, 2.4 g. total fat, 1.3 g. saturated fat, 7 mg. cholesterol, 266 mg. sodium

Corn Cakes

Adapted from *RSVP*
JUNIOR LEAGUE OF PORTLAND

You can serve these corn cakes with either sweet or savory toppings to suit your fancy. Try reduced-calorie maple-flavored syrup or a sprinkle of powdered sugar for sweetness. To highlight the corn cakes' savory note, top with reduced-fat sour cream or salsa.

1 egg
1 tablespoon skim milk
1 tablespoon all-purpose flour
2½ teaspoons sugar
½ teaspoon baking powder
¼ teaspoon salt
Pinch of ground black pepper
2 packages (10 ounces each) frozen whole kernel corn, thawed and drained
2 egg whites

In a large bowl, beat together the egg and milk until combined. Stir in the flour, sugar, baking powder, salt and pepper. Then add the corn and stir until coated.

In a small bowl, beat the egg whites until stiff peaks form. Then gently fold the egg whites into the corn mixture.

Lightly coat an unheated griddle or large skillet with no-stick spray. Then heat the griddle over medium heat. For each cake, drop a rounded tablespoon of the corn mixture onto the griddle and cook about 1 minute or until golden brown. Turn the cakes over and cook about 1 minute more or until golden brown.

Makes 20; 5 servings.

ба PER 4 CAKES: 129 calories, 1.1 g. total fat, 0.3 g. saturated fat, 43 mg. cholesterol, 181 mg. sodium

Roasted Corn

Adapted from *The Cotton Country Collection*
JUNIOR LEAGUE OF MONROE

Butter can fit into a healthy diet—as long as you're smart about how you use it. Each of these cobs is brushed with 1 teaspoon of butter blend, which is lower in saturated fat than regular butter. Believe it or not, 1 teaspoon is enough to give each cob a rich, buttery taste.

4   ears corn, with husks
4   teaspoons reduced-calorie butter blend, melted
4   teaspoons finely chopped fresh chives
4   teaspoons finely chopped fresh parsley
⅛   teaspoon salt
    Pinch of ground black pepper

Pull back the husks, without removing them, and remove the silks from each ear of corn.

Brush each cob with 1 teaspoon of the butter blend. Sprinkle each cob with 1 teaspoon each of the chives and parsley. Then sprinkle with the salt and pepper. Pull the husks back up over the corn to cover.

Light the grill according to the manufacturer's directions. Check the temperature for grilling; the temperature should be "hot" or 2 seconds that the palm of your hand can withstand the heat (see tip on page 131). Place the rack on the grill.

Place the corn on the rack over the hot coals. Grill, uncovered, for 15 to 18 minutes or until the corn is tender. Turn it frequently. Remove the husks before serving.

TEST KITCHEN TIP: You could also roast the corn in the oven. Totally remove the husks and silks from the ears. Brush with the butter blend and the seasonings as directed. Wrap each cob in a piece of heavy foil. Preheat the oven to 400°. Place the wrapped corn on the center rack in the oven. Roast about 30 minutes or until tender.

Makes 4 servings.

PER SERVING: 148 calories, 4.3 g. total fat, 0.8 g. saturated fat, 0 mg. cholesterol, 104 mg. sodium

Eggplant Casserole

Adapted from *Cookbook 25 Years*
MADISON COUNTY FARM BUREAU WOMEN'S COMMITTEE

The common way to extract bitter juices from eggplant is to generously salt it and let it drain for at least 20 minutes. To achieve the same results without salt, we cooked the eggplant in the microwave and then pressed the slices nearly dry before using them in this side-dish casserole.

SAUCE

1	can (16 ounces) tomatoes (with juice)
¼	cup chopped onions
3	tablespoons tomato paste
½	teaspoon sugar
¼	teaspoon salt
1	clove garlic, minced
¼	teaspoon dried oregano leaves, crushed
¼	teaspoon ground black pepper

EGGPLANT

1	medium eggplant (1–1¼ pounds)
½	cup (2 ounces) finely shredded reduced-fat mozzarella cheese
2	tablespoons finely shredded fresh Parmesan cheese (optional)

FOR THE SAUCE: In a small saucepan, stir together the tomatoes (with juice), onions, tomato paste, sugar, salt, garlic, oregano and pepper. Bring to a boil, then reduce the heat. Simmer, uncovered, for 15 to 20 minutes or until thick, stirring frequently.

FOR THE EGGPLANT: Meanwhile, cut and discard the stem and bottom end from the eggplant. Then cut off and discard the peel. Cut the eggplant into ½"-thick slices. Place the slices in a 1-quart microwave-safe casserole. Cover and cook in a microwave oven on high power for 6 to 8 minutes or just until tender, rotating the casserole a quarter turn after every 2 minutes. Drain.

Transfer the slices to a large plate lined with paper towels. Place additional paper towels on top and press down, applying gentle pressure, to remove the excess moisture.

Madison County Farm Bureau Women's Committee

The era of the small family-run farm may be drawing to a close, but agriculture will always play a crucial role in the survival of every American community. The 8,600 members of the Madison County Farm Bureau want to remind us that our milk still comes from a cow, not a carton, and our meat still comes from farm animals, not from the refrigerator case in our local markets.

Illinois' Madison County Farm Bureau is tireless in its support of farmers in its area. The bureau promotes legislation that helps farmers continue to make a living in agriculture, gives farm families a hand in day-to-day matters, awards scholarships to students who plan to study agriculture in college, supports the local 4-H organization and does much more.

In addition, the bureau helps make life a little more pleasant for its members by sponsoring various sports and other activities and offering discounted tickets to amusement parks and area events. Sales from the Bureau's 25th-anniversary cookbook, *Cookbook 25 Years*, are earmarked for the group's scholarship fund.

To assemble, place one layer of the eggplant in a flat serving dish. Top with half each of the sauce and mozzarella. Then repeat the layers using the remaining eggplant, sauce and mozzarella. If desired, sprinkle the Parmesan over the top. Serve immediately.

Makes 6 servings.

ù PER SERVING: 71 calories, 1.8 g. total fat, 1 g. saturated fat, 0 mg. cholesterol, 209 mg. sodium

Ratatouille

Adapted from *The Cotton Country Collection*
JUNIOR LEAGUE OF MONROE

Traditional recipes for ratatouille call for the eggplant, zucchini and other vegetables to be simmered in lots of oil. This low-fat version, however, achieves the same saucy consistency by sautéing the vegetables in a small amount of water, then baking them in a covered casserole.

1   eggplant (1 pound), peeled and sliced ¼" thick
1   pound zucchini, sliced ¼" thick
2   tablespoons water
1   small onion, very thinly sliced and separated into rings
1   small green pepper, thinly sliced
2   cloves garlic, halved
1   pound tomatoes (3–4 tomatoes), peeled, seeded and sliced
1   teaspoon dried basil leaves, crushed
¼   teaspoon salt
¼   teaspoon dried thyme leaves, crushed
⅛   teaspoon freshly ground black pepper
1   bay leaf

In a large skillet, combine the eggplant, zucchini and water. Cover and cook over medium heat for 2 minutes. Turn the vegetables over and cook about 3 minutes more or until tender. Remove the vegetables from the skillet and discard the liquid.

Lightly coat the skillet with no-stick spray. Add the onions, green peppers and garlic. Cook and stir over medium heat about 5 minutes or until the onions are very tender. Remove and discard the garlic. Add the tomatoes and toss until combined.

Preheat the oven to 350°. In a 2-quart casserole, layer half each of the eggplant mixture, tomato mixture, basil, salt, thyme and black pepper. Add the bay leaf, then repeat the layers with the remaining eggplant mixture, tomato mixture and seasonings. Cover and bake for 1 hour. Remove and discard the bay leaf before serving.

TEST KITCHEN TIP: Even though this recipe makes quite a lot (about 5 cups), this hot vegetable dish is also delicious served cold as a salad or appetizer.

Makes 10 servings.

ва PER SERVING: 32 calories, 0.3 g. total fat, 0 g. saturated fat, 0 mg. cholesterol, 60 mg. sodium

---

Greek Potato Wedges

Adapted from *Rogue River Rendezvous*
JUNIOR SERVICE LEAGUE OF JACKSON COUNTY

These potatoes resemble french fries but are a lot lower in fat.

4   large potatoes (1½ pounds total)
1   tablespoon olive oil
    Paprika (to taste and color)
½   teaspoon salt

Preheat the oven to 450°. Cut each potato into 6 lengthwise wedges.

Place the potatoes in a large bowl. Drizzle the oil over the potatoes, then toss until coated. Sprinkle with the desired amount of paprika, then toss again.

Lightly coat a baking sheet with no-stick spray. Then arrange the potatoes on the baking sheet in a single layer. Sprinkle with the salt. Bake for 15 minutes. Using a spatula, turn the wedges over and bake for 10 to 15 minutes more or until tender and slightly crispy.

TEST KITCHEN TIP: There's an endless array of flavor possibilities for these potatoes. Try garlic, onion or seasoned salt instead of regular salt. If you're watching your sodium intake, omit the paprika and salt and sprinkle the potatoes with a salt-free blend such as lemon-herb, garlic-and-herb or lemon-pepper seasoning.

Makes 24; 6 servings.

ва PER 4 WEDGES: 132 calories, 2.4 g. total fat, 0.3 g. saturated fat, 0 mg. cholesterol, 186 mg. sodium

Sweet Red Pepper Tart

Adapted from *A Taste of New England*
JUNIOR LEAGUE OF WORCESTER

Serve this quichelike tart as a side dish with grilled chicken or salmon. Or make it into a main dish by serving larger portions.

PASTRY

1¼ cups all-purpose flour
     Pinch of salt
2   tablespoons stick margarine (not reduced-calorie)
2   tablespoons canola oil
2–3 tablespoons skim milk
1   tablespoon Dijon mustard

VEGETABLE FILLING

1   tablespoon tub-style reduced-calorie margarine
2   small onions, finely chopped
1   clove garlic, minced
3   large sweet red peppers, chopped
1   green pepper, chopped
1   cup (4 ounces) finely shredded reduced-calorie Swiss cheese
2   tablespoons finely chopped fresh parsley or basil, chopped

EGG FILLING

1   can (12 ounces or 1½ cups) evaporated skim milk
½   cup fat-free egg substitute
2   eggs
2   teaspoons cornstarch
½   teaspoon salt
¼   teaspoon freshly ground black pepper
     Pinch of ground nutmeg
     Pinch of ground red pepper

FOR THE PASTRY: Preheat the oven to 450°. In a medium bowl stir together the flour and salt. Using a pastry blender, cut in the margarine. In a custard cup, stir together the oil and 2 tablespoons of the milk. Drizzle the oil mixture over the flour mixture. Using a fork, toss and stir lightly until the dry ingredients are moistened. If necessary, add enough of the remaining 1 tablespoon milk to moisten. Then, using your hands, gently shape the mixture into a ball.

Place the ball of dough between two 12"-square pieces of wax paper. Gently roll out the dough to a 12" circle. Remove the top piece of wax paper. Then invert the dough onto a 9" pie plate. Remove the remaining piece of wax paper and gently fit the dough into the pan. Fold the edges of pastry under and flute. Do not prick the pastry.

Line the pastry shell with a double thickness of heavy foil. Bake for 5 minutes, then remove the foil and bake for 5 to 7 minutes more or until the pastry is almost golden. Remove from the oven and reduce the oven temperature to 325°. Brush the bottom of the pie shell with the mustard and set aside.

FOR THE VEGETABLE FILLING: Lightly coat an unheated large skillet with no-stick spray. Add the margarine and melt. Then add the onions and garlic. Cook and stir over medium heat about 3 minutes or until tender. Add the red peppers and green peppers. Cook and stir about 5 minutes more or until tender. Using a slotted spoon, transfer the vegetables to a large plate lined with paper towels. Blot the top of the vegetables with additional paper towels, then cool slightly.

Spread the vegetable mixture on the bottom of the crust, then sprinkle with the Swiss and parsley or basil.

FOR THE EGG FILLING: In a medium bowl, lightly beat together the milk, egg substitute, eggs, cornstarch, salt, black pepper, nutmeg and red pepper.

Pour the egg mixture evenly over the vegetables. Bake for 30 to 40 minutes or until the top is golden brown and a knife inserted in the center comes out clean. Cool for 10 minutes before cutting and serving.

TEST KITCHEN TIP: You can easily microwave leftovers for a quick, light lunch. You could also freeze the tart for future use. Wrap individual pieces in heavy foil and freeze them. To thaw and reheat, remove the foil from a piece and place the tart on a microwave-safe plate. Cover with wax paper and cook on high power for a total of 2 minutes, until heated through; rotate the plate a quarter turn every 30 seconds.

Makes 10 servings.

 PER SERVING: 212 calories, 9.4 g. total fat, 2.3 g. saturated fat, 51 mg. cholesterol, 261 mg. sodium

Twice-Baked Yams

Adapted from *The Philadelphia Orchestra Cookbook*
WEST PHILADELPHIA COMMITTEE FOR THE PHILADELPHIA ORCHESTRA

These yams are perfect for holiday dinners, especially since you can assemble and refrigerate them ahead of time. Just before serving, heat them in the oven about 20 minutes.

4	medium yams (6–8 ounces each)
1	tablespoon tub-style reduced-calorie margarine
⅓	cup apricot preserves
2	teaspoons fresh orange juice
½	teaspoon salt
2–4	teaspoons skim milk
	Pinch of ground nutmeg

Preheat the oven to 350°. Use a fork to prick the yams. Place the yams on the oven rack and bake for 40 to 50 minutes or until tender.

Cut a thin slice in the top of each yam. Scoop out the pulp, being careful not to break the skin. Place the pulp in a medium bowl. Using a potato masher or fork, mash the pulp. Stir in the margarine until melted. Add the preserves, orange juice and salt. Stir in enough of the milk to moisten.

Spoon the pulp mixture into the empty yam shells. Sprinkle with the nutmeg. Place the yams on a baking sheet and bake in the 350° oven for 15 to 20 minutes until heated through.

Makes 4 servings.

    PER SERVING: 295 calories, 2.7 g. total fat, 0.3 g. saturated fat, 0 mg. cholesterol, 314 mg. sodium

West Philadelphia Committee for the Philadelphia Orchestra

The Revolutionary War years were lean ones for music lovers. In 1757, the first public concert in Philadelphia's recorded history was held. Admission: $1. The war put a damper on public enjoyment of music, though, and it was not until 1820 that the founding of the Philadelphia Musical Fund Society brought orchestral music to the public again.

From the seeds planted by the Musical Fund Society, the Philadelphia Orchestra eventually formed, holding its first performance in 1900 in the city's lavish Academy of Music. By 1907, under the direction of Maestro Fritz Scheel, the orchestra was widely acclaimed. The beloved conductor Eugene Ormandy continued the orchestra's renown during his 46 years as Musical Director. Ormandy passed on his baton at the end of the 1980–1981 season, but the Philadelphia Orchestra continues to be held in high regard.

The Philadelphia Orchestra Cookbook showcases finely tuned recipes contributed by members of the orchestra and their families as well as area chefs and other culinary notables. Proceeds from the book help support the orchestra.

Butternut Squash Soufflé

Adapted from *Two and Company*
ST. THOMAS CHURCH

By slightly increasing the orange juice in this recipe, we were able to make two savings—in butter and in sugar. The additional juice replaces moistness that was contributed by butter and sweetness that came from additional sugar.

1   butternut squash (1½ pounds)
1   tablespoon tub-style reduced-calorie margarine
2   egg whites
1   egg
½   cup orange juice
⅓   cup nonfat dry milk
¼   cup sugar
⅛   teaspoon salt
     Pinch of ground cinnamon

Preheat the oven to 350°. To bake the squash, cut the squash in half lengthwise. Remove the seeds. Place the halves, cut side down, in an 8″ × 8″ baking dish. Cover with foil and bake for 30 minutes. Turn the pieces over. Cover and bake about 30 minutes more or until tender.

Scoop the pulp out of the squash and transfer the pulp to a food processor (or large bowl). Discard the squash shells. Add the margarine and process (or mash by hand) until nearly smooth.

In a small bowl, beat together the egg whites, egg, orange juice, milk, sugar, salt and cinnamon. Add the egg mixture to the squash. Process with on/off pulses until just combined. (Or, stir the egg mixture into the mashed squash.)

Coat a 1-quart soufflé dish or casserole with no-stick spray. Transfer the squash mixture to the dish. Bake for 50 to 60 minutes or until a knife inserted in the center comes out clean.

TEST KITCHEN TIP: To shave minutes from your preparation time, you can cook the squash in the microwave. Place the squash halves, cut side down, in a microwave-safe baking dish. Cover with plastic wrap and vent the wrap by pulling back a corner. Cook on high power for a total of 10 minutes or until tender; rearrange the squash halves halfway through cooking.

Makes 8 servings.

> &. PER SERVING: 93 calories, 2 g. total fat, 0.3 g. saturated fat, 27 mg. cholesterol, 88 mg. sodium

---

Mock Hollandaise Sauce

Adapted from *Talk about Good!*
JUNIOR LEAGUE OF LAFAYETTE

This creamy lemon sauce from the Junior League of Lafayette is much lower in fat than its classic cousin. Serve it over fish or vegetables such as asparagus, broccoli or cauliflower.

    1   container (8 ounces) soft-style light cream cheese
    ¼   cup fat-free egg substitute
    2   tablespoons fresh lemon juice
        Pinch of salt (optional)
        Pinch of ground white pepper
  1–2   teaspoons skim milk or fresh lemon juice (optional)

In a small, heavy saucepan, stir together the cream cheese and egg substitute until well-combined. Then stir in the 2 tablespoons lemon juice, salt, if desired, and pepper.

Cook and stir over low heat until heated through. If necessary, stir in enough of the milk or additional lemon juice to make a desired pouring consistency.

TEST KITCHEN TIP: Leftover sauce will keep, covered, in the refrigerator for up to 1 week. Before serving, reheat it over low heat or in the microwave.

Makes 1 cup; 8 servings.

> &. PER 2 TABLESPOONS: 65 calories, 5.1 g. total fat, 3 g. saturated fat, 10 mg. cholesterol, 173 mg. sodium

Creamy Sour Cream Sauce for Vegetables

Adapted from *A Cook's Tour of the Azalea Coast*
THE AUXILIARY TO THE NEW HANOVER–
PENDER COUNTY MEDICAL SOCIETY

This creamy, sweet-and-tangy sauce is virtually fat-free because it contains nonfat sour cream instead of regular sour cream. Serve it over steamed broccoli, brussels sprouts or cabbage.

   ¼   cup chopped onions
1½   teaspoons all-purpose flour
   ¼   cup skim milk
1½   teaspoons packed brown sugar
   ¼   teaspoon dry mustard
       Pinch of salt
   ½   cup fat-free sour cream
   2   teaspoons finely chopped fresh parsley (optional)

Lightly coat an unheated small skillet with no-stick spray. Add the onions. Cook and stir over medium heat about 3 minutes or until the onions are tender.

In a small bowl, use a wire whisk to stir together the flour and milk. Then slowly stir the mixture into the onions. Add the brown sugar, mustard and salt. Cook and stir over medium heat until the mixture begins to thicken and just comes to a boil.

Reduce the heat to low and stir in the sour cream. Cook and stir just until heated through.

To serve, pour the sauce over cooked vegetables and gently toss until coated. If desired, sprinkle with the parsley to garnish.

Makes ¾ cup; 6 servings.

   PER 2 TABLESPOONS: 38 calories, 0.2 g. total fat, 0 g. saturated fat, 0 mg. cholesterol, 23 mg. sodium

Happy
Endings

Apricot Nectar Cake

Adapted from *River Feast*
JUNIOR LEAGUE OF CINCINNATI

Cake mixes are among the easiest baked products to make over. Just substitute an equal amount of applesauce for the oil and use two egg whites for each whole egg called for.

CAKE

1 tablespoon all-purpose flour
8 egg whites
½ cup unsweetened applesauce
1 package 2-layer yellow cake mix (without pudding)
⅓ cup sugar
1 cup apricot nectar

GLAZE

½ cup sugar
⅓ cup nonfat buttermilk
2 tablespoons tub-style reduced-calorie margarine
¼ teaspoon vanilla

FOR THE CAKE: Preheat the oven to 350°. Lightly coat a 12-cup Bundt pan with no-stick spray. Dust the pan with the flour. Set aside.

In a large bowl, use an electric mixer to beat the egg whites until foamy. Stir in the applesauce. Then stir in the cake mix and sugar.

Slowly drizzle the apricot nectar into the egg white mixture while beating the mixture on low speed. Then beat the mixture on medium speed for 4 minutes. Spread the batter in the prepared pan. Bake for 45 to 50 minutes or until a toothpick inserted near the center comes out clean. Cool the cake in the pan on a wire rack for 10 minutes.

FOR THE GLAZE: In a small saucepan, stir together the sugar, buttermilk, margarine and vanilla. Bring to a boil, without stirring. Reduce the heat and gently boil for 1 minute.

Invert the cake onto a serving platter and remove the pan. While the cake is still warm, use a toothpick to poke holes in it. Then pour the glaze over the cake. Cool before serving.

To store, cover the cake and refrigerate.

Makes 12 servings.

ટ⬥ PER SERVING: 277 calories, 5.7 g. total fat, 1.2 g. saturated fat, 0 mg. cholesterol, 345 mg. sodium

Chocolate Lover's Chocolate Cake

Adapted from *Charleston Receipts*
JUNIOR LEAGUE OF CHARLESTON

Fat-free mayonnaise makes a great substitute for butter in this chocolate cake.

2   cups all-purpose flour
1   cup sugar
¼   cup Dutch-process or regular unsweetened cocoa powder
1½   teaspoons baking soda
1   teaspoon baking powder
1   cup fat-free mayonnaise
1   cup cold water
3   tablespoons powdered sugar

Preheat the oven to 350°. Lightly coat a 13″ × 9″ baking pan with no-stick spray and set aside.

In a large bowl, stir together the flour, sugar, cocoa powder, baking soda and baking powder.

In a small bowl, stir together the mayonnaise and water. Then add the mayonnaise mixture to the flour mixture. Stir just until well-combined.

Transfer the batter to the prepared pan. Bake for 30 to 35 minutes or until a toothpick inserted in the center comes out clean. Cool the cake in the pan on a wire rack. Just before serving, sift the powdered sugar over the cake.

TEST KITCHEN TIP: For a special occasion, turn this delicious chocolate cake into a 2-layer cake by cutting it crosswise in half. Assemble the 2 layers with a store-bought reduced-fat frosting and top with fresh raspberries.

Makes 16 servings.

   PER SERVING: 121 calories, 0.3 g. total fat, 0 g. saturated fat, 0 mg. cholesterol, 289 mg. sodium

Pineapple Cake

Adapted from *Come and Get It*
JUNIOR WELFARE LEAGUE OF TALLADEGA

Even though sugar plays an important role in the texture of baked products, we were able to reduce the amount by half and not notice a difference in this cake.

PINEAPPLE CAKE

 2 eggs
 1 can (20 ounces) crushed pineapple (packed in juice)
 ¾ cup sugar
 ⅔ cup packed brown sugar
 2 teaspoons baking soda
 2 cups all-purpose flour
 ⅔ cup toasted and chopped nuts

CREAM CHEESE GINGER FROSTING

 4 ounces light cream cheese, softened
 2 tablespoons tub-style reduced-calorie margarine
 1 teaspoon vanilla
 ½ teaspoon ground ginger
 1¾ cups powdered sugar

FOR THE PINEAPPLE CAKE: Preheat the oven to 350°. Lightly coat a 13″ × 9″ baking pan with no-stick spray and set aside.

In a large bowl, use an electric mixer to beat the eggs on high speed for 3 minutes. Use a spoon to stir in the pineapple (with juice), sugar, brown sugar and baking soda. Add the flour and stir just until combined. Then gently stir in the nuts.

Transfer the batter to the prepared pan. Bake for 35 to 40 minutes or until a toothpick inserted in the center comes out clean. Cool the cake in the pan on a wire rack before spreading on the frosting.

FOR THE CREAM CHEESE GINGER FROSTING: In a medium bowl, use an electric mixer to beat together the cream cheese and margarine until well-combined. Beat in the vanilla and ginger. Then beat in the powdered sugar. Continue beating until light and smooth. Spread the frosting on top of the cake.

Makes 16 servings.

& PER SERVING: 257 calories, 6.3 g. total fat, 1.3 g. saturated fat, 29 mg. cholesterol, 170 mg. sodium

Date-Nut Cake Roll

Adapted from *Simple Elegance*
OUR LADY OF PERPETUAL HELP WOMEN'S GUILD

Here's a fat-free cake that relies on cooked dates for its richness and moistness. Be sure to buy whole dates and finely snip or chop them yourself. Many brands of ready-chopped dates are coated with sugar and are not cut fine enough for this cake.

CAKE

1   cup pitted whole dates, finely snipped
¾   cup water
¾   cup sugar
¼   teaspoon + ⅛ teaspoon salt
1   cup all-purpose flour
1   teaspoon baking powder
½   teaspoon allspice
2   egg whites
2   eggs
½   cup chopped walnuts
     Powdered sugar

FILLING

1   package (8 ounces) light cream cheese, softened
½   teaspoon vanilla
1   cup sifted powdered sugar

FOR THE CAKE: Preheat the oven to 375°. Then lightly coat a 15″ × 10″ baking pan with no-stick spray. Line the bottom of the pan with wax paper, then coat the wax paper with no-stick spray. Set the pan aside.

In a small saucepan, combine the dates, water, ¼ cup of the sugar and ¼ teaspoon of the salt. Bring to a boil, then reduce the heat to low. Cook and stir for 5 to 10 minutes or until thickened. Remove the saucepan from the heat and let stand at room temperature for 5 minutes or until cool.

Meanwhile, in a small bowl, stir together the flour, baking powder, allspice and the remaining ⅛ teaspoon salt; set aside.

In a large bowl, use an electric mixer to beat the egg whites and eggs on medium-high speed for 5 minutes. Beat in the remaining ½ cup sugar, 1 tablespoon at a time.

(continued)

OUR CAUSE

Our Lady of Perpetual Help Women's Guild

Simple things like a good meal and lively conversation help keep us centered in this busy turn-of-the-century time. But simplicity doesn't have to mean plain. The women of Our Lady of Perpetual Help Women's Guild know that, and it shows in *Simple Elegance,* their cookbook to benefit their parish and the community of Germantown in southwestern Tennessee. The recipes in this collection are, indeed, simple. But every one is a dish that you would proudly serve to company.

The guild has a 44-year history of service to the community. Among its activities are the assistance and support of the religious, educational and social functions of the parish as well as reaching out to those in need.

Proceeds from *Simple Elegance* benefit Our Lady of Perpetual Help's Family Life Center and local women and children.

Fold or gently stir the flour mixture into the egg mixture. Then fold in the date mixture. Spread the batter evenly in the prepared pan. Sprinkle with the walnuts. Bake for 12 to 15 minutes or until no imprint remains when the cake is lightly touched in the center.

Meanwhile, lightly sift the powdered sugar on one side of a clean dish towel.

Immediately loosen the cake from the sides of the pan and invert it onto the towel. Remove the wax paper and roll up the towel and cake together, jellyroll fashion, starting from a short end. Transfer to a wire rack, seam side down, and cool completely.

FOR THE FILLING: In a small bowl, beat together the cream cheese and vanilla until combined. Beat in the powdered sugar.

Unroll the cake. Spread the filling on the cake to within ½" of its edges. Then roll up the cake without the towel. Transfer it to a serving platter. Cover with plastic wrap and chill in the refrigerator for at least 1 hour before serving. Store in the refrigerator.

Makes 10 servings.

    PER SERVING: 305 calories, 10.2 g. total fat, 4 g. saturated fat, 60 mg. cholesterol, 196 mg. sodium

Creamy Chocolate Roll

Adapted from *Cultivated Palate*

THE ARBORETUM FOUNDATION, WASHINGTON PARK ARBORETUM

Each serving of this luscious cake roll gets only 19 percent of its calories from fat.

CAKE

¾ cup all-purpose flour
¼ cup unsweetened cocoa powder
1 teaspoon baking powder
¼ teaspoon salt
1 egg
1 cup sugar
⅓ cup water
1 teaspoon vanilla
3 egg whites
5 tablespoons powdered sugar

RICOTTA FILLING

2 cups part-skim ricotta cheese
3 tablespoons powdered sugar
¼ cup finely chopped candied orange peel or 2 teaspoons finely shredded orange peel
½ teaspoon almond extract

FOR THE CAKE: Preheat the oven to 375°. Then lightly coat a 15″ × 10″ baking pan with no-stick spray. Line the bottom of the pan with wax paper, then coat the wax paper with no-stick spray. Set the pan aside.

In a small bowl, stir together the flour, cocoa powder, baking powder and salt. Set the flour mixture aside.

In a large bowl, use an electric mixer to beat the egg on high speed about 1½ minutes or until thick and lemon-colored. Slowly beat in the sugar. Then beat on medium-high speed, scraping down the sides of the bowl often, about 2 minutes, or until the mixture is creamy and pale in color.

Beat in the water and vanilla until well-combined. Then fold or gently stir in the flour mixture and set aside.

Wash and dry the beaters. In a medium bowl, beat the egg whites

(continued)

on high speed until they form stiff peaks. Fold or gently stir the egg whites into the chocolate mixture.

Gently spread the mixture evenly in the prepared pan. Bake about 10 minutes or until no imprint remains when lightly touched in the center.

Meanwhile, lightly sift 3 tablespoons of the powdered sugar on one side of a clean dish towel.

Immediately loosen the cake from the sides of the pan and invert it onto the towel. Remove the wax paper and roll up the towel and cake together, jelly-roll fashion, starting from a short end. Transfer to a wire rack, seam side down, and cool completely.

FOR THE RICOTTA FILLING: In a small bowl, use the electric mixer to beat together the ricotta, powdered sugar, orange peel and almond extract until well-combined.

Unroll the cake. Spread the filling on the cake to within ½″ of its edges. Then roll up the cake without the towel. Transfer it to a serving platter. Cover it with plastic wrap and chill in the refrigerator for at least 2 hours or up to 24 hours before serving.

Before serving, sift the remaining 2 tablespoons powdered sugar over the top of the cake. Store any remaining cake in the refrigerator.

Makes 10 servings.

* PER SERVING: 227 calories, 4.7 g. total fat, 2.6 g. saturated fat, 36 mg. cholesterol, 175 mg. sodium

Kiwi Sorbet

Adapted from *The Fine Art of Cooking*

THE WOMEN'S COMMITTEE OF THE PHILADELPHIA MUSEUM OF ART

This frozen fruit dessert is customarily served after a meal or between courses as a palate refresher. For a variation, the Women's Committee of the Philadelphia Museum of Art suggests substituting 2 peeled and chopped mangoes for the kiwis.

1½	cups fresh orange juice
3	ripe kiwifruits, room temperature, peeled and chopped
1	banana, sliced
9	strawberries (optional)

In a food processor, combine the orange juice, kiwifruit and bananas; process for 25 seconds. Stop and scrape down the sides of the container. Then process about 20 seconds more or until just pureed. (Do not overprocess the mixture.)

Transfer the mixture to a 2-quart ice-cream freezer and freeze according to the manufacturer's instructions. (For best texture, do not freeze for more than 2 hours before serving, or it will become too hard to scoop.)

Serve the sorbet in stemmed glasses. If desired, garnish each with a strawberry.

Makes 3 cups; 9 servings.

PER ⅓ CUP: 46 calories, 0.2 g. total fat, 0 g. saturated fat, 0 mg. cholesterol, 2 mg. sodium

Raisin Bread Pudding

Adapted from *Talk about Good!*
JUNIOR LEAGUE OF LAFAYETTE

Raisin bread makes this bread pudding special. If you don't have raisin bread on hand, use whole-wheat or French bread along with a handful of raisins.

8–10	slices raisin bread, lightly toasted
1	tablespoon tub-style reduced-calorie margarine, melted
4	egg whites, lightly beaten
1	egg, lightly beaten
1	can (12 ounces or 1½ cups) evaporated skim milk
1½	cups skim milk
⅓	cup + 2 tablespoons sugar
½	teaspoon vanilla
½	teaspoon ground cinnamon

Coat an 8″ × 8″ baking dish with no-stick spray.

Brush the toast with the margarine, then cut the toast in half. Arrange the pieces in the bottom of the baking dish, slightly overlapping if necessary.

In a medium bowl, stir together the egg whites, eggs, evaporated milk, skim milk, ⅓ cup of the sugar and vanilla. Pour the egg mixture over the toast. Using a spatula, lightly press the toast so it absorbs the egg mixture. Let stand for 10 minutes at room temperature.

Meanwhile, preheat the oven to 350°. In a custard cup, stir together the remaining 2 tablespoons sugar and cinnamon.

Sprinkle the cinnamon mixture on top of the egg mixture. Bake for 30 to 35 minutes or until a knife inserted in the center comes out clean. Serve warm.

TEST KITCHEN TIP: For a caramel-flavored bread pudding, use packed light brown sugar instead of white sugar.

Makes 6 servings.

ફ• PER SERVING: 254 calories, 4 g. total fat, 0.8 g. saturated fat, 39 mg. cholesterol, 289 mg. sodium

Lemon Meringue Squares

Adapted from *Recipe Jubilee!*
JUNIOR LEAGUE OF MOBILE

These cookie bars have a tender lemon-flavored crust with a nutty meringue topping. The crust uses a combination of margarine and light-style cream cheese instead of the usual shortening. The margarine adds flavor, and the cream cheese reduces the fat.

CRUST

- ¼ cup tub-style margarine (not reduced-calorie)
- 2 ounces light cream cheese, softened
- ¼ cup powdered sugar
- 2 tablespoons finely shredded lemon peel
- 1 cup all-purpose cake flour
- 1–3 teaspoons skim milk

TOPPING

- 2 egg whites
- 1 tablespoon fresh lemon juice
- ½ cup sugar
- ⅓ cup toasted and finely chopped walnuts

FOR THE CRUST: Preheat the oven to 350°. Coat an 11″ × 7″ baking dish with no-stick spray and set aside.

In a medium bowl, use an electric mixer to beat together the margarine, cream cheese, powdered sugar and lemon peel until well-combined. Using a pastry blender, mix in the flour until the mixture resembles coarse crumbs. Sprinkle with 1 teaspoon of the milk. Using a fork, stir lightly just until the ingredients are moistened enough to stick together. If necessary, add enough of the remaining 2 teaspoons milk to moisten.

Pat the mixture in a thin, even layer in the prepared dish. Bake for 10 minutes.

FOR THE TOPPING: Meanwhile, wash and dry the medium bowl and beaters. Add the egg whites to the bowl and beat with the electric mixer on high speed until foamy. Add the lemon juice. Then beat on medium speed until the egg whites form soft peaks. Add the sugar, 1 tablespoon at a time, and continue beating on medium speed until the egg whites form stiff peaks but are not dry. Fold in the walnuts.

(continued)

Spread the egg white mixture on top of the crust. Then bake at 350° for 20 to 25 minutes or until golden. Cool in the pan on a wire rack for 3 minutes. Then cut into pieces and cool completely before serving. Store, tightly covered, in the refrigerator or freezer.

Makes 30 bars.

> ❧ PER BAR: 56 calories, 2.7 g. total fat, 0.5 g. saturated fat,
> 1 mg. cholesterol, 35 mg. sodium

Lemon Pecan Dainties

Adapted from *Impressions*
AUXILIARY TO THE MEMPHIS DENTAL SOCIETY

These slice-and-bake cookies are really easy to prepare. They're especially good for the holidays.

1	cup sugar
6	tablespoons stick margarine (not reduced-calorie)
¼	cup fat-free egg substitute
1	tablespoon finely shredded lemon peel
1	tablespoon fresh lemon juice
1	teaspoon baking powder
2	cups all-purpose flour
⅔	cup toasted and finely chopped or ground pecans

In a large bowl, use an electric mixer to beat together the sugar and margarine until light and fluffy. Then beat in the egg substitute, lemon peel and lemon juice.

Beat in the baking powder. Then beat in the flour just until combined. Stir in pecans.

Divide the dough. Then shape each portion into a roll, 2" in diameter. Wrap the rolls in plastic wrap and chill in the freezer for 2 to 3 hours or until firm.

Preheat the oven to 350°. Lightly coat 2 baking sheets with nostick spray. Unwrap the rolls and cut into ¼" slices. Place the slices on the baking sheet 2" apart. Bake for 10 to 12 minutes or until lightly golden.

Makes 48 cookies.

> ❧ PER COOKIE: 57 calories, 2.5 g. total fat, 0.4 g. saturated fat,
> 0 mg. cholesterol, 25 mg. sodium

Walnut Spice Kisses

Adapted from *Forum Feasts*
FRIENDS OF THE FORUM SCHOOL

We cut the amount of walnuts in half in these meringue cookies and replaced the nuts with low-fat granola.

2	egg whites
⅔	cup low-fat granola without raisins
½	cup toasted and ground walnuts
½	cup sugar
1½–2	teaspoons ground cinnamon
¼	teaspoon ground nutmeg
¼	teaspoon ground cloves

Place the egg whites in a medium bowl and let stand at room temperature for 30 minutes.

Meanwhile, place the granola in a blender or food processor. Process with on/off pulses until finely ground. Stir in the walnuts and set the granola mixture aside.

Preheat the oven to 250°. Line 2 baking sheets with parchment paper. Lightly coat the paper with no-stick spray.

In a small bowl, stir together the sugar, cinnamon, nutmeg and cloves. Using an electric mixer, beat the egg whites on high speed until they form soft peaks. Add the sugar mixture, 1 tablespoon at a time, and beat on medium speed until the egg whites form stiff peaks but are not dry.

Fold the granola mixture into the egg white mixture. Drop tablespoons of the mixture 1″ apart onto the prepared baking sheets. Bake for 35 to 40 minutes or until lightly browned. Remove the cookies from the paper and let cool on a wire rack. When the cookies are cooled, store them in a tightly covered container.

TEST KITCHEN TIP: If you like, you can omit the walnuts altogether. Just increase the granola to 1⅓ cups and use only 1 teaspoon cinnamon.

Makes 24 cookies.

  ❧ PER COOKIE: 33 calories, 2 g. total fat, 0.5 g. saturated fat,
    0 mg. cholesterol, 11 mg. sodium

Rogue Pears

Adapted from *Rogue River Rendezvous*
JUNIOR SERVICE LEAGUE OF JACKSON COUNTY

This dessert features pears, one of Oregon's finest fruits from the orchards along the Rogue River. The Bosc pear is an ideal variety for this recipe because it holds its shape well when poached.

SUGARED ORANGE PEELS (optional)

- 1 orange
-   Sugar

POACHED PEARS

- 1 tablespoon butter
- 4 large firm pears (Bosc preferred), peeled, cored and thinly sliced lengthwise
- ¼ cup packed light brown sugar
- ¼ cup orange liqueur or light rum (see tip)
- 1 teaspoon finely shredded orange peel
- 3 tablespoons fresh orange juice
- 1 quart (4 cups) frozen fat-free vanilla yogurt

FOR THE SUGARED ORANGE PEELS: If desired, for the garnish, use a vegetable peeler or sharp knife to cut 6 narrow 2½"-long orange peel slices. Use only the outer layer of the orange, not the white layer. Place the peels in a shallow bowl or pie plate. Cover with the sugar until serving time. To make the garnishes, remove the peels from the sugar and twist attractively.

FOR THE POACHED PEARS: In a large skillet, melt the butter. Add the pears. Cook over low heat about 20 minutes or until the slices are golden, stirring occasionally.

Meanwhile, in a small bowl, stir together the brown sugar, liqueur or rum, orange peel and orange juice.

Add the orange mixture to the pears. Bring to a boil over high heat. Boil for 2 to 3 minutes or until the sauce begins to cling to the pears. Cool slightly.

Spoon the warm pears and sauce over individual servings of the frozen yogurt. If desired, garnish each serving with a sugared orange-peel twist.

OUR CAUSE

Junior Service League of Jackson County

From Crater Lake National Park to the Pacific Ocean, the Rogue River tumbles its way through three full counties, across miles of beautiful southern Oregon. What spot could have served better as a meeting place for early explorers of the West?

The territory was lush with forests. The river teemed with salmon and trout. Riverside meadows were ripe with berries and other fruits. Every year, in classic Old West tradition, traders, trappers, settlers, Indians and merchants met to trade goods and to feast on the bounty of natural foods that the Rogue River Valley provided.

From those meetings, known as rendezvous, comes the flavor of today's southern Oregon cuisine, with its emphasis on all things fresh and natural. *Rogue River Rendezvous* tells in lyrical text and colorful photographs the story of the Rogue River Valley.

The recipes blend the classic flavors of Oregon with the contemporary flair of today's Pacific Northwest. The book serves as a fund-raiser for the Junior Service League of Jackson County and the many community projects it is involved in, particularly programs for children and teens.

TEST KITCHEN TIP: For a nonalcoholic version, use ¼ cup unsweetened white grape juice or prepared pear-apple cider frozen concentrate.

Makes 6 servings.

&❧ PER SERVING: 269 calories, 2.3 g. total fat, 1.2 g. saturated fat, 5 mg. cholesterol, 116 mg. sodium

Congo Bars

Adapted from *Our Favorite Recipes*
ST. JOHN'S GUILD

*Dried apricots replace part of the chocolate chips in this recipe—
which is essentially chocolate-chip cookie dough baked in a pan.*

- ⅓ cup chopped dried apricots
- 2⅔ cups all-purpose flour
- 2½ teaspoons baking powder
- ¼ teaspoon salt
- 2 cups packed brown sugar
- ⅓ cup tub-style reduced-calorie margarine
- ⅓ cup unsweetened applesauce
- 2 eggs
- 2 egg whites
- ⅔ cup toasted and chopped walnuts
- ⅔ cup mini chocolate chips

Pour boiling water over the apricots and let stand about 5 minutes or until softened. Then drain well and set aside.

Preheat the oven to 350°. Lightly coat a 15½″ × 10½″ baking pan with no-stick spray. Set the pan aside.

In a small bowl, stir together the flour, baking powder and salt. Set the flour mixture aside.

In a large saucepan, combine the brown sugar, margarine and applesauce. Cook and stir over medium-low heat just until the sugar and margarine are melted. Remove from the heat and cool.

Add the eggs, one at a time, and beat with a spoon until combined. Then beat in the egg whites. Add the flour mixture and stir just until moistened. Then stir in the apricots, walnuts and chocolate chips.

Transfer the batter to the prepared pan. Bake for 25 to 30 minutes or until a toothpick inserted in the center comes out clean. Partially cool in the pan on a wire rack, then cut into pieces. Cool completely before serving.

Makes 40.

    PER BAR: 122 calories, 3.9 g. total fat, 0.3 g. saturated fat, 11 mg. cholesterol, 59 mg. sodium

Orange-Apple Strudel

Adapted from *Cultivated Palate*

THE ARBORETUM FOUNDATION, WASHINGTON PARK ARBORETUM

Many strudel recipes call for lots of butter between the layers of phyllo dough. This recipe from the University of Washington Arboretum Foundation, however, uses only a small amount of margarine and supplements it with butter-flavored no-stick spray.

STRUDEL

2	pounds Granny Smith apples or other tart cooking apples, peeled, cored and thinly sliced
⅓	cup packed brown sugar
¼	cup all-purpose flour
2	teaspoons finely shredded orange peel
1	teaspoon ground cinnamon
½	teaspoon ground nutmeg
3	sheets phyllo dough
1½	teaspoons reduced-calorie margarine, melted

ORANGE SAUCE

1	tablespoon cornstarch
1	tablespoon water
1	cup fresh orange juice
¼	cup low-sugar orange marmalade

FOR THE STRUDEL: Preheat the oven to 375°. Coat a baking sheet with no-stick spray, then set aside.

Place the apples in a large bowl. In a small bowl, stir together the brown sugar, flour, orange peel, cinnamon and nutmeg. Add the flour mixture to the apples, then toss until coated. Set the apples aside.

Place 1 sheet of the phyllo dough on a large piece of wax paper. Coat the dough with butter-flavored no-stick spray. Repeat layering and spraying the dough 2 more times with the remaining 2 sheets dough.

Spoon the apple mixture in a strip down a long side of the phyllo, 1½" from the edge and 1" from the ends. Fold the ends of the phyllo over the filling, then fold the edge of the phyllo over the filling; roll up, jelly-roll fashion. Transfer the strudel to the prepared baking sheet, then brush with the margarine.

(continued)

Bake about 45 minutes or until golden. Cool the strudel on the baking sheet on a wire rack. Serve warm or at room temperature.

FOR THE ORANGE SAUCE: In a small saucepan, use a wire whisk to stir together the cornstarch and water. Then stir in the orange juice and marmalade. Bring to a boil, stirring constantly. Reduce the heat to low. Cook and stir for 2 minutes more. If desired, cool before serving.

To serve the strudel, cut it crosswise into 10 slices. Pour about 2 tablespoons of the sauce over each slice.

Makes 10 servings.

> ❧ PER SERVING: 136 calories, 1.3 g. total fat, 0.2 g. saturated fat, 0 mg. cholesterol, 10 mg. sodium

---

Raspberry Pie

Adapted from *Family Secrets*
LEE ACADEMY

Underneath the red raspberry layer of this pie is a creamy layer of cheesecake. By switching from regular to light cream cheese, we whittled away 39 grams of fat.

CRUST

1⅓	cups low-fat graham crackers crushed to fine crumbs
3	tablespoons powdered sugar
1	egg white, lightly beaten
2½	tablespoons tub-style reduced-calorie margarine, melted and cooled

FILLING

1	package (8 ounces) light cream cheese, softened
⅓	cup sugar
1	egg
2	egg whites
1	teaspoon clear vanilla

TOPPING

   3   tablespoons sugar

   2   tablespoons cornstarch

   1   package (10 ounces or 2¼ cups) frozen unsweetened red raspberries, thawed

   1   container (8 ounces) fat-free and sugar-free vanilla-flavored yogurt or 1 cup thawed, reduced-fat frozen whipped topping (optional)

FOR THE CRUST: In a small bowl, stir together the cracker crumbs and powdered sugar. In a custard cup, stir together the egg whites and margarine. Add the egg white mixture to the crumb mixture and stir until well-mixed.

Lightly coat a 9″ pie plate with no-stick spray. Pat the crumb mixture into the bottom and up the sides to form an even crust. Set the crust aside.

FOR THE FILLING: Preheat the oven to 300°. Use an electric mixer to beat the cream cheese, sugar, egg, egg whites and vanilla until well-combined.

Spread the mixture evenly in the pie shell. Bake for 25 to 28 minutes or until the center is almost set. Cool the pie on a wire rack.

FOR THE TOPPING: Meanwhile, in a small saucepan, stir together the sugar and cornstarch. Set the saucepan aside.

In a blender or food processor, puree the raspberries. Add the raspberries to the saucepan. If desired, to remove the seeds, push the mixture through a sieve into the saucepan; discard the seeds. Stir until the raspberries and sugar are well-combined.

Cook and stir over medium heat until the mixture begins to thicken and just comes to a boil. Then cook and stir for 2 minutes more. Cool to room temperature.

Stir the raspberry mixture, then carefully spread it on the cheese filling. If desired, top each serving with a spoonful of the yogurt or whipped topping.

Makes 8 servings.

    PER SERVING: 276 calories, 9.4 g. total fat, 4.5 g. saturated fat, 47 mg. cholesterol, 323 mg. sodium

Summer Strawberry Pie

Adapted from *The Golden Taste of South Carolina*
SOUTH CAROLINA FARM BUREAU FEDERATION

We used phyllo dough to make a low-fat flaky crust. You can use this crust idea for your own no-bake pies.

¾ cup sugar
3   tablespoons cornstarch
1   cup water
½   teaspoon sugar-free strawberry-flavored gelatin
     (half a 4-serving-size package)
3½ cups medium fresh strawberries, stems removed
1   baked 9-inch phyllo pastry shell (see tip)
1   cup thawed, reduced-fat frozen whipped topping

In a small saucepan, stir together the sugar and cornstarch until well-combined. Then stir in the water. Cook and stir over low heat just until the sugar and cornstarch dissolve and the mixture becomes clear.

Stir in the gelatin. Cook and stir over low heat until the gelatin dissolves. Then cook and stir over medium heat until the mixture begins to thicken and just comes to a boil. Cook and stir for 2 minutes more. Remove from the heat and cool until slightly warm.

Meanwhile, arrange the strawberries in the pastry shell, stem ends down. Carefully pour the gelatin mixture over the strawberries. Chill in the refrigerator for 3 to 4 hours or until set. Serve with dollops of the whipped topping.

TEST KITCHEN TIP: To make the crust, drape one 13" × 9" sheet of phyllo dough across a 9" pie plate. Press the phyllo into the plate and fold the overhanging edges toward the center, crumpling them slightly to fit. Lightly coat the dough with no-stick spray. Slightly rotate the plate and drape another sheet of phyllo on top of the first; spray and crimp it as before. Add 2 more layers to make a crust that's evenly thick around the edges.

OUR CAUSE

South Carolina Farm Bureau Federation

Half a century ago, a small group of progressive farmers in South Carolina got together to try to improve the economic, professional and social welfare of the state's agricultural community. Today, the South Carolina Farm Bureau represents the interests of more than 100,000 members statewide. The bureau helps on both large- and small-scale levels, from lobbying for legislation that improves farmers' lives to providing needed agricultural supplies and equipment.

The Women's Committee of the bureau celebrated the bureau's anniversary with *The Golden Taste of South Carolina*. Proceeds from the book benefit two programs dear to the group: the American Farm Bureau Research Foundation and the bureau's Agriculture in the Classroom Program, an ambitious national effort to improve the "agricultural literacy" of American students.

The classroom program helps educators teach students about the vital role of farming in America today. The Farm Bureau hopes that, no matter what career paths those students eventually choose, they will have the knowledge to understand the support programs and policies that benefit American agriculture.

Bake the crust in a 375° oven for 5 to 7 minutes or until the shell is golden. Transfer the pie plate to a wire rack to cool the crust before filling it.

Makes 8 servings.

❧ PER SERVING: 115 calories, 2.2 g. total fat, 0 g. saturated fat, 0 mg. cholesterol, 29 mg. sodium

Praline Pumpkin Pie

Adapted from *Necessities and Temptations*
JUNIOR LEAGUE OF AUSTIN

The praline layer gives this pumpkin pie a nutty, caramel flavor.

PRALINE LAYER

2	teaspoons tub-style reduced-calorie margarine
¼	cup packed brown sugar
1	tablespoon reduced-calorie maple-flavored syrup
⅓	cup chopped pecans
1	9″ unbaked pie shell (see tip)

PUMPKIN LAYER

4	egg whites, lightly beaten
1	cup cooked and mashed pumpkin or canned pumpkin
½	cup packed brown sugar
½	teaspoon ground ginger
½	teaspoon ground cinnamon
¼	teaspoon ground cloves
⅛	teaspoon ground mace
1	can (5 ounces or ⅔ cup) evaporated skim milk

FOR THE PRALINE LAYER: Preheat the oven to 450°. In a small bowl, use your fingers to rub the margarine into the brown sugar. Stir in the syrup until well-combined. Then stir in the pecans. Press the mixture into the bottom of the pie shell. Bake for 10 minutes. Reduce the oven temperature to 325°.

FOR THE PUMPKIN LAYER: In a medium bowl, stir together the egg whites and pumpkin. Then stir in the brown sugar, ginger, cinnamon, cloves and mace. Add the milk. Using a rotary beater or wire whisk, beat just until combined.

Carefully pour the pumpkin mixture over the praline layer. Bake in the 325° oven about 45 minutes or until a knife inserted in the center comes out clean.

TEST KITCHEN TIP: Most pie crusts are made with lard, shortening or butter, all of which contain a fair amount of saturated fat. This version of a traditional pastry uses canola oil, which is high in healthy monounsaturated fat.

In a medium bowl, stir together 1¼ cups all-purpose flour and a pinch of salt. Using a pastry blender, cut in 1 tablespoon stick margarine (not reduced-calorie). In a custard cup, stir together 3 tablespoons canola oil and 2 tablespoons skim milk. Drizzle the oil mixture over the flour mixture. Using a fork, toss and stir lightly until the dry ingredients are mostened. If necessary, add 1 to 3 teaspoons additional skim milk to moisten. Use your hands to gently shape the mixture into a ball.

Place the ball of dough between two 12"-square pieces of was paper. Gently roll out the dough into a 12" circle. Remove the top piece of was paper. Invert the dough onto a 9" pie plate. Remove the remaining piece of wax paper and gently fit the dough into the pan. Fold the edges of pastry under and flute them.

Makes 8 servings.

&. PER SERVING: 278 calories, 10.7 g. total fat, 1 g. saturated fat,
    1 mg. cholesterol, 83 mg. sodium

Fruit Crisp

Adapted from *A Cook's Tour of the Azalea Coast*
THE AUXILIARY TO THE NEW HANOVER–
PENDER COUNTY MEDICAL SOCIETY

Choose your fruit—peaches or apples—for this healthier version of an old-time favorite.

FILLING

3 tablespoons sugar
1 teaspoon ground cinnamon
4 cups peeled and sliced peaches or apples
2 teaspoons fresh lemon juice

TOPPING

¾ cup quick-cooking rolled oats
¼ cup all-purpose flour
¼ cup packed brown sugar
2 tablespoons tub-style reduced-calorie margarine
Frozen fat-free vanilla yogurt (optional)

FOR THE FILLING: Preheat the oven to 350°. In a medium bowl, stir together the sugar and cinnamon. Add the peaches or apples and drizzle with the lemon juice. Toss until combined. Spread the fruit mixture evenly in an 8″ × 8″ baking dish.

FOR THE TOPPING: In a small bowl, stir together the oats, flour and brown sugar. Use a pastry blender to cut in the margarine until the mixture resembles coarse crumbs. Sprinkle the mixture evenly on top of the filling. Bake about 40 minutes or until the fruit is tender and the topping is golden. If desired, serve warm with the frozen yogurt.

Makes 6 servings.

&. PER SERVING: 232 calories, 4.8 g. total fat, 0.6 g. saturated fat, 0 mg. cholesterol, 43 mg. sodium

Menu
Sampler

Menu Sampler

Would you like to take a culinary journey across America—and taste the wonderful regional specialties that different communities have to offer? You can! And you can do it without even leaving home.

We've created 16 festive menus that capture the essence of this country's various regions. You can use them for entertaining, for family meals or even just to give yourself a lift. We've included details about serving sizes and a one-serving nutritional analysis with each menu so that you can easily keep tabs on how these meals fit into your daily eating plan.

Unless otherwise noted, the portion size for recipes featured in this book is one serving. Remember that you can be generous with ingredients such as lettuce, tomatoes, cucumbers, melons and other vegetables and fruits, which are very low in calories and have no fat or cholesterol.

Enjoy your trip!

Busy Morning Southern Brunch

Cantaloupe slices wrapped with thinly sliced ham
Praline French Toast Casserole (page 86)
Orange-mint tea

For each serving, plan on 1 slice cantaloupe wrapped with 1 very thin slice ham.

    PER SERVING: 374 calories, 8.5 g. total fat, 1.4 g. saturated fat, 76 mg. cholesterol, 484 mg. sodium

Missouri Country Breakfast

Good-Taste Waffles (page 91)
Sliced peaches
Plain yogurt drizzled with honey and sprinkled with pecans
Coffee

For each serving, plan on 2 waffles, 1 peach, ½ cup fat-free plain yogurt with 2 teaspoons honey and 2 teaspoons toasted and chopped pecans.

&- PER SERVING: 376 calories, 3.8 g. total fat, 0.5 g. saturated fat, 3 mg. cholesterol, 190 mg. sodium

Colorado Ghost-Town Summer Lunch

Trout Almondine (page 176)
Roasted Corn (page 237)
Sliced tomatoes
Parmesan Primavera (page 200)
Watermelon

For each serving, plan on 1 cob corn, 1 sliced tomato and 2 cups watermelon chunks.

&- PER SERVING: 655 calories, 21 g. total fat, 3.6 g. saturated fat, 69 mg. cholesterol, 200 mg. sodium

Picnic on the Great Plains

Herb-Basted Cornish Hens (page 162)
Cooked wild rice
Health Bread (page 96)
Tossed salad
Slenderized Roquefort Dressing (page 228)
Apples

For each serving, plan on ½ cup rice, 1 slice bread, 1 cup mixed salad greens with tomato and cucumber slices, 2 tablespoons dressing and 1 apple.

&- PER SERVING: 569 calories, 15 g. total fat, 3 g. saturated fat, 94 mg. cholesterol, 606 mg. sodium

Northwestern Swordfish Dinner for Four

Swordfish with Mushroom and Tomato Sauce (page 179)
Steamed rice
Spinach Salad (page 217)
Light Yogurt Crescent Roll (page 94)
Poached pears

For each serving, plan on ½ cup cooked rice, 1 roll and 1 pear.

&ampnbsp;❧ PER SERVING: 650 calories, 15 g. total fat, 2 g. saturated fat,
45 mg. cholesterol, 333 mg. sodium

New England Thanksgiving Dinner for Eight

Crudités
Florentine Dip (page 57)
Roast Turkey Breast (page 168)
Sweet Potato Casserole (page 48)
Apricot Nectar Salad (page 33)
Mixed salad greens
Slenderized Roquefort Dressing (page 228)
Brown-and-serve rolls
Baked apples with maple syrup and vanilla yogurt

For each serving, plan on a variety of raw vegetables (such as
julienned carrots, turnips and rutabagas), 2 tablespoons dip, 1 cup
mixed greens, 2 tablespoons dressing, 1 roll and 1 apple with
1 tablespoon maple syrup and ¼ cup fat-free vanilla yogurt.

❧ PER SERVING: 827 calories, 15.4 g. total fat, 2.8 g. saturated fat,
101 mg. cholesterol, 697 mg. sodium

Kentucky Derby Picnic

Crispy Baked Chicken (page 159)
Bibb lettuce with fat-free honey Dijon salad dressing
Canned baked beans
Cornbread
Lemon Pecan Dainties (page 260)
Apricots or peaches

For each serving, plan on 1 cup lettuce, 2 tablespoons dressing,
½ cup baked beans, 1 piece cornbread, 1 cookie and 1 piece of
fruit.

> &ᴥ PER SERVING: 697 calories, 13 g. total fat, 4 g. saturated fat,
> 106 mg. cholesterol, 1,379 mg. sodium

Chesapeake Bay Dinner

Crab Cakes (page 188)
Pasta with Lemon Cream Sauce (page 199)
Steamed asparagus
Mixed salad greens with olive oil vinaigrette
Summer Strawberry Pie (page 268)

For each serving, plan on ½ cup steamed asparagus and 1 cup
mixed salad greens with 1 tablespoon vinaigrette.

> &ᴥ PER SERVING: 563 calories, 19 g. total fat, 4.6 g. saturated fat,
> 152 mg. cholesterol, 606 mg. sodium

Pennsylvania Dutch Dinner

Holiday Stuffed Ham (page 143)
Pennsylvania Dutch Potato Dressing (page 47)
Green Beans with Basil (page 231)
Fresh Broccoli-Cauliflower Salad (page 214)
Raisin Bread Pudding (page 258)
Coffee

For each serving, plan on 1 serving of each of the dishes.

> 🍴 PER SERVING: 618 calories, 14.6 g. total fat, 3.7 g. saturated fat,
> 82 mg. cholesterol, 772 mg. sodium

West Virginia Summer Dessert Party

Praline Cheesecake (page 52)
Lemon Pecan Dainties (page 260)
Chocolate Lover's Chocolate Cake (page 251)
Mixed fresh fruit chunks or watermelon slices
Iced mint tea

*For each serving, plan on half a piece of the cheesecake, 1 cookie
and 1 cup fruit or 1 slice watermelon.*

> 🍴 PER SERVING: 352 calories, 9 g. total fat, 2.8 g. saturated fat,
> 26 mg. cholesterol, 526 mg. sodium

Texas-Style Ranch Dinner

Cold Marinated Tenderloin (page 130)
Buffet rolls
Dijon or honey-Dijon Mustard
Sour Cream Potato Salad (page 40)
Mixed salad greens
Fat-free salad dressing
Rice pudding

*For each serving, plan on 1 roll, 1 tablespoon mustard, 1 cup salad
greens with 2 tablespoons dressing and ½ cup rice pudding.*

> 🍴 PER SERVING: 690 calories, 18 g. total fat, 6 g. saturated fat,
> 100 mg. cholesterol, 1,395 mg. sodium

Tex-Mex Potluck Fiesta

Mexican Cheese Soup (page 103)
Picadillo Dip (page 12)
Baked corn tortilla chips
Raw carrot, celery and sweet pepper sticks
Jalapeño Cornbread and Ground Meat Casserole (page 123)
Assorted fresh fruit

For each serving, plan on ¼ cup dip, 6 chips, lots of vegetable sticks and 1 piece of fruit.

> PER SERVING: 898 calories, 21.4 g. total fat, 4.4 g. saturated fat, 101 mg. cholesterol, 1,703 mg. sodium

Iowa Pork Lovers' Feast

Pork Loin Roast with Orange Barbecue Sauce (page 142)
Baked potatoes
Corn
Mixed salad greens with tomatoes
Reduced-calorie French dressing
Cracked wheat bread
Layered Strawberry Gelatin Salad (page 35)

For each serving, plan on 1 potato, ½ cup corn, 1 cup salad greens with tomato slices and 2 tablespoons dressing and 1 slice bread.

> PER SERVING: 897 calories, 24 g. total fat, 8.8 g. saturated fat, 83 mg. cholesterol, 1,132 mg. sodium

Louisiana Creole Dinner

Log House Gumbo (page 118)
Mr. Tim's Baked Hush Puppies (page 82)
Mixed salad greens
Reduced-calorie, reduced-fat French dressing
Summer Strawberry Pie (page 268)

For each serving, plan on 2 hush puppies and 1 cup salad greens with 2 tablespoons dressing.

> PER SERVING: 617 calories, 12 g. total fat, 1.6 g. saturated fat, 136 mg. cholesterol, 797 mg. sodium

Florida Sunset Dinner Party

Rich Hot Crab Dip (page 60)
Celery stalks
Reduced-fat, low-salt crackers
Florida Chicken Salad (page 226)
Citrus Couscous with Basil and Apricots (page 195)
Kiwi Sorbet (page 257)

For each serving, plan on ¼ cup dip with lots of celery and 4 crackers.

> **PER SERVING:** 619 calories, 15 g. total fat, 4.6 g. saturated fat, 72 mg. cholesterol, 823 mg. sodium

An Arabia-in-Philadelphia Dinner Party

Hummus (page 58)
Pita bread
Moroccan Lamb (page 149)
Cooked rice
Cucumber salad
Walnut Spice Kisses (page 261)
Dates
Turkish coffee

For each serving, plan on ¼ cup hummus, 1 pita bread, ½ cup cooked rice, ½ cup sliced cucumbers mixed with 2 tablespoons chopped onions and ¼ cup fat-free plain yogurt, 2 cookies and 3 dates.

> **PER SERVING:** 666 calories, 12.5 g. total fat, 2.9 g. saturated fat, 47 mg. cholesterol, 663 mg. sodium

Directory

We chose the recipes in *Healthy Hometown Favorites* from a cross-section of community cookbooks nationwide. The organizations that publish those books raise money for good causes. If you would like to help support their causes by ordering any of their books, write to the addresses below. Postage and handling are included in the prices listed. If additional state sales tax is required, it is noted in the entry.

A Cook's Tour of the Azalea Coast
The Auxiliary to the New
    Hanover–Pender County Medical
    Society
P.O. Box 5303
Wilmington, NC 28403

Send a check for $17.95 payable to *A Cook's Tour of the Azalea Coast*
Proceeds benefit: Health education and medical needs of the community and "Straight Talk," a hotline for teenagers
Recipes: Creamy Sour Cream Sauce for Vegetables, page 248; Fruit Crisp, page 272; Roast Turkey Breast, page 168

Among Friends
Junior Auxiliary of Russellville
P.O. Box 1011
Russellville, AR 72801

Send a check for $17.45 payable to *Junior Auxiliary of Russellville*
Proceeds benefit: Service projects for children
Recipes: Country Pork Ribs, page 136; Exceptional Macaroni and Cheese, page 203; Holiday Stuffed Ham, page 143

A Taste of Aloha
Junior League of Honolulu, Inc.
1802A Keeaumoku Street
Honolulu, HI 96822

Send a check for $24.95 payable to *JLH Commercial Publications* (Hawaii residents add $0.80 state sales tax)
Proceeds benefit: Projects to end domestic violence and promote positive parenting
Recipes: Florentine Dip, page 57; Gingered Carrots, page 233; Russian Raspberry Cream Mold, page 34

A Taste of New England
Junior League of Worcester, Inc.
71 Pleasant Street
Worcester, MA 01609

Send a check for $20.95 payable to *Junior League of Worcester, Inc.*
Proceeds benefit: Programs supported by the League, including Good Start (training for first-time parents) and scholarships for young women
Recipes: Crispy Baked Chicken, page 159; Moussaka, page 146; Sweet Red Pepper Tart, page 242

A Touch of Atlanta
Marist Parents' Club
3790 Ashford-Dunwoody Road NE
Atlanta, GA 30319-1899

Send a check for $17.95 payable
to *A Touch of Atlanta*
Proceeds benefit: Projects for the
Marist School
Recipes: Tabbouleh, page 218;
Turkey Piccata, page 165; Walnut
Chicken, page 158

Bay Leaves
Junior Service League of Panama
    City, Inc.
P.O. Box 404
Panama City, FL 32402

Send a check for $15.95 payable
to *Bay Publications* (Florida residents
add $0.98 state sales tax)
Proceeds benefit: Service projects of
the League
Recipes: Patio Cassoulet, page 160;
Springtime Vegetable Soup,
page 110

Between Greene Leaves
Greene County Homemakers
    Extension Association
c/o Mrs. Kathy Harms
R.R. 1, Box 216
Carrollton, IL 62016

Send a check for $10.50 payable
to *Greene County Homemakers
Extension Association* (Illinois
residents add $0.54 state sales tax)
Proceeds benefit: Continuing
education for homemakers and 4-H
members in Greene County
Recipes: Harvard Beets, page 232;
Three-Bean Bake, page 43

*The Black Family Dinner Quilt
    Cookbook*
Simon and Schuster/Fireside Books
1230 Avenue of the Americas
New York, NY 10020

Send a check for $12.00 payable
to *Wimmer Books Plus*
Proceeds benefit: National Council of
Negro Women
Recipes: Crispy Oven-Fried Fish
Fingers, page 177; Mr. Tim's Baked
Hush Puppies, page 82

Calico Cupboards
Junior Auxiliary of Benton
P.O. Box 851
Benton, AR 72018

Send a check for $19.00 payable
to *Calico Cupboards*
Proceeds benefit: Projects assisting
the children of Saline County
Recipes: Brunswick Stew, page 116;
Sauerbraten with Gingersnap Gravy,
page 128; Spanish Rice, page 191

California Kosher
Women's League of Adat Ari El
    Synagogue
12020 Burbank Boulevard
North Hollywood, CA 91607

Send a check for $22.45 payable
to *Women's League of Adat Ari El
Synagogue* (California residents add
$1.65 state sales tax)
Proceeds benefit: The expansion of
Jewish education and community ac-
tivities of the League, including their
interfaith food pantry and programs
for the developmentally disabled
Recipes: Challah, page 92; Chocolate
Chip Coffee Cake, page 83

California Sizzles
Junior League of Pasadena, Inc.
149 South Madison Avenue
Pasadena, CA 91101

Send a check for $24.45 payable
to *Junior League of Pasadena, Inc.*
(California residents add $1.65 state
sales tax)
Proceeds benefit: Projects assisting
children
Recipes: Black Bean Salad, page 220;
Carrot-Ginger Soup, page 106;
Newport Clam Chowder, page 113

Candlelight and Wisteria
Lee-Scott Academy
2307 East Glenn Avenue
Auburn, AL 36830

Send a check for $19.95 payable
to *Lee-Scott Academy*
Proceeds benefit: Lee-Scott Academy
and construction of its fine-arts auditorium
Recipes: Crystal's Coleslaw, page 37;
Rich Hot Crab Dip, page 60

Cane River Cuisine
Service League of Natchitoches, Inc.
P.O. Box 2206
Natchitoches, LA 71457

Send a check for $15.95 payable
to *Cane River Cuisine*
Proceeds benefit: Projects and
programs of the League
Recipes: Chicken Breasts Parmesan,
page 157; Trout Almondine, page 176

Charleston Receipts
Junior League of Charleston, Inc.
51 Folly Road
Charleston, SC 29407

Send a check for $13.50 payable
to *Junior League of Charleston, Inc.*
Proceeds benefit: Projects of the
League, including organization of
conferences and seminars to prevent
child abuse, and funding and volunteering time to establish a parenting
coalition
Recipes: Chocolate Lover's Chocolate
Cake, page 251

Come and Get It!
Junior Welfare League
of Talladega
P.O. Box 331
Talladega, AL 35160

Send a check for $17.45 payable
to *Junior Welfare League of
Talladega* (Alabama residents add
$1.20 state sales tax)
Proceeds benefit: Projects of the
League, such as Meals on Wheels
and Dial-a-Story
Recipes: Breakfast Pizza, page 209;
Meatball Chowder, page 16;
Pineapple Cake, page 252

Cookbook 25 Years
Madison County Farm Bureau
Women's Committee
900 Hillsboro Avenue
P.O. Box 10
Edwardsville, IL 62025

Send a check for $18.95 payable
to *Madison County Farm Bureau*
Proceeds benefit: Scholarships for
agricultural students at local junior
colleges
Recipes: Cheese Meat Loaf,
page 126; Eggplant Casserole,
page 238

Cordonbluegrass
Junior League of Louisville, Inc.
627 West Main Street
Louisville, KY 40202

Send a check for $18.95 payable
to *Junior League of Louisville, Inc.*
(Kentucky residents add $1.02 state
sales tax)
Proceeds benefit: Community
projects of the League, including the
Sister-to-Sister program
Recipes: Cheese-Sauced Cauliflower,
page 234; Cold Marinated Tenderloin, page 130; Pumpkin Mincemeat
Bread, page 79

The Cotton Country Collection
Junior League of Monroe, Inc.
2811 Cameron Street
P.O. Box 7138
Monroe, LA 71211-7138

Send a check for $20.45 payable
to *Cotton-Bayou Publications*
(Louisiana residents add $0.68 state
sales tax)
Proceeds benefit: Service projects of
the League, including the YWCA
Safe House for battered women and
children
Recipes: Ratatouille, page 240;
Roasted Corn, page 237

Cranbrook Reflections
Cranbrook House & Gardens
    Auxiliary
380 Lone Pine Road
P.O. Box 801
Bloomfield Hills, MI 48303

Send a check for $23.45 payable
to *Cranbrook Reflections* (Michigan
residents add $0.80 state sales tax)

Proceeds benefit: The preservation
and restoration of Cranbrook House,
a national historic landmark, and its
surrounding gardens
Recipes: Good-Taste Waffles,
page 91; London Broil on the Grill,
page 132; Pasta with Lemon Cream
Sauce, page 199

Cultivated Palate
The Arboretum Foundation,
    Washington Park Arboretum
c/o University of Washington,
    XD-10
Seattle, WA 98195

Send a check for $24.95 payable
to *The Arboretum Foundation*
(Washington residents add $2.05
state sales tax)
Proceeds benefit: The Washington
Park Arboretum
Recipes: Creamy Chocolate Roll,
page 255; Orange-Apple Strudel,
page 265; Salmon Tart, page 182;
Swordfish with Mushroom and
Tomato Sauce, page 179

Deep in the Heart
Dallas Junior Forum
800 East Campbell Road
Suite 114
Richardson, TX 75081

Send a check for $19.95 payable
to *Dallas Junior Forum*
Proceeds benefit: Community
projects, such as The Kids on the
Block Puppetry, Juliette Fowler
Homes, Ronald McDonald House
and Children's Cancer Fund of Dallas
Recipes: Black-Eyed Pea Salad,
page 39; Golden Rice, page 190

Desert Treasures
Junior League of Phoenix, Inc.
2600 North Central Avenue #750
P.O. Box 10223
Phoenix, AZ 85064

Send a check for $21.45 payable
to *The Junior League of Phoenix, Inc.*
Proceeds benefit: The project,
"Healthy Touch: Good Touch–Bad
Touch," for elementary school
children
Recipes: Hearts of Palm with Tangy
Lemon Dressing, page 219; Pork
Loin Roast with Orange Barbecue
Sauce, page 142; Turkey with
Raspberry Sauce, page 166; Wild
Rice Soup, page 107

Family and Company
Junior League of Binghamton, Inc.
55 Main Street
Binghamton, NY 13905

Send a check for $21.45 payable
to *Junior League of Binghamton, Inc.*
Proceeds benefit: Community
projects of the League
Recipes: Barbecued Pork on a Bun,
page 22; Saffron Risotto, page 193;
Salmon Filling for Hors d'Oeuvres,
page 13; Vegetable Pizza, page 64

Family Secrets
Lee Academy
415 Lee Drive
Clarksdale, MS 38614

Send a check for $17.45 payable
to *Family Secrets*
Proceeds benefit: Lee Academy, a college preparatory school
Recipes: Mexican Cheese Soup,
page 103; Raspberry Pie, page 266

Fast and Fancy
Saddle River Day School Parents'
Guild
147 Chestnut Ridge Road
Saddle River, NJ 07458

Send a check for $10.00 payable
to *Saddle River Day School
Cookbook, Attn: M. Jaehnee*
Proceeds benefit: Saddle River Day
School
Recipes: Rolled Fillets of Flounder
with Lemon Sauce, page 174; Shrimp
Mélange, page 227

The Fine Art of Cooking
The Women's Committee of the
Philadelphia Museum of Art
P.O. Box 7646
Philadelphia, PA 19101

Send a check for $24.95 payable
to *Philadelphia Museum of Art
Cookbook* (Pennsylvania residents
add $1.32 state sales tax)
Proceeds benefit: The Philadelphia
Museum of Art
Recipes: Barley and Pine Nut Casse-
role, page 196; Kiwi Sorbet, page 257

Forum Feasts
Friends of the Forum School
P.O. Box 43
Waldwick, NJ 07463

Send a check for $17.45 payable
to *Forum Feasts Cookbook* (New
Jersey residents add $0.90 state sales
tax)
Proceeds benefit: Children with special needs at the Forum School
Recipes: Raisin Harvest Coffee Cake,
page 84; Walnut Spice Kisses,
page 261

The Golden Taste of South Carolina
South Carolina Farm Bureau
   Federation
P.O. Box 754
Columbia, SC 29202

Send a check for $17.50 payable to *South Carolina Farm Bureau Federation*
Proceeds benefit: The project, "Agriculture in the Classroom"
Recipes: Cookies and Cream Cheesecake, page 53; Enchilada Casserole, page 125; Slow-Cooker Pepper Steak, page 135; Summer Strawberry Pie, page 268

Gracious Goodness . . . Charleston!
Bishop England High School
203 Calhoun Street
Charleston, SC 29401-3522

Send a check for $19.95 payable to *Gracious Goodness . . . Charleston!* (South Carolina residents add $1.02 state sales tax)
Proceeds benefit: Bishop England High School Endowment
Recipes: Chinese Oven-Fried Pork Chops, page 138; Garlic Bread Twists, page 100; Hummus, page 58; Praline Cheesecake, page 52

The Gulf Gourmet
Westminster Academy PTA, Inc.
5003 Lawson Avenue
Gulfport, MS 39507

Send a check for $15.45 payable to *The Gulf Gourmet* (Mississippi residents add $0.91 state sales tax)
Proceeds benefit: Projects and programs at the Westminster Academy, a small elementary school

Recipes: Jalapeño Cornbread and Ground Meat Casserole, page 123

Heart and Soul
Junior League of Memphis, Inc.
3475 Central Avenue
Memphis, TN 38111

Send a check for $23.45 payable to *Junior League of Memphis Publications* (Tennessee residents add $1.65 state sales tax)
Proceeds benefit: Community projects assisting families and children
Recipes: Chicken Cashew Salad, page 32; Delta Beef and Rice, page 20; Jazzy Orange Roughy, page 170

Holy Cow, Chicago's Cooking
Women of the Church of the Holy
   Comforter
222 Kenilworth Avenue
P.O. Box 168
Kenilworth, IL 60043

Send a check for $20.20 payable to *Women of the Church of the Holy Comforter* (Illinois residents add $1.32 state sales tax)
Proceeds benefit: Chicago's metropolitan outreach organizations for the hungry, homeless and families at risk
Recipes: Citrus Couscous with Basil and Apricots, page 195; Red Pepper Sauce for Pasta, page 198; Salmon in Parchment, page 180

Hospitality
North Shore Medical Center
   Auxiliary
Salem Hospital Aid Association
81 Highland Avenue
Salem, MA 01970

Send a check for $22.95 payable
to *AKA North Shore Medical
Center Auxiliary* (Massachusetts
residents add $1.00 state
sales tax)
Proceeds benefit: Area hospitals, by
providing diagnostic and lifesaving
patient equipment
Recipes: Apple Pancakes with
Apricot Butter, page 88; Indonesian
Grilled Chicken Breasts, page 154;
Wonton Soup, page 108

Impressions
Auxiliary to the Memphis Dental
    Society
P.O. Box 17272
Memphis, TN 38187-0272

Send a check for $16.95 payable
to *Impressions* (Tennessee residents
add $1.40 state sales tax)
Proceeds benefit: The Dr. Mike
Overbey Dental Health Exhibit
at the Children's Museum of
Memphis
Recipes: Fresh Broccoli-Cauliflower
Salad, page 214; Grilled Catfish with
Dijon Sauce, page 172; Lemon Pecan
Dainties, page 260

The Kitchen Connection
National Council of Jewish Women,
    Omaha Section
13007 Frances Street
Omaha, NE 68144

Send a check for $10.00 payable
to *National Council of Jewish
Women, Omaha Section* (Nebraska
residents add $0.65 state sales tax)
Proceeds benefit: Child care and
educational projects
Recipes: Popover Pizza, page 122;
Spinach Ricotta Tart, page 206

Land of Cotton
John T. Morgan Academy
P.O. Drawer P
Selma, AL 36702

Send a check for $15.45 payable
to *Land of Cotton* (Alabama
residents add $0.98 state sales tax)
Proceeds benefit: Educational
programs at the John T. Morgan
Academy
Recipes: Beef Burgundy Stroganoff,
page 127; Layered Strawberry Gelatin
Salad, page 35; Picadillo Dip, page 12

The League Sampler
Clarksburg League for Service
R. #1, Box 167D
Lost Creek, WV 26385

Send a check for $5.00 payable to
Clarksburg League for Service
Proceeds benefit: Community
projects for the underprivileged,
including Mother's Clinic, Baby
Clinic and scholarships
Recipes: Caramel Apple Dip, page
56; Yippee Yogurt Pops, page 70

Lone Star Legacy
Austin Junior Forum
P.O. Box 26628
Austin, TX 78755

Send a check for $19.45 payable
to *AJF Publications*
Proceeds benefit: Community organizations and programs for children
Recipes: Arroz con Salsa Verde, page
192; Dill Dip with Rye Bread, page 9

The Maine Collection
Portland Museum of Art Guild
P.O. Box 6128
Falmouth, ME 04105

Send a check for $21.45 payable
to *Portland Museum of Art Guild*
(Maine residents add $1.14 state
sales tax)
Proceeds benefit: The restoration of
the McLellan-Sweat House
Recipes: Green Beans with Basil,
page 231

Merrymeeting Merry Eating
Mid Coast Hospital/Brunswick
   Auxiliary
58 Baribeau Drive
Brunswick, ME 04011

Send a check for $18.95 payable
to *Mid Coast Hospital/Brunswick
Auxiliary* (Maine residents add $0.96
state sales tax)
Proceeds benefit: The Mid Coast
Hospital and scholarships for
students in pursuit of health careers
Recipes: Danish Apple Bars, page 50;
Sweet Potato Casserole, page 48

Necessities and Temptations
Junior League of Austin, Inc.
5416 Parkcrest, Suite 100
Austin, TX 78731

Send a check for $23.45 payable
to *The Junior League of Austin, Inc.*
(Texas residents add $1.60 state sales
tax)
Proceeds benefit: Projects and
programs of the League
Recipes: Praline Pumpkin Pie,
page 270; Spinach Salad, page 217;
Turkey Quiche with Stuffing Crust,
page 164

Only in California
Children's Home Society of
   California
7695 Cardinal Court
San Diego, CA 92123

Send a check for $20.95 payable
to *Children's Home Society of
California* (California residents add
area state sales tax)
Proceeds benefit: The Children's
Home Society of California (CHS)
and programs responsive to the needs
of vulnerable families and children in
local communities
Recipes: Dilly Cheese Bread, page 98

Our Country Cookin'
Junior Social Workers of Chickasha
P.O. Box 355
Chickasha, OK 73023

Send a check for $16.43 payable
to *Our Country Cookin'* (Oklahoma
residents add $1.36 state sales tax)
Proceeds benefit: Community needs
and projects
Recipes: Breakfast Ring, page 95;
Chicken Cordon Bleu, page 155;
Cranberry-Orange Bread, page 78

Our Favorite Recipes
St. John's Guild
c/o June Spielman
809 South Sixth Avenue
West Bend, WI 53095

Send a check for $14.95 payable
to *St. John's Guild*
Proceeds benefit: Various projects,
including scholarships for St. John's
students and assisting the aging and
handicapped
Recipes: Banana Bread, page 77;
Congo Bars, page 264

The Pasquotank Plate
Christ Episcopal Churchwomen
200 McMorrine Street
Elizabeth City, NC 27909

Send a check for $20.70 payable
to *The Pasquotank Plate* (North
Carolina residents add $1.08 state
sales tax)
Proceeds benefit: The Northeastern
Children's Co-Op, various community outreach projects and other
charitable works of the Episcopal
Churchwomen
Recipes: Chicken Tetrazzini, page 24;
Hash Brown Potato Casserole,
page 46; Light Yogurt Crescent Rolls,
page 94

Peachtree Bouquet
Junior League of DeKalb County, Inc.
716 West Trinity Place
Decatur, GA 30030

Send a check for $17.45 payable
to *JLD Publications* (Georgia
residents add $0.75 state sales tax)
Proceeds benefit: The DeKalb Rape
Crisis Center and other community
projects
Recipes: Roasted Pepper and Tomato
Soup, page 104; Smoked Sausage
Salad Medley, page 224

The Philadelphia Orchestra
    Cookbook
West Philadelphia Committee for the
    Philadelphia Orchestra
P.O. Box 685
Bryn Mawr, PA 19010

Send a check for $19.00 payable
to *The Philadelphia Orchestra
Cookbook* (Pennsylvania residents
add $0.96 state sales tax)

Proceeds benefit: The Philadelphia
Orchestra
Recipes: Moroccan Lamb, page 149;
Twice-Baked Yams, page 244

Pow Wow Chow
The Five Civilized Tribes Museum
Agency Hill on Honor Heights Drive
Muskogee, OK 74401

Send a check for $15.95 payable
to *The Five Civilized Tribes Museum*
(Oklahoma residents add $1.00 state
sales tax)
Proceeds benefit: The Five Civilized
Tribes Museum
Recipes: Cold Beef Salad, page 221;
Health Bread, page 96; Scramble
Mix, page 14

Prairie Potpourri
Immanuel Medical Center Auxiliary
6901 North 72nd Street
Omaha, NE 68122

Send a check for $18.20 payable
to *Immanuel Medical Center Auxiliary* (Nebraska residents add $1.04
state sales tax)
Proceeds benefit: Immanuel Medical
Center Auxiliary Hospitality House
Recipes: Oven-Baked Beef Stew,
page 114; Shrimp Creole, page 185

Preserving Our Italian Heritage
Sons of Italy Florida Foundation
87 NE 44th Street, Suite 5
Ft. Lauderdale, FL 33334

Send a check for $17.95 payable
to *Sons of Italy Florida Foundation*
Proceeds benefit: Sons of Italy
Florida Foundation scholarship pro-
gram and various charities, including
Cooley's Anemia

Recipes: Fresh Tomato Salad, page 215; Pepperoni Bread, page 99

Rave Reviews
Junior League of North Little Rock
216 West Fourth Street
P.O. Box 9043
Main Street Station
North Little Rock, AR 72119-9043

Send a check for $16.95 payable to *Junior League of North Little Rock*
Proceeds benefit: The League's community projects, grants and scholarships
Recipes: Asparagus Eleganté, page 230; Little Links in Oriental Sauce, page 15

Recipe Jubilee!
Junior League of Mobile, Inc.
P.O. Box 7091
Mobile, AL 36607

Send a check for $18.45 payable to *Mobile Junior League Publications* (Alabama residents add $0.60 state sales tax; Mobile residents add an additional $0.60 city tax; Mobile County residents add an additional $0.15 county tax)
Proceeds benefit: Community education, cultural and welfare projects of the League
Recipes: Lemon Meringue Squares, page 259; Pennsylvania Dutch Potato Dressing, page 47

River Feast
Junior League of Cincinnati
3500 Columbia Parkway
Cincinnati, OH 45226

Send a check for $17.70 payable to *Junior League of Cincinnati* (Ohio residents add $0.80 state sales tax)
Proceeds benefit: Projects of the League
Recipes: Apricot Nectar Cake, page 250; Buffalo Chicken Wings, page 10; Greek Beef Stew, page 115; Light-Hearted Cincinnati Chili, page 120

Rogue River Rendezvous
Junior Service League of Jackson County
526 East Main Street
Medford, OR 97504

Send a check for $22.95 payable to *Rogue River Rendevous*
Proceeds benefit: Community projects assisting children, troubled families and at-risk teens; drug education and cultural events
Recipes: Greek Potato Wedges, page 241; Northwest Blueberry Muffins, page 75; Rogue Pears, page 262

RSVP
Junior League of Portland, Inc.
P.O. Box 477
Portland, ME 04101

Send a check for $17.95 payable to *Junior League of Portland, Inc.*
Proceeds benefit: Community projects and programs, such as Prevention of Child Abuse and Neglect and Portland Ministry-at-Large Teen Center

Recipes: Blueberry-Corn Cakes, page 90; Corn Cakes, page 236

Savannah Style
Junior League of Savannah, Inc.
P.O. Box 1864
Savannah, GA 31402

Send a check for $19.45 payable to *Savannah Style* (Georgia residents add $1.02 state sales tax)
Proceeds benefit: Various community projects, including the Coastal Children's Advocacy Center
Recipes: Low Country Shrimp Boil, page 186; Marinated Pork Tenderloin, page 140; Skewered Fish Mediterranean, page 178

Savoring the Southwest
Roswell Symphony Guild
P.O. Box 3078
Roswell, NM 88202

Send a check for $21.70 payable to *Roswell Symphony Guild Publications* (New Mexico residents add $1.37 state sales tax)
Proceeds benefit: The Roswell Symphony Orchestra and the Roswell Symphony Orchestra Foundation Trust
Recipes: Baked Stuffed Mushrooms, page 66; Chicken à l'Orange, page 152; Lamb Pilaf with Apricots, page 148

Sea Island Seasons
Beaufort County Open Land Trust
P.O. Box 75
Beaufort, SC 29901

Send a check for $14.70 payable to *Sea Island Seasons* (South Carolina residents add $0.65 state sales tax)
Proceeds benefit: Support of the Beaufort Open Land Trust
Recipes: Sour Cream Potato Salad, page 40; Wild Rice Pecan Casserole, page 194

Seasoned with Sun
Junior League of El Paso, Inc.
520 Thunderbird Drive
El Paso, TX 79912

Send a check for $19.70 payable to *Junior League of El Paso, Inc.*
Proceeds benefit: Community projects of the League
Recipes: Black Bean Soup, page 112; Chili Corn, page 42; Tortilla Pinwheels, page 62

Sensational Seasons
Junior League of Fort Smith, Inc.
P.O. Box 3266
Fort Smith, AR 72913

Send a check for $19.95 payable to *JLFS Sensational Seasons*
Proceeds benefit: Various community projects, including the Adolescent Pregnancy Clinic, Community Free Dental Clinic and Literacy for Adults program
Recipes: Croutons with Tomato and Pesto, page 63; Grilled Chicken Salads with Corn, Peppers and Tortilla Chips, page 222; Log House Gumbo, page 118

Settings
Junior League of Philadelphia, Inc.
P.O. Box 492
Bryn Mawr, PA 19010

Send a check for $27.95 payable to *Junior League of Philadelphia, Inc.* (Pennsylvania residents add $1.50 state sales tax)
Proceeds benefit: Community projects of the League
Recipes: Chinese Dumplings, page 68; Lemon Glazed Muffins, page 72; Roast Chicken Stuffed with Mushrooms, page 161

The Shadows-on-the-Teche Cookbook
The Shadows Service League
317 East Main Street
New Iberia, LA 70560

Send a check for $18.95 payable to *The Shadows-on-the-Teche Cookbook*
Proceeds benefit: The preservation, maintenance and improvement of the Shadows-on-the-Teche, a historic house museum of the National Trust for Preservation
Recipes: Crab Ball, page 59; Parmesan Primavera, page 200

Simple Elegance
Our Lady of Perpetual Help Women's Guild
8151 Poplar Avenue
Germantown, TN 38183

Send a check for $19.45 payable to *Our Lady of Perpetual Help Women's Guild* (Tennessee residents add $1.40 state sales tax)
Proceeds benefit: Assistance to Our Lady of Perpetual Help Family Life Center, St. Jude Children's Research Hospital and the YWCA Women's Abuse Shelter
Recipes: Date-Nut Cake Roll, page 253

Simply Simpático
Junior League of Albuquerque, Inc.
2920 Yale Boulevard, SE
Albuquerque, NM 87106

Send a check for $16.95 payable to *Simply Simpático*
Proceeds benefit: Women and children in need
Recipes: Baked Chili Rellenos, page 208; Slenderized Roquefort Dressing, page 228

Some Like It Hot
Junior League of McAllen, Inc.
P.O. Box 2465
McAllen, TX 78502

Send a check for $19.95 payable to *Junior League of McAllen, Inc.*
Proceeds benefit: Various projects for the children and youth in the community
Recipes: Carrot-Orange Muffins, page 73; Mexican Pork Chops, page 137

Southern Elegance
Junior League of Gaston County
2950 Union Road
Suite A
Gastonia, NC 28054

Send a check for $16.45 payable to *Southern Elegance* (North Carolina residents add $0.84 state sales tax)
Proceeds benefit: Community projects, such as Habitat House for Humanity, Preschool for at-risk preschoolers and Teen Outreach (a drop-out prevention program)
Recipes: Country Pot Roast, page 133; Smoked Sausage and Pasta Jambalaya, page 145

Specialties of the House
Kenmore Association, Inc.
1201 Washington Avenue
Fredericksburg, VA 22401

Send a check for $25.00 payable
to *Kenmore Association, Inc.*
Proceeds benefit: Restoration
of the Kenmore Museum and
Gardens
Recipes: Boston Brown Bread,
page 76; Papaya-Coconut Bread,
page 80

Still Fiddling in the Kitchen
National Council of Jewish Women
30233 Southfield Road
Suite 100
Southfield, MI 48076

Send a check for $18.00 payable
to *National Council of Jewish
Women* (Michigan residents add
$0.90 state sales tax)
Proceeds benefit: All the group's
projects, particularly those meeting
the needs of children and families
Recipes: Low-Fat Noodle Kugel,
page 202; Praline French Toast
Casserole, page 86

Still Gathering
Auxiliary to the American
   Osteopathic Association
142 East Ontario Street
Chicago, IL 60611

Send a check for $22.95 payable
to *Auxiliary to the American
Osteopathic Association*
Proceeds benefit: National and
local projects and programs for promoting public health education and
providing scholarships and funds for
students
Recipes: Baked White Beans,
page 44; Oven-Fried Vegetables,
page 67

Talk about Good!
Junior League of Lafayette, Inc.
100 Felecie Street
Lafayette, LA 70506

Send a check for $18.50 payable
to *Junior League of Lafayette, Inc.*
Proceeds benefit: Children's
programs in the areas of substance
abuse, child abuse prevention and
educational enrichment
Recipes: Black-Eyed Pea Jambalaya,
page 23; Mock Hollandaise Sauce,
page 247; Raisin Bread Pudding,
page 258

Thymes Remembered
Junior League of Tallahassee, Inc.
404 East Sixth Avenue
P.O. Box 13428
Tallahassee, FL 32317

Send a check for $21.95 payable
to *Thymes Remembered Cookbook*
(Florida residents add $1.33 state
sales tax)

Proceeds benefit: Projects and programs assisting local citizens with special needs and providing educational and artistic opportunities to the community
Recipes: Apricot Nectar Salad, page 33; Herb-Basted Cornish Hens, page 162; Paella Salad, page 30; Simply Delicious Scallops, page 184

Tropical Seasons
Beaux Arts of the Lowe Art Museum
    of the University of Miami, Inc.
Lowe Art Museum
1301 Stanford Drive
Coral Gables, FL 33146

Send a check for $20.95 payable to *Beax Arts* (Florida residents add $1.17 state sales tax)
Proceeds benefit: The Lowe Art Museum of the University of Miami
Recipes: Assorted Fruit with Banana Poppy Seed Dressing, page 212; Florida Chicken Salad, page 226; Tortilla Turkey Soup, page 111

Two and Company
St. Thomas Church
232 St. Thomas Lane
Owings Mills, MD 21117

Send a check for $19.45 payable to *St. Thomas Church Cookbook*

Proceeds benefit: Projects to feed the hungry
Recipes: Butternut Squash Soufflé, page 246; Crab Cakes, page 188; Scrambled Egg Casserole, page 27

Uptown Down South
Junior League of Greenville, Inc.
17 West North Street
Greenville, SC 29601

Send a check for $17.20 payable to *Junior League of Greenville Publications*
Proceeds benefit: Community projects of the League
Recipes: Chicken Lasagna, page 26; Layered Salad Supreme, page 38; Spinach-Mushroom Stuffed Pork Tenderloin, page 139

Vintage Vicksburg
Vicksburg Junior Auxiliary, Inc.
P.O. Box 86
Vicksburg, MS 39181

Send a check for $18.95 payable to *Vintage Vicksburg* (Mississippi residents add $1.02 state sales tax)
Proceeds benefit: Projects assisting the children of Warren County
Recipes: Blintz Soufflé, page 204; Homemade Herb Cheese, page 8

Virginia Seasons
Junior League of Richmond, Inc.
205 West Franklin Street
Richmond, VA 23220

Send a check for $20.95 payable to *Virginia Seasons* (Virginia residents add $0.76 state sales tax)
Proceeds benefit: The Metro Literacy Council of Richmond and Sacred Heart Family Resource Center

Recipes: Lamb Chops en Papillote, page 150; Overnight Chicken Soufflé, page 28

Yesterday, Today and Tomorrow
Baddour Memorial Center, Inc.
P.O. Box 69
Senatobia, MS 38668

Send a check for $19.00 payable to *Baddour Memorial Center, Inc.*
Proceeds benefit: Mentally disabled residents at the Baddour Center
Recipes: Chili Supreme, page 18; Cream of Fresh Asparagus Soup, page 102

Index